Multimedia Literacy

Fred T. Hofstetter

University of Delaware

With CD-ROM by

Patricia Fox

McGRAW-HILL

New York St. Louis San Francisco Auckland Bogotá Caracas
Lisbon London Madrid Mexico Milan Montreal New Delhi
Paris San Juan Singapore Sydney Tokyo Toronto

McGraw-Hill

Multimedia Literacy

1 2 3 4 5 6 7 8 9 0   DOW DOW   9 0 9 8 7 6 5 4

P/N 029380-5

Order Information
ISBN 0-07-911956-5 (text with accompanying CD-ROM)

Sponsoring Editor: Frank Ruggirello
Editorial Assistant: Debra Colon
Technical Reviewer: Stephanie Chenault
Production Supervisor: Richard DeVitto
Project Manager: Jane Granoff
Copyeditor: Madhu Prasher
Interior designer: Gary Palmatier, Ideas to Images
Cover designer: Tom Trujillo
Compositor: Ideas to Images
Printer and binder: R.R. Donnelley & Sons

Library of Congress Card Catalog No. 94-77893

Dedication

Throughout this project my wife, Laura, provided a constant source of inspiration and support. She applied her computing skills to test the tutorial sections and install the multimedia products reviewed throughout this book.

During our courtship in 1979, when Laura was head of the PLATO mainframe computer in Belgium and I directed one in the United States, we would log on during off-peak times and exercise our system privileges to use the inter-continental PLATO satellite link for two-way interactive conversations. My proposal that we marry filled eleven screens. This book is dedicated to the memory of the day she typed y-e-s.

Brief Contents

Part One   **Understanding Multimedia**   1

   1   Definitions   2

   2   Taxonomy of Multimedia Objects   15

Part Two   **A Survey of Multimedia Applications**   29

   3   Business and Industry   30

   4   Education   46

   5   Entertainment   76

   6   Government   88

   7   Medicine and Nursing   99

   8   Encyclopedic Resources   107

   9   Application Development Packages   117

Part Three   **Selecting Multimedia Hardware**   127

   10 Competing Multimedia Standards   128

   11 Multimedia Computer Components   133

   12 Multimedia Computer Buyer's Checklists   146

   13 Configuring a Multimedia Computer   150

Part Four   **Looking into the Future of Multimedia**   157

   14 Multimedia Frontiers   158

   15 Emerging Technology   162

   16 Societal Issues   168

   17 How to Keep Up   183

HANDS-ON TUTORIAL

Part Five **Multimedia Tools and Techniques** **195**

18 Text 196

19 Graphics 205

20 Triggering 217

21 Waveform Audio Recording 223

22 CD Audio Clipmaking 228

23 MIDI Sequencing 233

24 Digital Video Recording 238

25 Videodisc Clipmaking 251

HANDS-ON TUTORIAL

Part Six **Creating a Simple Multimedia Application** **257**

26 The History of Flight Picture Menu 258

27 1920's Barnstorming 262

28 The Flying Fortress 266

29 The Blue Angels 270

30 Jumbo Jets 274

HANDS-ON TUTORIAL

Part Seven **Creating an Advanced Multimedia Application** **277**

31 Designing Advanced Applications 278

32 Creating the Information Superhighway Screen 287

33 Defining the Internet 292

34 Providing a Graceful Way to Exit 295

35 Internet Resources 298

36 Interesting Gopher Servers 304

37 Weather Satellite Images 311

38 Electronic News Feed 314

39 Cable News Network Live Video Feed 318

40 Distributing Your Multimedia Application 320

Contents

Part One
Understanding Multimedia   1

Chapter 1   Definitions   2

What Is Multimedia? 3

Why Is It Important? 3

How Fast Is It Growing? 4

How Is It Changing the World? 8

Mergers and Alliances 8 ▪ Telecommuting 9 ▪ Home Shopping 9 ▪ Electronic Publishing 9 ▪ Teaching and Learning 10 ▪ Mass Market Use of Information Services 10

Who Needs to Know About It? 11

What Is a Multimedia PC? 11

RAM and MB 11 ▪ Processor and Mhz 12 ▪ Hard Drive 12 ▪ CD-ROM 13 ▪ 8-Bit and 16-Bit Sound 13 ▪ Synthesizer and MIDI Playback 13 ▪ 640x480 14 ▪ Pixels and Megapixels 14 ▪ 64 KB Buffer 14 ▪ Bandwidth 14

EXERCISES 14

Chapter 2   Taxonomy of Multimedia Objects   15

Text 16

Printed Text 16 ▪ Scanned Text 16 ▪ Electronic Text 16 ▪ Hypertext 18

Graphics 18

Bitmaps 18 ▪ Clip Art 18 ▪ Digitized Pictures 23 ▪ Hyperpictures 23

Sound 24

Waveform Audio 24 ▪ CD Audio 24 ▪ MIDI 26 ▪ Hyperaudio 26 ▪ Video 26 ▪ Live Video Feeds 26 ▪ Videotape 27 ▪ Videodisc 27 ▪ Digital Video 27 ▪ Hypervideo 28

EXERCISES 28

Part Two
A Survey of Multimedia Applications   29

Chapter 3   **Business and Industry**   30

Interactive Multimedia Merchandising   31

Florsheim Shoes 31 ▪ MusicWriter's NoteStation 31 ▪
Video Merchandising 32 ▪ Virtual Shopping 33

Desktop Video Conferencing   33

Multimedia Travel Systems   34

Financial Services   35

Real Estate   35

Corporate Training   36

Just-In-Time Training   39

Pilot Training   40

Advertising and Electronic Brochures   40

Mass Market Applications   42

EXERCISES 45

Chapter 4   **Education**   46

Art   47

Biology   49

Chemistry   51

Civics   53

Foreign Languages   54

Geography   56

History   59

Videodisc 59 ▪ History Textbooks 60 ▪ Multimedia History
Titles 60 ▪ Wars 60 ▪ The Assassination of JFK 61 ▪ Internet
Resources for Historians 62

Music   63

Physics   65

Science   66

Elementary Education   68

Reading   70

Preschool   72

EXERCISES 74

Chapter 5   **Entertainment**   **76**

Cinema   77

Morphing 77 ▪ **Superimposition** 78 ▪ **Animation** 78 ▪
Digital Recasting 79

Video Games   79

Interactive Movies   79

Virtual Reality   82

EXERCISES 87

Chapter 6   **Government**   **88**

Public Service Kiosks   89

Electronic Town Meetings   92

Internet and the National Information Superhighway   92

Safeguarding National Interests   93

Warfare   93

Olympic Bidding   93

Virtual Campaigning   96

Consumer Information   97

EXERCISES 98

Chapter 7   **Medicine and Nursing**   **99**

Medical Training   100

Anatomy and Physiology   102

Virtual Surgery   103

Video Conferencing Network   104

Life Support Skills   104

Online Resources   105

National Health Insurance   105

EXERCISES 106

Chapter 8   **Encyclopedic Resources**   **107**

Multimedia CD-ROMs   108

Internet Resources   115

Library of Congress 115 ▪ **Smithsonian** 115 ▪ **Museums** 115
▪ **Encyclopedia Britannica** 116

EXERCISES 116

Chapter 9   **Application Development Packages**   117

Presentation Packages   118

PowerPoint   118 ▪ Harvard Graphics   119

Hypermedia Programs   121

ToolBook   121 ▪ PODIUM   121

Authoring Systems   122

Authorware Professional   122 ▪ IconAuthor   123 ▪ Quest   124

EXERCISES 126

Part Three
Selecting Multimedia Hardware   127

Chapter 10   **Competing Multimedia Standards**   128

Multi Multimedia   129

Microsoft's MCI   129 ▪ Apple's QuickTime   130 ▪ IBM Ultimedia   130
▪ Intel's Digital Video Interactive (DVI)   130 ▪ Philips' CD-I   131

Coping with Multi Multimedia   131

EXERCISES 132

Chapter 11   **Multimedia Computer Components**   133

System Unit   134

Central Processor   134 ▪ RAM   134 ▪ Color Display   134
▪ Pointing Device   135

Multimedia Accessories   136

CD-ROM   136 ▪ Digital Audio   136 ▪ Audio Speakers   136 ▪
Video Overlay   137 ▪ Digital Video   139 ▪ TV Tuner   139 ▪
MIDI   139 ▪ Videodisc   140

Multimedia Read/Write Storage   140

Hard Disk   140 ▪ SCSI   141 ▪ Read-Write Optical Disk   141 ▪
Writable CD-ROM   142 ▪ PCMCIA Cards   142

Communication Options   142

Modems   142 ▪ Networks   142 ▪ Internet Connections   143

Auxiliary Input   143

Hand-Held Scanners   143 ▪ Flatbed Scanners   144 ▪
Slide Scanners   144 ▪ Digital Cameras   144

Printers   145

EXERCISES 145

Chapter 12   **Multimedia Computer
              Buyer's Checklists**   146

              Low-Budget System 147 ▪ **Mid-Range System** 147 ▪
              High-End System 148

                   EXERCISES 149

Chapter 13   **Configuring a Multimedia Computer** 150

              Feature Cards 151

              Audio Connections 151

              Audio Wiring 151 ▪ **Audio Mixing** 152

              Video Connections 154

              A Low-Cost Audio/Video Switch 154

                   EXERCISES 155

Part Four
Looking into the Future of Multimedia   157

Chapter 14   **Multimedia Frontiers**   158

              Electronic Publishing 159

              The Information Superhighway 159

              Rural Datafication 160

              Virtual Reality 160

                   EXERCISES 160

Chapter 15   **Emerging Technology**   162

              Fad or Future Trend? 163

              Digital Video 163 ▪ **HDTV** 163 ▪ **ISDN** 164 ▪ **Video Dial
              Tones** 164 ▪ **Holography** 165 ▪ **Pen Computing** 165 ▪
              Voice Recognition 165 ▪ **Telecomputing** 165 ▪ **Wireless
              Communications** 166 ▪ **Knowbots** 166 ▪ **Multimedia** 166

                   EXERCISES 167

Chapter 16   **Societal Issues**   168

Human Impact   169

Violence and Game Addiction 169 ■ Sex 170 ■ Pornography and Obscenity 170

Regulation   171

Privacy 172 ■ Encryption and the Clipper Chip 172 ■ Censorship 173 ■ Protectionism 173

Multimedia and the Law   174

Patents 174 ■ Copyright 176 ■ Fair Use 176

Equity, Cost, and Universal Access   178

Entitlement 178 ■ Cost 179 ■ Usability 179 ■ Access 180 ■ The Technological Underclass 180 ■ Employment 181 ■ Sizing 181

EXERCISES 182

Chapter 17   **How to Keep Up**   183

Periodicals   184

NewMedia 184 ■ Morph's Outpost 184 ■ Multimedia Today 184 ■ Internet World 184 ■ T.H.E. Journal 185 ■ Technology & Learning 185 ■ The Videodisc Compendium 185 ■ CD-ROM World 185 ■ Virtual Reality World 185 ■ Higher Education Product Companion 186 ■ Communications Industries Report 186 ■ Cinefex 186

Multimedia CDs   186

Nautilus 186 ■ Medio Magazine 186 ■ Substance.digizine 187 ■ CD-ROMs in Print 187

Catalogs   187

Directory of Multimedia Equipment, Software & Services 187 ■ NewMedia Source Book 187 ■ CD-ROMs in Print 188

Professional Associations   188

AECT 188 ■ SALT 188 ■ ICIA 188

Conferences and Exhibits   189

INFOCOMM 189 ■ COMDEX 189 ■ CeBit 189 ■ InterMedia 189 ■ NewMedia Expo 189 ■ Virtual Reality Expo 190 ■ Ed-Media 190 ■ NAB Multimedia World 190 ■ National Net 190 ■ Interactive Healthcare 190 ■ National Demonstration Laboratory 190

Networked Resources   191

EDUPAGE 191 ■ Electronic Frontier Foundation 191 ■ Internet Resources Listserve 191 ■ FTP Sites 191 ■ Whole Internet Catalog 192 ■ HOTT 192 ■ Lucas Newsletter 193

EXERCISES 193

Part Five   *HANDS-ON TUTORIAL*

Multimedia Tools and Techniques   195

Chapter 18   **Text**   196

Creating a Directory 197 ▪ **Starting a New Screen** 198
▪ **The PODIUM Toolbox** 198 ▪ **Entering Text** 199 ▪
Positioning Text 200 ▪ **Sizing Text** 200 ▪ **Centering
Text** 200 ▪ **Editing Text** 200 ▪ **Selecting Fonts** 201 ▪
Coloring Text 201 ▪ **Changing the Background Color** 202
▪ **Shadowing Text** 202 ▪ **Cloning Text** 203 ▪ **Building Text** 203

EXERCISE 204

Chapter 19   **Graphics**   205

Graphic Backdrops 206 ▪ **Hanging Pictures** 207 ▪
Positioning Graphics 208 ▪ **Capturing and Converting Graphics** 208
▪ **Picture Takers** 210 ▪ **Still Video Cameras** 211 ▪ **Kodak's
Photo CD** 211 ▪ **Digital Chalk** 212 ▪ **Compressing Bitmaps** 212
▪ **Controlling Palettes** 213

EXERCISES 216

Chapter 20   **Triggering**   217

Hypertext 218 ▪ **Hyperpictures** 219 ▪ **Buttons** 220 ▪
Editing Links 220 ▪ **Triggers in Backdrops** 221 ▪
Applications As Objects 221 ▪ **Deleting Objects** 222 ▪
Undoing Deletes and Edits 222

EXERCISES 222

Chapter 21   **Waveform Audio Recording**   223

PODIUM's Waveform Audio Tool 224 ▪ **Making Your First
Recording** 224 ▪ **Editing Waveform Audio Recordings** 224 ▪
Adjusting the Quality of Waveform Audio Recordings 225 ▪
Sound Under Stills 226

EXERCISES 227

Chapter 22   **CD Audio Clipmaking**   228

Running the CD Audio Clipmaker 229 ▪ **Play Lists** 230 ▪
Recording Compact Disc Audio to Your Hard Drive 231

EXERCISE 232

Chapter 23   **MIDI Sequencing**   233

Launching Band-in-a-Box 234 ▫ **How Band-in-a-Box Works** 235 ▫ **Creating a Twelve-Bar Blues** 235 ▫ **Setting the Length and Number of Choruses** 236 ▫ **Choosing a Style** 236 ▫ **Playing the Blues** 237 ▫ **Saving the Blues** 237

EXERCISES 237

Chapter 24   **Digital Video Recording**   238

How Digital Video Works 239 ▫ **Preparing Your Hard Drive** 240 ▫ **Running the VidCap Program** 240 ▫ **Setting the Capture File** 241 ▫ **Viewing the Video and Checking the Audio** 241 ▫ **Grabbing a Palette** 242 ▫ **Setting the Capture Options** 242 ▫ **Capturing the Video** 243 ▫ **Editing the Video** 244 ▫ **Compressing the Video** 245 ▫ **Rehearsing the Video** 246 ▫ **Cutting Video Windows into PODIUM Screens** 246 ▫ **Putting Frames Around the Windows** 247 ▫ **Controlling Video Palettes** 247

EXERCISES 250

Chapter 25   **Videodisc Clipmaking**   251

Videodisc Formats 252 ▫ **Running the Videodisc Clipmaker** 252 ▫ **Locating the Clip Start and Stop Points** 253 ▫ **Linking the Videodisc Clip** 253 ▫ **Showing Videodisc Slides** 253 ▫ **Using Videodisc Slides As Backdrops** 254 ▫ **Videodisc Special Effects** 254

EXERCISES 255

Part Six   *HANDS-ON TUTORIAL*

Creating a Simple Multimedia Application   257

Chapter 26   **The History of Flight Picture Menu**   258

Creating the Flight Directory 259 ▫ **Making the Home Screen** 259 ▫ **Titling the Home Screen** 260 ▫ **Making the Backdrop** 260 ▫ **Positioning Text** 261

Chapter 27   **1920's Barnstorming**   262

Making the Link 263 ▫ **Triggering the Link** 263 ▫ **Entering the Biplane Text** 263 ▫ **Making the Biplane Backdrop** 264 ▫ **Adjusting the Text** 264 ▫ **Rehearsing the Link** 264 ▫ **Linking the Motion Sequence** 265 ▫ **Testing the Motion Sequence** 265

Chapter 28   **The Flying Fortress**   266

Making the Link 267 ▪ **Triggering the Link** 267 ▪
Entering the Flying Fortress Text 267 ▪ **Making the Flying
Fortress Backdrop** 268 ▪ **Adjusting the Text** 268 ▪
Rehearsing the Link 268 ▪ **Linking the Motion Sequence** 269
▪ **Testing the Motion Sequence** 269

Chapter 29   **The Blue Angels**   270

Making the Link 271 ▪ **Triggering the Link** 271 ▪
Entering the Blue Angels Text 271 ▪ **Making the Blue Angels
Backdrop** 271 ▪ **Rehearsing the Link** 272 ▪ **Linking the Motion
Sequence** 272 ▪ **Testing the Motion Sequence** 273

Chapter 30   **Jumbo Jets**   274

Creating the Jumbo Jet Link 275 ▪ **Entering the Jumbo
Jet Text** 275 ▪ **Making the Jumbo Jet Backdrop** 275 ▪
Rehearsing the Link 276 ▪ **Linking the Motion Sequence** 276 ▪
Testing the Motion Sequence 276 ▪ **Self-Assessment** 276

Part Seven *HANDS-ON TUTORIAL*
Creating an Advanced Multimedia Application   277

Chapter 31   **Designing Advanced Applications**   278

Design Paradigms 279 ▪ **Content Definition** 281 ▪
Navigational Metaphor 283 ▪ **Visualizing a Structure** 283

EXERCISES 286

Chapter 32   **Creating the Information
Superhighway Screen**   287

Entering the Text 288 ▪ **Making the Backdrop** 289 ▪ **Positioning
Text** 290 ▪ **Layering Icons** 290 ▪ **Backing Up Your Work** 291

EXERCISE 291

Chapter 33   **Defining the Internet**   292

Making Hypertext 293 ▪ **Triggering the Link** 293 ▪
Creating the Definition 293 ▪ **Default Navigation Options** 294

EXERCISES 294

Chapter 34   **Providing a Graceful Way to Exit**   295

Activating the Exit Sign 296 ▪ **Testing the Exit Sign** 296
▪ **Customizing the Navigation** 296 ▪ **Disabling the Default
Navigation** 296

EXERCISES 297

Chapter 35   **Internet Resources**   298

Linking the Submenu 299 ▪ **Creating the Internet
Services Submenu** 299 ▪ **Making Secondary Links** 300 ▪
Testing 301 ▪ **Navigating** 303

EXERCISES 303

Chapter 36   **Interesting Gopher Servers**   304

Linking to the Gopher Server Menu 305 ▪ **Adding a Server That
Interests You** 305 ▪ **Getting Connected** 306 ▪ **Domain Names** 307
▪ **Configuring Your PODIUM Gopher Connection** 307 ▪ **Using the
Internet Gopher Tool** 308 ▪ **Pasting Internet Links from the
Clipboard** 309 ▪ **Downloading Objects from the Internet** 309

EXERCISES 310

Chapter 37   **Weather Satellite Images**   311

Making the Weather Icon Hyper 312 ▪ **Using the Virtual Slide
Tray** 312 ▪ **Downloading Images from the Weather Machine** 312

EXERCISES 313

Chapter 38   **Electronic News Feed**   314

Gophering to the Electronic Newsstand 315 ▪
Testing the Electronic News Feed Connection 315

EXERCISES 317

Chapter 39   **Cable News Network
Live Video Feed**   318

Creating the Television Trigger 319 ▪ **Triggering the Video** 319
▪ **Sizing the Video** 319

EXERCISES 319

Chapter 40   **Distributing Your Multimedia Application**   320

Packaging Your Application for CD-ROM 321 ▪ **Rolling Your Own CD** 323 ▪ **Compact Disc Service Bureaus** 323 ▪ **Zipping Applications for Publication** 324 ▪ **Zipping Applications to Diskettes** 324 ▪ **Zipping Applications for the Information Superhighway** 325 ▪ **Sending Zipped Applications Through E-Mail** 326 ▪ **Distributing Zipped Applications via FTP** 327 ▪ **Marketability of Multimedia Titles** 328

EXERCISES 329

Appendix A   **PODIUM Licensing and Ordering Information**   330

Personal PODIUM   331

Retail PODIUM   332

Runtime PODIUM   333

Appendix B   **Paint Shop Pro Order Form**   334

Appendix C   **PKZIP Order Form**   335

Glossary   336

Bibliography   340

For Further Information   343

Application Software 343 ▪ **Conferences and Exhibits** 344 ▪ **Education and Training Systems** 345 ▪ **Hardware** 345 ▪ **Internet Service Providers** 345 ▪ **Multimedia and the Law** 346 ▪ **Multimedia Resources** 346 ▪ **Multimedia Titles** 346 ▪ **Networked Resources** 349 ▪ **Professional Associations** 350 ▪ **Publications: Catalogs, Journals, and Publishing Organizations** 350 ▪ **Virtual Reality** 351

Credits   352

Index   353

Introduction

As chairman of Chrysler Corporation, Lee Iacocca said, "Lead, follow, or get out of the way." So it is with multimedia. Never has an industry grown so quickly or had such an impact on the way we receive, process, and communicate ideas.

This book is designed to teach you about the world of multimedia—how multimedia is changing the world we live in, how to use it effectively, why it became a multibillion dollar industry so quickly, and the impact it will have on your way of life. This book will also teach you how to tell when someone is using multimedia, how to see through the hype, and most important, how to do it yourself—how to create your own multimedia applications and make them sizzle with effectiveness.

This book defines and teaches the basic skills of multimedia. Skills that will enable you to create beautifully typeset text, full-color pictures, animation, audio commentary, motion video clips, and stereo sound tracks. Skills that let you browse, receive, and send multimedia objects on the Information Superhighway. Skills that let you put any word or picture any place on your computer screen and make any part of the screen into a trigger that you can link to any object on your computer. When a user selects one of the triggers, the object of the link will appear. This object can be text, a picture, a sound, a movie, an animation, or an application on your computer or network.

Think about the power this provides: once you can display an object on your computer screen and link it to any other object on your computer, you have gained control over all your computer's capabilities. You can have your computer provide you with instant access to every note you ever took, every talk you ever gave, and every slide you ever photographed. You can create an effective presentation that includes instant access to all of your company's information when your boss asks you for a report. You can author a multimedia title and publish it on a CD-ROM or distribute it over the Information Superhighway. Would you like to be able to do some of these things? Then this is the book for you.

Organization

The book and its accompanying CD-ROM are built around seven main parts. The first four are conceptual, dealing with definitions, principles, applications, hardware, future trends, and social issues; the last three are tutorials, in which you learn to use multimedia application creation tools to create a simple and an advanced multimedia application. The CD-ROM brings what you read to life through color pictures, stereo sound, animation, and full-motion video clips.

Part One defines multimedia, tells you who uses it for what, describes how it is changing the world, tells you who needs to know about it, and provides a taxonomy of multimedia objects that you can use when creating your own applications.

Part Two deals with multimedia applications. Dozens of full-color screen prints and photos illustrate how multimedia is being used in classrooms, board rooms, homes, retail stores, just-in-time training, cinema, video arcades, government, and industry. The CD-ROM that comes with this book includes demonstrations of these applications that you can run on any multimedia PC under Microsoft Windows 3.1 or higher. The CD also demonstrates several of the development packages that were used to create these applications.

Part Three focuses on multimedia hardware. Remember how the VHS and Beta videotape standards competed for market share when home VCRs were invented? There are even more competing multimedia standards today; Part Three tells you what they are, recommends the one to follow, and provides a checklist of features to look for when buying a multimedia computer.

Part Four looks into the future of multimedia and discusses how it will impact us all. Acknowledging the rapid rate at which the technology is advancing, it describes how you can keep up with this fascinating field, continue to increase your multimedia skills, and help influence future uses of multimedia.

Part Five provides you with a multimedia toolkit. Step-by-step tutorials guide you through the creation of text, graphics, sound, and video using the multimedia authoring software PODIUM, which is included on the CD-ROM. You will learn how to enter text, import clip art, digitize existing pictures, create new pictures, record sound, create MIDI sequences, make CD Audio clips, edit digital video, and make videodisc clips.

Part Six teaches you how to create hypermedia, in which you link multimedia objects to make presentations and applications. Using the hypermedia application generator on the enclosed CD-ROM, you will make a simple multimedia application on the History of Flight.

Part Seven is a more advanced tutorial in which you create a multimedia application about the Information Superhighway. You will also learn how to distribute your multimedia application on CD-ROM, diskettes, and on the Information Superhighway itself.

In addition to letting you complete the tutorials, the version of the authoring software PODIUM included on the CD-ROM lets you create small applications with up to seven original screens. However, to create longer applications you will need to order a retail copy of the software. See Appendix A for ordering information.

Also included at the back of the book is a section called "For Further Information." This section contains contact information for many of the products (software, hardware, publications, and other resources) discussed in this book.

The book concludes with a glossary that defines the terms a multimedia-literate person should know. The author has coined a new term that combines the words "multimedia" and "literate" into the adjective *multiliterate*, which is what you will be when you finish this book:

> **mul-ti-lit-er-ate** \ ˌməl-ti-ˈlit-ə-rət, ˈli-trət \ *adj* : understanding the principles of multimedia, its impact on the world, and how to use it for attaining business, professional, educational, and personal objectives

Interactive CD-ROM Brings the Book to Life

The CD-ROM packaged with this book is known as the *Multiliteracy CD*. The CD is tied to each chapter in the book and includes:

- Hundreds of examples, vividly illustrated with pictures, animation, and full-motion video clips

- Demonstrations of many of the most popular commercial multimedia packages available today

- A step-by-step tutorial on how to build multimedia applications using PODIUM, which is included on the CD

- Two separate projects that allow the user to build complete, working multimedia applications on the History of Flight and the Information Superhighway

- An electronic version of the glossary, with hypermedia links to the multimedia materials that were used to present it initially

The book and the CD are designed to serve either as a course of instruction that can be used in more formal settings, or for self-study by those learning more informally. The reading level and computer skills required are appropriate for any business professional, teacher, executive, college student, marketing rep, audiovisual professional, or high school student.

- Chapter 1 illustrates how multimedia impacts everyone's way of life, with charts and graphs that show why it's to anyone's advantage to become multiliterate.

- Chapter 2 provides a taxonomy of multimedia, and the CD-ROM brings the taxonomy to life with multimedia examples in full color with stereo sound, animation, and full-motion video clips.

- Chapters 3 through 8 survey multimedia applications in business, education, entertainment, government, health, and public information. The book provides a comprehensive overview of these applications while the CD contains demonstrations of selected applications supplied by multimedia publishers. These allow you to take a product for a "test drive" and consider whether you would like to purchase a retail copy.

- Chapter 9 profiles several of the development packages that were used to create these applications. The book explains the purposes of the different packages, and the CD demonstrates their features.

One of the most important issues in multimedia is deciding what hardware to buy.

- Chapter 10 reviews the competing multimedia standards and recommends the one to follow.

- Chapter 11 presents the components of a multimedia computer.

- Chapter 12 provides a checklist that will come in handy when you buy a multimedia computer.

- Chapter 13 shows you how to configure a multimedia computer so that all of the audio and video mixing can be done by your software, without the need for an external video or audio mixer.

- The CD illustrates all of this in full color, providing a multimedia hardware presentation that can be used to present and discuss these materials in class.

The next four chapters look into the future of multimedia:

- Chapter 14 explores the multimedia frontiers of electronic publishing, fiber optic superhighways, rural datafication, and virtual reality.

- Chapter 15 reviews emerging video, voice, and datacommunication technologies and shows how they are creating a new use of multimedia called *telecomputing*.

- Chapter 16 addresses the issues raised by the impact multimedia is having on our sensibilities and moralities, questions who is in control of it, describes the problems that multimedia is causing, and suggests what you can do about them.

- Chapter 17 offers suggestions for staying abreast of new developments in this fast-paced field, and how to contribute your own ideas to its continued evolution.

- The CD contains a multimedia presentation that will not only help instructors present this material in class, but also provide individual readers with a quick online reference.

Hands-on Tutorial and Projects

The rest of the book is a hands-on tutorial you complete on your multimedia computer.

- Chapters 18 through 25 cover multimedia tools and techniques. The book provides step-by-step instructions for the tools and techniques that you will use to create beginning and advanced projects.

- The CD includes hypermedia software that lets you create these applications, along with an "answer section" that shows one correct way of completing them.

- Chapters 26 through 30 contain a project in which you will create a simple multimedia application on the History of Flight. You will use multimedia on the CD to make the aircraft come to life with full-color slides, audio clips, and full-motion video.

- In Chapters 31 through 39 you will create a more advanced application on the Information Superhighway. If your computer is not connected to the Information Superhighway, the CD will simulate its presence, allowing you to complete the tutorial as if you were online.

- The project culminates in Chapter 40, where you learn how to distribute your application on a multimedia CD, on diskettes, or on the Information Superhighway itself.

Instructor's Guide

An Instructor's Guide accompanies *Multimedia Literacy*. The guide includes strategies and teaching tips for using the text and CD in class, suggested course outlines, hints for helping students when they encounter difficulties, and a test bank.

System Requirements

The software on the *Multiliteracy CD* will run on any computer that meets or exceeds the following specifications:

- 4 megabytes of RAM
- 386SX processor
- hard disk drive with 4 megabytes of storage free
- CD-ROM drive
- 8-bit waveform audio
- 640x480 color display

In general, the faster your processor and the more RAM you have, the faster your software will run. More detailed information about multimedia hardware selection is provided in Part Three of this book.

How to Install the Software on the CD-ROM

The CD that comes with this book is known as the *Multiliteracy CD*. The software on it is very easy to install on any computer that has Windows 3.1 or higher. Simply insert the CD into your CD-ROM drive and run the install program you will find in the root directory of the CD. Here are detailed instructions that show how to perform the installation:

1. If your computer is not already running Windows, type **WIN** and press Enter.

2. From the Windows Program Manager, pull down the File menu and select Run. The Run dialog will appear.

3. In the Command Line field, you must tell your computer to run the install program from the root directory of the CD. Assuming your CD-ROM is drive *D*, here is the command to type: **D:\install**

4. Click the OK button, and a PODIUM installation dialog will appear. All of the software on the CD is accessed via PODIUM.

5. The installation dialog will ask you just one question: on what drive do you wish to install PODIUM? You should respond by typing the letter of your hard drive, which will probably be *C.*

6. The installation creates a very important directory called *wnpodium* to provide PODIUM with a read/write workspace on your hard drive.

7. When the installation is done you will find a PODIUM icon in the PODIUM group on your Windows desktop. The name of the icon is *Multimedia Literacy.* To start the CD, double-click on this icon. You will find that much of this book is available in a multimedia format on the CD. The CD is self-explanatory; go ahead and explore it.

Acknowledgments

Creating this book is one of the most exciting projects I have worked on. While researching it I made many new friends, and the brainstorming that ensued inspired new ideas and innovations.

I wish to acknowledge and thank all of my students, who continue to teach me a lot.

Carl Jacobson, Director of Management Information Services at the University of Delaware, inspired the Gopher connection in the Information Superhighway tutorial. Thanks to Carl's insight and advice, it became possible for the tutorial to take users online on the Internet in a simple yet powerful way.

University of Delaware Research Professor L. Leon Campbell provided valuable service as the author's "intelligent agent" on the Internet. Almost daily, Leon sent the author information about new media from his extensive surfing of the network. Leon is a valued friend and colleague.

Paul Evan Peters, executive director of the Coalition for Networked Information, read and commented on the section on Copyright and Fair Use of new media, as did Carol Race, Director of Instructional Technology at Northeast Missouri State University, and Susan Brynteson, Director of Libraries at the University of Delaware. I am grateful for the guidance, corrections, and citations they provided.

Pat Fox, Trident Technical College's professor of computer graphics and CD-ROM designer par excellence, made the *Multiliteracy CD* easy to use. She designed it so that users always realize where they are and how to navigate elsewhere. When you try the CD you will surely agree that Pat is an expert in making hypermedia easy to use.

As the McGraw-Hill senior multimedia editor who managed this project, Frank Ruggirello made many contributions. It was his idea to include both beginning and advanced tutorials, and he provided the resources for Pat Fox to create the *Multiliteracy CD.* Frank also worked several minor miracles to remove obstacles to this book's timely publication.

At the University of Delaware my assistant, Denise Methven, coordinated hundreds of contacts with the vendors who provided products for review and illustration. George Harding, who is one of the world's best multimedia hardware engineers, reviewed and commented on references to hardware. Pat Sine, who manages the Instructional Technology Center (ITC), read and commented on the entire document, especially the section on the Information Superhighway. ITC network administrator George Mulford, a linguist, gave the manuscript a most careful reading, and I am grateful for his many comments.

Many reviewers provided helpful suggestions, insights, and constructive criticisms of the manuscript and early versions of the CD-ROM. I would like to thank:

James Ames, Virginia Commonwealth University; Howard Baker, Ambassador College; Harvey Blessing, Essex Community College; Stephanie Chenault, The College of Charleston; Jo Elliot, Prince George's Community College; Katherine Forney, Spokane Falls Community College; Amita Goyal, Virginia Commonwealth University; Nancy Greenwood, St. Charles County Community College; Mona Hamilton, Tallahassee Community College; M. J. Patricia Harley, Howard Community College; Lynn Heinrichs, Western Carolina University; Sharon Hill, University of Maryland; Joe Howell, Gulf Coast Community College; Phyllis Kane, Prince George's Community College; Fred Klappenberger, Anne-Arundel Community College; Billy Lim, Illinois State University; John McKinney, University of Cincinnati; Pat O'Hara, New York University; Jeffrey Olson, Coastal Carolina University; Brian Scarbeau, Miami Dade Community College; Sue Zulauf, Sinclair College.

Finally, the 1994 Multimedia class of the National Computer Educator's Institute spent two weeks under the expert tutelage of Pat Fox, working with a rough draft of the manuscript and an early version of the CD-ROM. Many improvements to the text and CD resulted from their intense 12 hour-a-day sessions with the package. We will always be grateful to:

Jacqueline Artmayer, Oklahoma City Community College; Sarah Baker, Ambassador College; Howard Baker, Ambassador College; Lorene Barbee, Howard College; William Barth, Cayuga Community College; Thomas Brodnax, East Texas State University; Mary Frances Craven, Alabama Southern Community College; Mindy Davis, Panhandle State University; Sandra Dzakovic, Niagra College; Martha Gattin, Hutchinson Community College; Nancy Greenwood, St. Charles County Community College; Patricia Harley, Howard Community College; Bill Hix, Motlow State Community College; James Holden, Clarion University of Pennsylvania; Alan Johnson, Clovis Community College; Dave Krohn, Virginia State University; Albert Leary, St. Charles County Community College; Mary Jean Lush, Delta State University; Denise Porter, Phillips County Community College; Diane Satterlee, AT&T; Elynor Seck, Hutchinson Community College; Larry Slack, Medicine Hat College; Ira Snead, Spartanburg Methodist College; Sandy Stephenson, Southwest Virginia College; Lesia Strong, Oklahoma State University; Mary Trail, McLennan Community College; Gary VanMeter, Moorehead State University; Marnel Wiedemann, AT&T; Stan Wilkinson, Appalachian State University; Dick Winslow, Central Wyoming College; Mark Workman, Frank Phillips College.

Part One

Understanding Multimedia

CONTENTS

Chapter 1
Definitions

Chapter 2
Taxonomy of Multimedia Objects

People retain only 20% of what they see and 30% of what they hear. But they remember 50% of what they see and hear, and as much as 80% of what they see, hear, and do simultaneously.

—Computer Technology Research, 1993.

Multimedia is the buzzword of the decade. Like most buzzwords, it has been used in many contexts. You find it on the covers of books, magazines, CD-ROMs, video games, and movies. It is used in advertising shoes, hairstyles, drugs, cars, computers, soft drinks, beer, kitchen floors, vacations, airplanes, televisions, telephones, houses, museums, newspapers, arcades, theme parks, olympic games, and shopping malls. Sometimes the term is used to add "hype" to products that have nothing to do with multimedia. The many uses and abuses of the word "multimedia" have led to confusion over just what multimedia is. For this reason, a book on multimedia literacy must begin by defining it.

CHAPTER

1

Definitions

OBJECTIVES

After completing this chapter, you will be able to:

- **Define multimedia, describe why it is effective, and explain how it will be important to life in the twenty-first century.**

- **Demonstrate how multimedia is changing the world through telecommuting, home shopping, electronic publishing, and computer-based education.**

- **Show how fast multimedia is growing in business, industry, homes, online services, and education.**

- **Identify and define the components of a Multimedia PC.**

To define multimedia properly, one must go beyond stating what it is and put the term in context. In this chapter, you will not only get a standard "textbook" definition of multimedia, but also learn why it is important, how fast it is growing, how it is changing the world, and who needs to know about it. The term **Multimedia PC** will also be defined, along with the nomenclature needed to understand the specifications of a multimedia computer.

What Is Multimedia?

Multimedia is the use of a computer to present and combine text, graphics, audio, and video with links and tools that let the user navigate, interact, create, and communicate.

This definition contains four components essential to multimedia. First, there must be a computer to coordinate what you see and hear, and to interact with. Second, there must be links that connect the information. Third, there must be navigational tools that let you traverse the web of connected information. Finally, since multimedia is not a spectator sport, there must be ways for you to gather, process, and communicate your own information and ideas.

If one of these components is missing, you do not have multimedia. For example, if you have no computer to provide interactivity, you have mixed media, not multimedia. If there are no links to provide a sense of structure and dimension, you have a bookshelf, not multimedia. If there are no navigational tools to let you decide the course of action, you have a movie, not multimedia. If you cannot create and contribute your own ideas, you have a television, not multimedia.

Why Is It Important?

Multimedia is fast emerging as a basic skill that will be as important to life in the twenty-first century as reading is now. In fact, multimedia is changing the nature of reading itself. Instead of limiting you to the linear presentation of text as printed in books, multimedia makes reading dynamic by giving words an important new dimension. In addition to conveying meaning, words in multimedia serve as triggers that readers can use to expand the text in order to learn more about a topic. This is accomplished not only by providing more text but by bringing it to life with sound, pictures, music, and video.

The more you learn about multimedia, the more books pale by comparison. For example, suppose you read a lengthy document and want to refer back to the page on which a certain idea was mentioned. You check the index, but the topic you want is not listed. A multimedia document can be searched automatically to find any topic or combination of topics, while a printed book makes this almost impossible. In fact, a multimedia document can refer not only to information within itself, but also to all the other documents to which it has been linked, and to all the documents to which they have been linked. Multimedia uses links to let you navigate the universe of connected information at the speed of light. Comparing this global network of multimedia to our highway system that lets motorists travel almost anywhere, the U.S. government has labelled it the Information Superhighway.

Multimedia is highly effective. As Computer Technology Research (CTR) reports, people retain only 20% of what they see and 30% of what they hear. But they remember 50% of what they see *and* hear, and as much as 80% of what they see, hear, and do *simultaneously*. That is why multimedia provides such a powerful tool for teaching and learning.

Multimedia will help spread the information age to millions of people who have not yet used a computer. A Roper survey sponsored by IBM found that more than half of the survey's respondents did not want a computer that required a manual to use it (*Washington Post* 12/27/93 Business: 13). Multimedia provides the computer industry with the key to reaching this untouched market, which will cause computer use to skyrocket.

How Fast Is It Growing?

As Figures 1-1 through 1-7 illustrate, multimedia is one of the fastest growing markets in the world today. According to Dataquest, 4.8 million CD-ROM players were sold in 1993, tripling the sales of the prior year. CTR (1992) projects that multimedia computers will grow by a compound average growth rate of 82% to

1-1

Projected growth of Multimedia PCs in the U.S.

1-2

Installed base of CD-ROM drives.

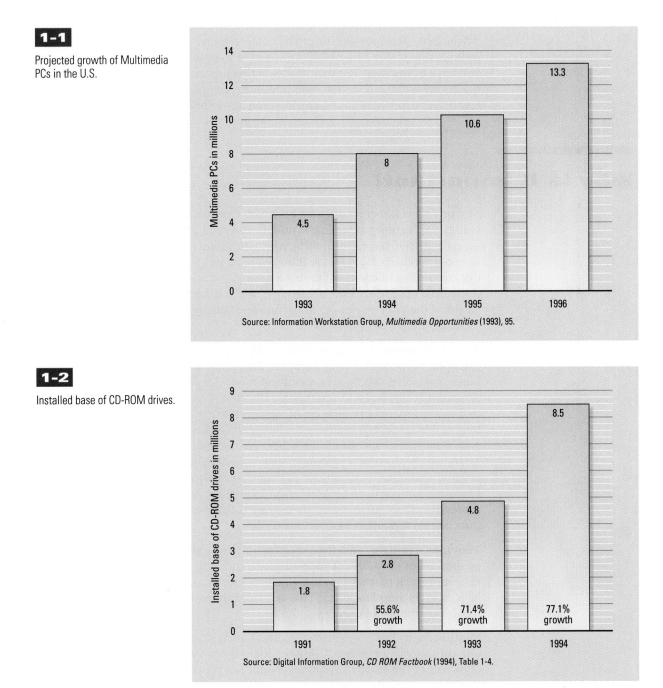

15.5 million systems in 1995. The Information Workstation Group (1993) forecasts that multimedia will be a $30 billion dollar industry by 1998: the top three applications will be entertainment ($9.1 billion), publishing ($4.7 billion), and education and training ($4.3 billion).

Fueling this growth are advances in technology (see Figure 1-8) and price wars that have dramatically lowered the cost of multimedia computers. The growing number of consumers has created a larger market for multimedia titles, and new tools are enabling more people to become developers. Noting how multimedia enables individuals to create productions that once required teams of specialists, Frost & Sullivan (1993) forecast a 50 percent growth rate for desktop video during each of the next seven years.

1-3

Projected growth of consumer videodisc players.

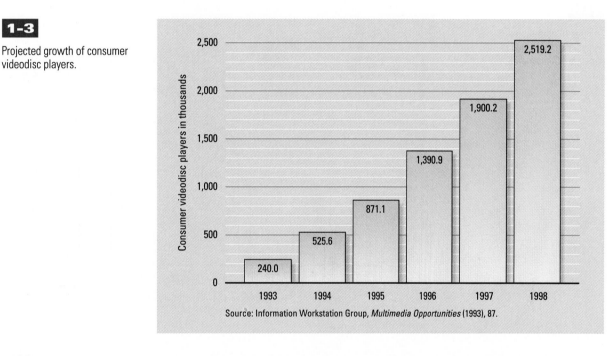

Source: Information Workstation Group, *Multimedia Opportunities* (1993), 87.

1-4

Projected growth of multimedia production services.

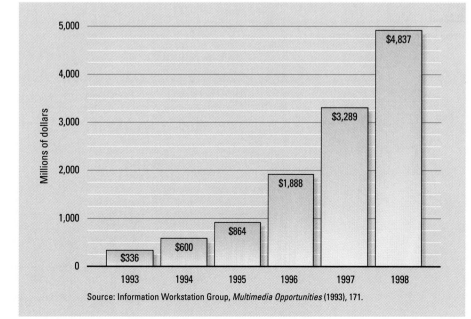

Source: Information Workstation Group, *Multimedia Opportunities* (1993), 171.

The home market for PCs is growing at a rate almost three times higher than the overall PC market. For the first time, computer electronics are growing faster than traditional consumer electronics. For example, growth in TV sales is forecast for 1994 at only 3% (down from 10% in 1993), while home computer sales are expected to grow 12%. According to Link Resources, 31% of U.S. homes had a PC in 1993, up from 26% in 1991, and 50% of homes will have PCs by 1998 (*Business Week* 11/22/93: 99).

Online multimedia services are booming. The number of subscribers jumped more than 28% in 1993, to four million. Forrester Research predicts that the service market will grow from its current size of $530 million in 1994 to $3 billion by 1998. Because only 13% of the 31 million home PC owners currently belong to a service,

Number of educational videodiscs catalogued in the *Videodisc Compendium*.

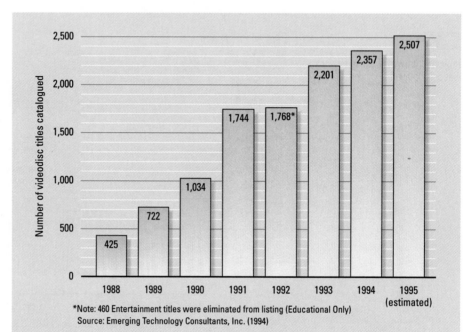

*Note: 460 Entertainment titles were eliminated from listing (Educational Only)
Source: Emerging Technology Consultants, Inc. (1994)

Home networks and integration.

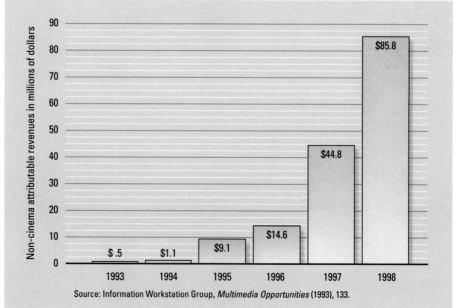

Source: Information Workstation Group, *Multimedia Opportunities* (1993), 133.

there is plenty of room for growth. And grow it will: Bell Atlantic has announced plans to serve multimedia to more than 8 million homes by the end of the decade (*Wall Street Journal* 12/2/93: B12).

1-7

Video conferencing services forecast.

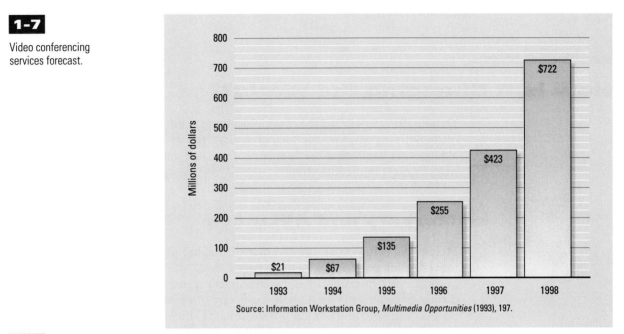

Source: Information Workstation Group, *Multimedia Opportunities* (1993), 197.

1-8

Intel's iCOMP index for i386 SX-20 through Pentium 66 processors. For comparison purposes, the i486 SX/25 is assigned a value of 100.

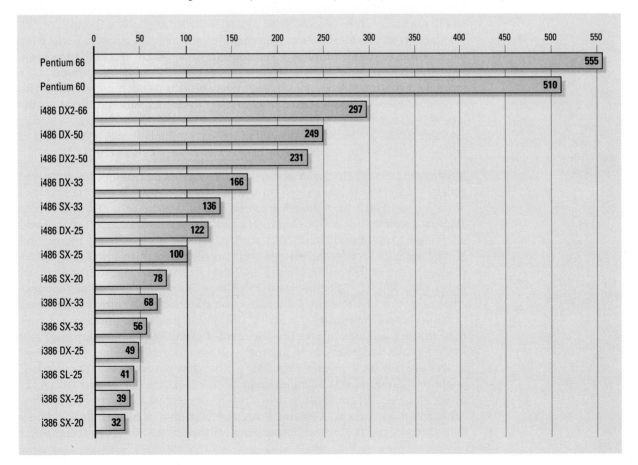

Educational use of multimedia is also skyrocketing. According to the Software Publishers Association, U.S. K-12 schools spent $2.1 billion on PC technology in 1993, a rise of 20% from the year before. Figure 1-5 shows how the number of educational videodiscs catalogued in the *Videodisc Compendium* grew from 425 in 1988 to 2,357 in 1994.

How Is It Changing the World?

Multimedia is redefining the communication system that forms a significant part of the infrastructure of our society. A large number of corporate mergers and alliances are combining the telephone, television, and personal computer into a mass market multimedia utility.

Mergers and Alliances

Multimedia is fueling an unprecedented number of mergers among companies jockeying for position in this fast-paced field. MCI and Jones Intercable have joined in a partnership to allow consumers to use cable TV for long-distance dialing, bypassing the local phone company (*Atlanta Constitution* 11/23/93: E3). Southwestern Bell and Cox Cable have formed a similar multibillion dollar alliance, and US West has partnered with Time Warner. Ameritech, the regional Bell company serving the midwestern United States, is spending $4.4 billion for video servers and fiber optic lines that will provide 1,000 channels of carrying capacity. Internet provider Performance Systems International (PSI) of Herndon, Virginia, and Continental Cablevision of New England in Portsmouth, New Hampshire, will offer access to the Information Superhighway through the standard television cable system in the Cambridge, Massachusetts area. Oracle and Bell Atlantic are providing interactive TV service in the Washington DC area. Oracle's database technology controls video servers that simultaneously transmit hundreds of movies to residential customers. Called Stargazer, the Oracle/Bell Atlantic alliance is the largest interactive video trial to date. Stargazer is expected to be commercially available to 250,000 homes by the end of 1994, 1.2 million homes in 1995, and 10 million households by the end of the century (*New York Times* 1/10/94: C4).

Multimedia alliances are not limited to the United States. Bell Atlantic has partnered with Italy's Stet SpA to bring video-on-demand services to the Italian market (*Wall Street Journal* 11/18/93: A16). US West has a joint venture with EDS and France Telecom Intelmatique to develop interactive financial transaction services and offer home banking and bill delivery services via modem, touchtone phone, and Minitel systems. Oracle has teamed with British Telecom to bring multimedia services to the British public (*New York Times* 3/3/94: C4). Microsoft has joined forces with Nippon Telegraph and Telephone Corporation to allow Japanese customers to receive multimedia services over telephone and computer networks (*Atlanta Journal-Constitution* 3/24/94: D3). Bell Canada has purchased a one-third interest in Jones Intercable. The Stentor group of phone companies and Kodak Canada have announced that they will form a strategic alliance to transmit images digitally via local-area networks, private data networks, and the switched public telephone network (*Toronto Globe & Mail* 12/03/93: B2; *Ottawa Citizen* 12/04/93: F8). The UBI consortium (Universal Bi-directional Interactive) of Quebec cable giant Videotron, Canada Post, the National Bank, Hydro-Quebec, Loto-Quebec, and the Hearst Corporation will launch a $750-million, eight-year project on Canada's first home electronic superhighway. With no hardware charge to consumers (charging only for services used), the first phase is to be in place early in 1995 and will offer direct-debit home shopping and banking, e-mail, advertising flyers, coupons, and tutoring (*Toronto Financial Post* 1/25/94: 1).

Telecommuting

Multimedia is also changing our place of work. According to a Deloitte & Touche report, telecommuting (working from home using computers, modems, and fax machines) accounted for 45% of all new jobs from 1987 to 1992 (*Atlanta Constitution* 1/2/94: E2). 1993 saw one million more people telecommute than during the year before, marking a 15% increase in company employees who work at home during normal business hours. According to a recent survey of more than 100 companies nationwide by Home Office Computing, 30% had some type of telecommuting program in place (*Miami Herald* 12/13/93: 24). A survey by Work/Family Directions found that 20% to 40% of employees would like to telecommute (*Wall Street Journal* 12/14/93: B1). The California earthquakes made many new converts to telecommuting, given the significant long-term damage to traffic routes around Los Angeles (*Investor's Business Daily* 1/27/94: 4). In addition to reducing traffic congestion, an Arthur D. Little study points out how telecommuting can cut pollution. For example, a 10-20% reduction in trips would save 3.5 billion gallons of gas yearly (*Atlanta Constitution* 12/2/93: A19). Telecommuting has also had an impact on the clothing industry, causing suit sales to plummet as more people work from home (*St. Petersburg Times* 1/3/94: 19).

Home Shopping

Multimedia is changing how the world shops. Instead of wearing yourself out trekking from store to store trying to find the size and style you like and then having to wait in line to pay for it, teleshopping services let you shop from home. A Yankelovich Partners survey found that 60% of respondents have tried either online or television shopping. Most cited convenient hours and a secure environment as the reasons they liked the service. Electronic home shopping sales have surged to more than $3 billion annually and are forecast to rise to anywhere from $30 billion to $250 billion in the next ten years (*Miami Herald* 1/18/94: C1). Market Vision (1993) predicts that by 1997 home shopping will comprise 62% of retail sales.

Electronic Publishing

Multimedia is changing how we read newspapers by eliminating the need for the paper and offering all the features of multimedia, including full-text search, graphics, audio, and video. For example, *ClariNews*, an electronic newspaper offered by ClariNet, uses MIME (Multipurpose Internet Mail Extensions) to deliver not only text, but also graphics, audio, and video. Read by more than 40,000 users worldwide, *ClariNews* offers world and national news, sports, financial news, stock quotations, and weather information. It also offers *Newsbytes*, a daily computer industry magazine, and syndicated columnists including Dave Barry and Mike Royko.

Dow Jones publishes an electronic version of its flagship *Wall Street Journal* and also offers an online service called *Personal Journal* that delivers selected stories based on customer demand (*Miami Herald* 12/9/93: C3). Imagine what a time-saver this is. Suppose you are an educator and you want the latest news in education, but you have little interest in sports. Instead of having a newspaper delivered that is 2% education and 40% sports, you get a news feed of all the educational articles from all of the "papers." Executives at Mercury Center, the electronic extension of the *San Jose Mercury News,* predict that reader loyalty will increase because electronic publishing gives a newspaper the tools to focus on small parts of the market, offering topics that may not interest a general audience (*New York Times* 2/7/94: C1).

USA Today, the *Washington Post,* the *New York Times,* and the *Los Angeles Times* are all available online. Their publisher, American Cybercasting Corporation, is developing teacher guides that coordinate these electronic newspapers into school curricula. Contact the American Cybercasting Corporation for detailed information.

According to The Kelsey Group, more than 2,700 newspapers are experimenting with electronic ventures, compared to only 42 in 1989; contributing to the need for these experiments is the fact that half of young people aged 18 to 24 do not read newspapers at all (*U.S.News & World Report* 5/16/94: 60).

Teaching and Learning

Electronic publishing is not the only way multimedia is changing how we teach and learn. Eiser (1992) describes how multimedia has proven so effective in education that the states of California and Texas have adopted videodiscs instead of textbooks, investing former textbook budgets in multimedia technology instead. After studying hundreds of controlled experiments in which computers were used in college and high school courses, elementary education, and adult high-school equivalency programs, Kulik (1985, 1986, 1991, and 1994) reports overall learning gains averaging more than a letter grade higher (effect size = .32), and significant reductions in the time required for students to learn (averaging 34% in college and 24% in adult education). Part Two of this book will survey some of these applications.

Mass Market Use of Information Services

The most strategic use of multimedia may be to help bring the public into the information age. In a society that depends so much on processing information, what could be more important? Multimedia relieves information overload and techno stress by engaging more of the senses. If one medium is not getting the message across, multimedia will engage more of the senses to make the communication more effective. Multimedia makes user interfaces easier, thereby providing much wider access to information services and making the whole market grow exponentially. This is why *Fortune Magazine* (2/21/94: 101) quotes Microsoft chairman Bill Gates' prediction that by the end of the decade, most of his company's revenues will come from home sales. When this book went to press, less than 4% of Microsoft sales were home-based. Imagine how different the information society will be when more than half of its computing is done from home instead of at work or school.

Who Needs to Know About It?

Ask yourself a few historical questions:

- Who needed to know how to read books after the printing press was invented?

- Who needed to know how to drive cars after highways where built?

- Who needed to know how to call someone when telephones were invented?

Now ask:

- Who needs to know how to use a multimedia computer to access the Information Superhighway?

Anyone who plans to learn, teach, work, play, govern, serve, buy, or sell in the information society needs to know about multimedia. Just imagine the consequences of not knowing about it. For example, suppose you are a journalist who cannot create a hypermedia document and transmit it across a network; how long do you think you will be employable? What about paramedics who cannot upload a picture of a wound and get expert advice on how to treat it? Or architects and designers who cannot use computers to simulate and troubleshoot products before they are built? Or merchandisers who do not know how to advertise products on the network? Or teachers who cannot use multimedia to bring their classrooms to life? Or businessmen who cannot access corporate data when it is needed to make the right decision? Or governments without the technology needed to detect and deter aggression?

To state the need succinctly: Everyone who plans to function productively in twenty-first century society needs to know about multimedia.

What Is a Multimedia PC?

In 1991, the Multimedia PC Marketing Council announced the Multimedia PC (MPC) standard. It defined the minimum hardware requirements for multimedia. Critics felt the MPC specification was not powerful enough. In the meantime, technological advances and price decreases enabled people to afford more powerful computers. In 1993, the Council established the Multimedia PC Level 2 specification, MPC2, which requires a more robust setup.

Table 1-1 compares the MPC and MPC2 specifications. In order to understand them, some terms need to be defined.

RAM and MB

RAM stands for Random Access Memory; it is the main memory at the heart of your computer in which multimedia programs execute. RAM is measured in megabytes (MB). Mega means a million, and byte is the unit of measure for computer memory. A byte can hold a single character, and a megabyte can hold a million characters. While some programs can run in smaller amounts of RAM, anyone serious about multimedia should have at least 8 MB.

640x480

If you look closely, you will see how your computer screen makes pictures by turning little dots on and off. **640x480** refers to this grid of dots, meaning that there are 640 dots across and 480 dots down the screen.

Pixels and Megapixels

The little dots on your screen are more properly referred to as pixels; the term **pixel** stands for picture element. **Megapixel** means a million pixels.

64 KB Buffer

KB stands for kilobyte, which means a thousand bytes. The **64 KB buffer** in the MPC specification is used to speed access to data coming off your CD-ROM. The buffer works like a staging area where data from the CD-ROM gets held until your computer needs it. Your computer can access data much more quickly from the buffer than from the CD-ROM.

Bandwidth

Bandwidth refers to the total amount of data that can be transferred in a given amount of time. The more bandwidth you have, the more data can be transferred.

E X E R C I S E S

1. Give examples of how multimedia has affected (a) the nation as a whole, (b) your local community, and (c) your personal life.

2. In your chosen career or profession, would telecommuting be appropriate? How would it help or hinder your work?

3. This chapter described how multimedia is changing the world through mergers and alliances, telecommuting, home shopping, electronic publishing, and computer-based learning. How else do you see multimedia changing the world?

4. Compare the advantages and disadvantages of home shopping as you see them. What impact will home shopping have on traditional stores and shopping malls?

5. Think of an example showing how a computer helped you learn something. What was the subject matter? What role did the computer play? Did you learn better because of the computer? Why or why not?

6. Of all the different kinds of occupations you can think of, which ones need multimedia the most? The least? What is your chosen occupation? Why will you need to know about multimedia to do well in your line of work?

7. The MPC is an evolving standard. In this chapter, you saw how the original MPC standard evolved into the MPC2 standard. What new features and capabilities do you think future MPC standards will include?

8. Rate your own computer or the one you use at school on the basis of the MPC standards provided in Table 1-1. In what ways does your computer surpass the standards? How does it need to be upgraded to meet the standards?

Taxonomy of Multimedia Objects

O B J E C T I V E S

After completing this chapter, you will be able to:

- **Define and recognize linked objects in a multimedia application.**

- **Understand the present-day limits of creating those objects.**

- **Think about what new kinds of objects there may be in the future as multimedia technology progresses.**

- **Consider whether the digitization of media is making communication better or worse, and to understand the appropriate role of technology.**

The definition of multimedia in the last chapter emphasized the important role that links play in giving users a way to interact and navigate. This chapter defines the objects of those links by providing a taxonomy of multimedia. There are four kinds of objects: text, graphics, sound, and video. The roles each kind plays in a multimedia system are described here.

Text

While it is possible to have multimedia without text, most multimedia systems use text because it is such an effective way to communicate ideas and provide instructions to users. There are four kinds of text.

Printed Text

Printed text, like the words in this paragraph, appears on paper. Suppose you want to use a printed text as the basis for a multimedia document. In order for a multimedia computer to read printed text, you need to transform the text into machine-readable form. The most obvious way to do this is to type the text into a word processor or text editor, but that is tedious and time-consuming. A faster way would be to scan the text.

Scanned Text

Low-cost scanners that can read printed texts and convert them into machine-readable form are widely available. There are two kinds of scanners: flatbed and hand-held. Flatbed scanners are more expensive because of the motors and pulleys that move the scanner over the paper. Hand-held scanners cost less because you move the scanner over the paper manually, thereby avoiding the cost of the flatbed enclosure and mechanism. Advances in the optical character recognition (OCR) software that comes with scanners have increased their accuracy.

For example, consider the newspaper article in Figure 2-1. Figure 2-2 shows it being scanned by the Caere Corporation's hand-held scanner, The Typist. You can see the results of the scan in Figure 2-3. Notice how a couple of characters have a ^ mark in front of them. The Caere software marks characters with a ^ when it is not sure whether it has accurately recognized them. However, if you compare Figure 2-3 to the original text in Figure 2-1, you will see that every character is correct.

The author used The Typist hand scanner extensively while writing this book. Instead of typing quotes from books and magazines, the author simply swiped the hand scanner over the quotes and flowed the scanned text into this document.

Electronic Text

A tremendous number of texts are available in machine-readable form because almost everyone who writes books or publishes manuscripts today does so with word processing and electronic publishing equipment. Because they can be read by a computer and transmitted electronically over networks, these texts are referred to as electronic texts. For example, this book was written with the WordPerfect word processor. In addition to being printed on the paper you are reading now, this book can also be used in its electronic form as the basis for multimedia documents. In fact, as you have already seen, large parts of it have been included on the CD enclosed with this book.

Electronic text was also used extensively in writing this book. Internet news feeds and other networked resources provided a rich store of information that would

A newspaper article from *USA TODAY*. Copyright 1994, USA TODAY. Reprinted with permission.

The newspaper article being scanned with a hand-held scanner.

USA TODAY · FRIDAY, JULY 1, 1994 · 9B

IDYEAR

Top trend so far: More big mergers

Deals have made a roaring comeback on Wall Street. Thursday alone, Nynex and Bell Atlantic said they'd merge their cellular phone operations; Burlington Northern and Santa Fe Pacific are teaming up in a $2.7 billion deal; and CBS says it's talking to QVC about a merger *(stories, 1B, 2B, 3B)*. The total value of mergers and acquisitions announced this year has ballooned to $117.7 billion compared with $99 billion the first half of last year. If the pace keeps up, 1994 could be the biggest year for M&A since 1989, the peak of the 1980s merger frenzy.

Why is M&A activity so hot? Strategic moves are behind the flurry of deals, analysts say. Companies are trying to add to market share or cut costs by selling a division or teaming up with a competitor. And interest rates, though rising, are still relatively low. That makes it cheap for companies to borrow for deals.

"We'll see a tremendous amount of activity the second half of the year," says Martin Sikora, editor of *Mergers & Acquisitions* magazine. The biggest deals have been in defense, health care, banking and telecommunications industries. Activity also has been hot in areas such as computer software, auto parts, business services and environmental companies.

Megadeals of '94
Biggest deals announced so far this year:

Buyer	Target	Price (billions)
Viacom	Blockbuster	$7.9
Roche Holding	Syntex	$5.3
Sandoz	Gerber	$3.7
Burlington Northern	Santa Fe Pacific	$2.7
Conseco	Kemper	$2.7

Source: *Mergers & Acquisitions*, USA TODAY research

The results of the scan. The ^ marks characters about which the scanner was unsure.

```
Notepad - MERGERS.TXT
File   Edit   Search   Help

Top trend so far:
More big mergers

Deals have made a roaring comeback on Wall Street. Thursday
alone, Nynex and Bell Atlantic said they'd merge their cellular
^phone operations; Burlington Northern and Santa Fe Pacific are
teaming up in a $2.7 billion deal; and CBS says it's talking to QVC
about a merger (stories, 1B, 2B, 3B). The total value of mergers
and acquisitions announced this year has ballooned to $117.7 bil-
lion compared with $99 billion the first half of last year. If the
pace keeps up, 1994 could be the biggest year for M&A since 1989,
the peak of the 1980s merger frenzy.

Why is M^&A activity so hot? Strategic moves are behind the
flurry of deals, analysts say. Companies are trying to add to mar-
ket share or cut costs by selling a division or teaming up with a
competitor. And interest rates, though rising, are still relatively
low. That makes it cheap for companies to borrow for deals.

"We'll see a tremendous amount of activity the second half of
the year," says Martin Sikora, editor of Mergers & Acquisitions
magazine. The biggest deals have been in defense, health care,
banking and telecommunications industries. Activity also has
been hot in areas such as computer software, auto parts, business
services and environmental companies.
```

otherwise have taken years to research. You will learn how to access this information later in the Information Superhighway tutorial.

Hypertext

The prefix "hyper" may be the most important word in this book, because it refers to the process of linking, which makes multimedia interactive. Hypertext is a word coined by Ted Nelson (1965). It refers to text that has been linked. When you view hypertext and click a word that has been linked, your computer launches the object of that link. Any one of the objects listed in this taxonomy of multimedia can be the object of such a link. The links give the text an added dimension, which is why it is called hyper.

To experience the power of hypertext, use the *Multiliteracy CD* to view this taxonomy as a hypertext. To do this, go to the Demonstrations section, select Textbook Examples, and click the Hypertext button. Notice how you can click the headings and subheadings to reveal more text, and even click individual words of the text to view figures and graphs. Imagine what it would be like if this entire book were available in such a form. Perhaps someday, when CD-ROMs become more popular than books, it will be.

Graphics

It has often been said that a picture is worth a thousand words. However, that is true only when you can show the picture you want when you need it. Multimedia lets you do this when graphics are the object of a link. Graphics often appear as backdrops behind text to create a pictorial framework for the text. Pictures can also serve as icons, intermixed with text, representing options that can be selected, or they can appear full-screen in place of text, with parts of the picture serving as triggers which, when selected, launch other multimedia objects or events.

Bitmaps

A bitmap is a picture stored as a set of pixels that correspond to the grid of dots on a computer screen. To display the picture, your computer sets each dot on the screen to the color specified for it in the bitmap. You can create bitmaps with any graphics editor, such as the Paintbrush program that comes free with Windows, or commercial drawing programs such as CorelDRAW! In the section on multimedia tools, you will learn how to capture into a bitmap any graphic displayed on your computer screen from any software program, including frames from live video feeds.

Clip Art

Creating graphics by hand is time consuming. To save time, there are extensive libraries of clip art that you can use in multimedia productions. After you purchase a clip art library, you can usually use the images in it royalty free, but make sure you read the license carefully because restrictions may apply.

The *Multiliteracy CD* that comes with this book contains bitmaps from several commercial clip art libraries. Their publishers provided these samples in return for our advertising their clip art libraries in this book. You can inspect these libraries by going to the Demonstrations section, selecting Textbook Examples, and clicking the Clip Art button.

The clip art library *Creative Backgrounds and Textures* (see Figure 2-4) contains 200 photographs of sunsets, skylines, bridges, and deserts plus various textures including brushed metal, broken tile, cliff face, and fiberglass. It is available from Gazelle Technologies on two Kodak Photo CDs. Figure 2-5 shows how Kodak's

The Creative Backgrounds and Textures CD-ROM.

The Kodak Photo CD Viewer lets you browse images on the *Creative Backgrounds and Textures* CD-ROM.

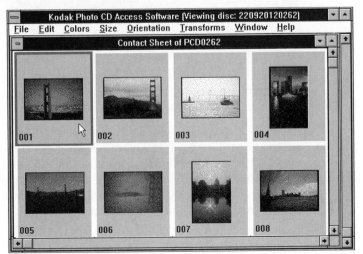

A photo from *Creative Backgrounds and Textures.*

A more abstract graphic from *Creative Backgrounds and Textures.*

Photo CD Viewer lets you view color thumbnails of every image, search by keyword, display color blow-ups (as shown in Figure 2-6 and Figure 2-7), or copy the photos directly to your hard drive.

Pixar One Twenty-Eight is a clip art library of 128 high-quality photographic textures on the CD-ROM shown in Figure 2-8. Pixar developed them for use in its own signature images and films. The textures include bricks, woods, metals, ground covers, animal skins, stones, sidings, fabrics, and roofs. As Figures 2-9 through 2-11 demonstrate, the textures are beautifully photographed and use a patented Pixar tiling technology that allows them to be combined seamlessly. A Windows program called Textile comes on the Pixar CD-ROM. Textile lets you seamlessly tile images into an area of any size. The Pixar CD also includes a tiling plug-in for

The *Pixar One Twenty-Eight*
CD-ROM.

Some of the textures on the
Pixar One Twenty-Eight
CD-ROM.

2-10

"Today's Menu" uses rattan for the background and figured mahogany for the masthead. Created by Pixar with *Pixar One Twenty-Eight.*

2-11

The Winter Garden book cover uses ivy as the background and railroad tie ends as the base. Created by Pixar with *Pixar One Twenty-Eight.*

the popular Photoshop graphics editor. The images are stored in TIFF format in 24-bit and 8-bit color. *Pixar One Twenty-Eight* is published by Pixar.

Aris Entertainment publishes a series of clip art and sound called *MediaClips* (see Figure 2-12). *MediaClips: Business Backgrounds* is a CD-ROM full of images, audio tracks and sound effects. *MediaClips: Money, Money, Money* contains images of international coins and currency and videos of money hot off the press. *MediaClips: Jets & Props* is a two-disc set of images of civilian and military aircraft, with rock sound tracks to complement jets and music with a foreign flair to accompany the props. Several pictures from *Jets & Props* are used in the History of Flight tutorial in Part Six of this book, courtesy of Aris Entertainment. *MediaClips: World View* contains 100 photos of the world from above as well as images from NASA space explorations, plus 100 sound tracks of new age piano music. *MediaClips: Majestic Places* contains photographs of many of the world's most spectacular vistas, including Mt. Everest and Mt. McKinley, with original contemporary music. *MediaClips: Wild Places* has stunning photographs of deserts, rocks, forests, and seascapes, with music composed to fit each picture. *MediaClips: Island Designs* includes vintage aloha and batik designs as well as playful and rare antique Hawaiian shirt patterns from the 1930's through the 1950's teamed with 100 sound tracks of early Hawaiian music. *MediaClips: Full Bloom* contains a variety of floral images, accompanied by piano audio clips. *MediaClips: Americana* features American scenes, from the purple mountains to the plains, and from big cities to small towns. *MediaClips: Animal Kingdom* features prides and gaggles, flocks and herds. *MediaClips: New York, NY* features the sights and sounds of the Big Apple, from the subways to the World Trade Center.

Collage of clip art from
MediaClips.

Digitized Pictures

Video digitizing boards let you connect a video camera, VCR, videodisc player, or live video feed to your computer and grab frames instantly into bitmaps that can be used in multimedia applications. Think of the pictorial breadth this technology provides: since video digitizers accept a video signal as input, they can digitize anything a video camera can see. Therefore, anything you can point a video camera at can become a bitmap for use in your multimedia production.

Thus, there is no limit to the visuals you can use in your multimedia application. Any photograph, slide, or picture from any book or magazine can be digitized in full color and linked into your multimedia application.

Hyperpictures

Just as words can serve as triggers in a hypertext, so also can parts of pictures. When parts of pictures are used to trigger multimedia events, they are called hyperpictures.

Figure 2-13 shows an example of a hyperpicture that you will find on the *Multiliteracy CD.* Try the hyperpicture now by going to the Demonstrations section, selecting Textbook Examples, and clicking the Hyperpictures button. Notice how the cursor changes shape as you move the mouse over a hot spot on the hyperpicture. Click the hot spots to trigger the linked objects.

As you will see when you learn how to make hyperpictures in the multimedia tools part of this book, there is virtually no limit to the number of triggers you can put on a hyperpicture.

3-7

Calibrating rectifier meters in AT&T's Regen Hut application.

3-8

Preparing for the discharge test in AT&T's Regen Hut application.

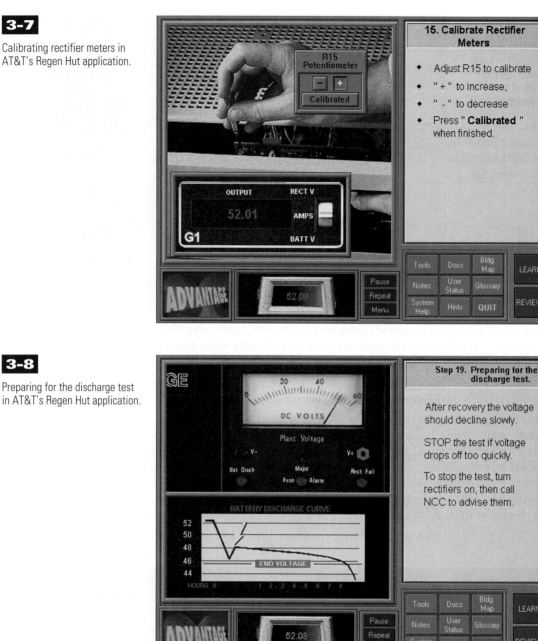

learning objectives. This mastery learning strategy has saved AT&T considerable costs by no longer requiring the company to fly 2,000 technicians to corporate headquarters for training.

Large libraries of multimedia training materials are available. For example, the Industrial Training Corporation publishes the ACTIV training system shown in Figure 3-9. ACTIV titles include lesson material on air compressor repair, electric motors, eye and face protection, forklift safety, hazardous waste, industrial hydraulic power, industrial lubrication, industrial pneumatic power, mechanical seals, pipefitting, respiratory protection, and valve repair. The Instrument Society of America publishes a series of interactive videodisc titles covering analyzers, control valves, digital instrumentation, electronic maintenance, industrial measurement, process control calibration, control safety, pneumatic maintenance,

The ACTIV training system.

and troubleshooting. Interactive Media Communications publishes an interactive videodisc *The Laboratory Safety Training Program.* It helps meet training requirements mandated by the OSHA Laboratory Standard "Occupational Exposure to Hazardous Chemicals in Laboratories."

Just-In-Time Training

Instruction called just-in-time training is required when something goes wrong and a worker must find out how to handle it quickly. Corporate downsizing has greatly increased the need for just-in-time training. With fewer employees on staff, chances are greater that a given worker will not know how to deal with a situation that specialists might have handled before losing their jobs due to downsizing. Explaining why training budgets are expected to increase tenfold by 1996, Tynan (1993) tells how rightsizing piles new responsibilities onto existing staff and requires hiring temporary staff that need just-in-time training. For example, CTR (page 57) reports on how Owens-Corning Fiberglass uses an interactive multimedia system to help factory workers diagnose and fix production line problems. After the computer performs the diagnosis based on input from workers, appropriate video sequences with instructional commentary show the workers how to correct the problem.

The Electric Power Research Institute has developed a similar system called Sa. Vant. Users describe problems in power plant turbines through the keyboard or a microphone, and Sa. Vant troubleshoots them, providing a diagnosis, associated wiring diagrams, photographs, and videos showing users how to fix the problem.

IBM claims an $800,000 annual savings from a just-in-time training system that guides employees step-by-step through factory processes at its Poughkeepsie, New York assembly plant. And Tynan (1993) reports that Xerox has a Generic Fault Analysis course that features schematic diagrams. "Trainees move an electronic version of a multimeter—a diagnostic tool that measures ohms and amperage—to different parts of the schematic, which then displays typical readings." He further reports how Alyeska, which operates the trans-Alaska pipeline, uses multimedia to prepare workers for dealing with emergencies such as leaks or fires so they know what valves to open or close, and what alarms to sound.

Pilot Training

Every major airline is using multimedia for pilot training. It saves costs by making pilot training more efficient and reducing the amount of time pilots spend in expensive flight simulators. CTR (page 65) notes how SAS Airlines used multimedia to reduce the time needed to train pilots by 35%. The SAS flight training system includes images of cockpit instrumentation, computer-generated instrument readings, and digitized audio clips that let pilots practice flight procedures before training on full-scale flight simulators.

Advertising and Electronic Brochures

The more you engage a potential customer with an advertisement, the greater the chance of making a sale. That is why multimedia provides such an effective way of advertising. Explaining why other forms of advertising are passive, Goldstein and Wittenstein (1993) note, "With multimedia, users have the ability to actively participate in the way they learn and make decisions. They can design their own car package, get company history, view customer's testimonials or celebrity endorsements, explore a piece of equipment, stopping at any point to receive related branching information, or navigate to any part of the presentation easily and logically."

The electronic brochure is a promotional and marketing tool that usually consists of a single diskette or CD-ROM sent to targeted audiences. General Motors, Ford, Chrysler, General Electronic, and Corning Glassware have marketed products this way. While the Direct Marketing Association considers a 1% return successful with paper brochures, electronic brochures draw a 12% response. CTR (page 50) reports how a followup survey by the Netherlands Foreign Investment Agency to 10,000 CD-ROMs they distributed (encouraging companies to locate in Holland) in anticipation of Europe 1992 indicated that 85% of the recipients looked at the CD. Paper direct mail examination on the other hand typically ranges from 2% to 4%.

Chrysler Corporation made an electronic brochure entitled *The Jeep and Eagle Adventure* (see Figure 3-10). It is distributed on diskette and costs $6.95. The disk has seven main parts: Models, Motion, Capability, Environment, Safety, Specs, and Pricing Option. Waltz (1993) describes the heart of the disk as "... an interactive price worksheet that calculates total cost and monthly payments—taking trade-ins, rebates and interest rates into account." Figures 3-11 through 3-13 show that the Chrysler disk comes with a wildlife photography adventure game called PhotoQuest. The user must locate a specific animal and snap its picture with enough time remaining to get back home. Chrysler included the game to encourage people to share the CD with friends; it also provides new ways to show off the cars'

3-10

The main menu of The Jeep and Eagle Adventure, a promotional electronic brochure from Chrysler Corporation.

3-11

The Jeep and Eagle Adventure includes the interactive game PhotoQuest in which players are given a photo assignment which requires driving to remote locations to find and photograph specific animals.

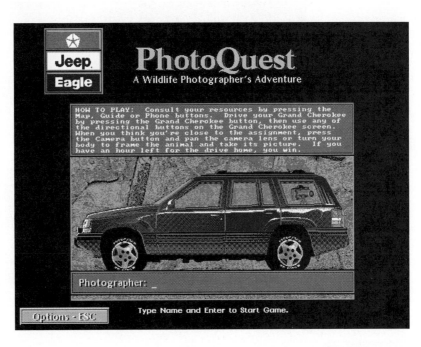

features. For example, there are places where the game advises the player to switch into four-wheel drive. The Demonstrations section of the *Multiliteracy CD* contains a demo of the Chrysler disk. You can try it by selecting Applications, then clicking the Jeep/Eagle button.

Corporations are also beginning to offer shareholders annual reports on CD-ROM. An executive at Oracle Corporation notes "The magic of CD-ROM is that you can make a little show of it" (*New York Times* 3/5/94: 21).

3-12

You, the player, get clues from a guide and a phone. You then use the map to navigate a Grand Cherokee to where the animal was last sighted. Once you find the animal, snap a photograph with the "camera" and complete the game.

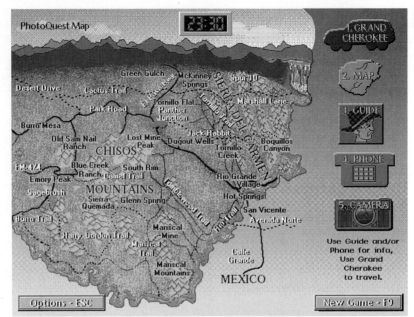

3-13

The player uses the directional buttons at the bottom of the screen to "drive" a Grand Cherokee to various locations.

Mass Market Applications

Multimedia is wide open for entrepreneurs who can make a lot of money dreaming up ways to use it in mass market applications. For example, nearly everyone is concerned about their appearance, and choosing hairstyles has mass market appeal. Figure 3-14 shows how New Image Industries has made clever use of multimedia to help you decide what hairstyle suits you best. They use a multimedia computer with a video capture board and a camera to digitize your head onto the computer screen. Then the operator uses the digitizing tablet and stylus pen shown in Figure 3-15 to remove your hair. The system proceeds to put other hairstyles on your head to show what you would look like in different

3-14

A Styles-On-Video system in action in a hair salon.

3-15

The Styles-On-Video system consists of a multimedia computer with video camera, digital video capture board, VCR, pen, and digitizing tablet.

fashions and hair colors, as shown in Figure 3–16. It creates a videotape that you can study privately or show friends to get their opinion on which style you should choose. According to the vendor, Styles-On-Video is the breakthrough business opportunity of the 90's.

Another mass market application has been developed by Mannington Resilient Floors. Coordinating floor colors with wall coverings, furniture, appliances, and cabinetry challenges every home maker. Mannington has created a touch-screen system that shows how vinyl flooring samples will look in rooms like yours (see Figures 3-17 and 3-18). You can choose a room that looks like yours from a photo library, and then change colors and flooring patterns to see what suits you best. According to CTR (page 51), "The system automatically performs market research, tabulating how many customers were looking at each color and pattern of flooring.

Styles-On-Video lets you explore your hairstyle fantasies.

The main menu from The Mannington Premiere Flooring Theatre.

It also includes a sales training program for teaching new employees techniques of the trade."

Any tennis player knows how much having the right size racket and grip affects your performance. CTR tells how the Racket Selector Company developed an interactive multimedia expert advisor to help customers choose a tennis racket

The user can see flooring selections in Mannington's gold, silver, or bronze product series.

that best fits their grip. After analyzing customer responses to ten questions, the system recommends and demonstrates five different racket models from a database of more than 100 rackets from all manufacturers.

EXERCISES

1. Have you ever used a point-of-sale kiosk? Where? Did it have multimedia? Compare the way it functioned to traditional shopping; did the kiosk complement, replace, or make traditional shopping unnecessary?

2. Find a point-of-sale kiosk in your local community. Describe its look and feel. Observe people using it and describe any problems or advantages you observe.

3. What are the obstacles to digital video replacing the VCR as the primary means of distributing video recordings? If your home has access to a digital video service, how has it impacted the use of your VCR? Do you rent more or fewer videotapes from your local video store? Why?

4. Visit your local Kinko's and ask to see their videoconferencing facilities. Do you think this will become a viable business at Kinko's? For whom and for what purpose? Would you use it in your line of work, or for personal things? Why?

5. Visit a local realtor and find out whether they use multimedia to sell homes. If so, ask what is the benefit; if not, find out why they do not use multimedia.

6. Visit a local business and find out whether they have ever used multimedia computers for just-in-time training. How is it used in your chosen profession?

7. Have you ever received an electronic brochure? What about? Was it effective? Examine the Chrysler Jeep/Eagle brochure on the *Multiliteracy CD*. Do you find it well designed? Effective? What would you add or change to sell more vehicles?

Education

After completing this chapter, you will be able to:

☐ **Understand how multimedia computers are being used across the curriculum in a wide range of subjects.**

☐ **Sample state-of-the-art applications on the enclosed *Multiliteracy CD*.**

☐ **Assess how up-to-date your local schools are in adopting these technologies.**

☐ **Question whether technology will make any major difference in the structure of schooling.**

As articulated by Brown, Collins, and Duguid (1989), skills and knowledge are too often taught out of context, as ends in and of themselves. To overcome this, teachers are using multimedia to bring into their classrooms real-life examples to provide the contextual framework so important for learning. Multimedia gives teachers instant access to thousands of slides, videos, sound tracks, and every lesson plan they ever wrote. These materials can be called up instantly, either as material for a lecture, or as a resource for cooperative learning, critical thinking, discussions, question-and-answer sessions, reviews, problem solving, or self study. Among educational researchers, the capability to demonstrate vividly and convincingly the real-world applicability of knowledge has become known as **anchored instruction** (The Cognition and Technology Group at Vanderbilt 1990).

The benefits of multimedia are well documented by Professor James Kulik (1985, 1986, 1991, and 1994) and his associates at the University of Michigan. During the past twenty years, they have analyzed hundreds of controlled experiments on the effectiveness of computer-based learning. Overall, the findings indicate that when multimedia is used effectively, average learning time has been reduced significantly (sometimes by as much as 80%), and achievement levels are more than a standard deviation higher (a full letter grade in school).

Networks add an important dimension to educational computing. The Information Superhighway is linking universities, colleges, schools, and homes into a continuum that is helping to break down distinctions between grade levels. Through cooperative learning on networks, students can collaborate on worldwide projects, share data and contribute findings to reach more immediate results.

Art

Art is a natural medium for multimedia because it is visual, and the ability to display more than 16 million colors lets computers exhibit artwork in true colors that rival those on the printed page. But unlike books, in which the pictures are static and unconnected, multimedia computers offer art educators all the advantages of hypermedia. For example, consider Ebook's CD-ROM *A Survey of Western Art* shown in Figure 4-1. It presents more than a thousand full-color photographs of western painting, sculpture, and architecture that span art history from ancient Egypt to modern America. Hypertext descriptions of the artwork are linked to detailed data cards and audio commentary on the extraordinary art images. This method provides a powerful teaching, learning, and research tool for scholars, teachers, students, and art enthusiasts.

Figure 4-2 shows how the Ebook software lets you browse the art database by artist, title, medium, date, object, and school. Clicking the View button on the data card displays the artwork, which has a Biography button you can press to see an artist's biography. Figure 4-3 shows the result of clicking these buttons for information on the artist Botticelli.

Title screen from Ebook's *A Survey of Western Art.*

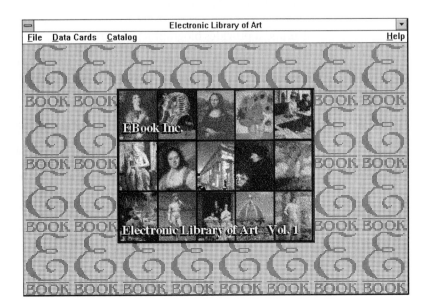

the Range Map button for the giraffe. Essays about the animals provide the equivalent of 600 pages of text.

In *The San Diego Zoo Presents The Animals!* from The Software Toolworks, users can explore a lively collection of animal sights, sounds, and statistics. More than 2,500 pages of articles and scientific data are embellished by more than an hour of full-motion video and 1,300 color photographs. The CD comes with a "Storybook Theater" and a "Kid's Corner" designed for younger explorers.

Dinosaurs! is a CD-ROM by Media Design Interactive. A multimedia encyclopedia on dinosaurs, it uses drawings, diagrams, movies, and narration to describe the age when the dinosaurs lived, teach you which animals they were related to and which ones might be their descendants, and present theories on how they may have become extinct. The section on fossils features videos of experts demonstrating the intricacies of fossil removal and dinosaur reconstruction. The dinosaur directory catalogs more than 100 dinosaurs and provides illustrations of each dinosaur, a description of its characteristics, a map showing where its bones were discovered, and a list of museums where the dinosaur's fossils can be viewed today. There is also an "Ask the Experts" screen that triggers movies of experts answering your questions.

Oceans Below is a simulated CD-ROM scuba diving adventure by Amazing Media. After checking your gear on the deck of the ship, reading a small guidebook that turns into a slide show on topics like altered depth perception and ocean conservation, and selecting one of seventeen dives (see Figure 4-6), you can view a fish chart like the plastic sheets real divers use (see Figure 4-7). Then, as you dive, the world beneath the waves emerges. You explore the depths with your mouse as many colorful images of sea creatures appear. For example, clicking on a picture of a lionfish lets you watch a video of it—within the frame of a face mask (see Figure 4-8)—and listen to a description.

4-6

The world map takes you to any one of 17 exciting dives in Amazing Media's *Oceans Below.*

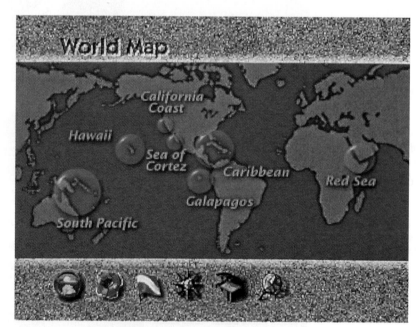

4-7

Narrated sea life charts identify the fish you encounter in *Oceans Below*.

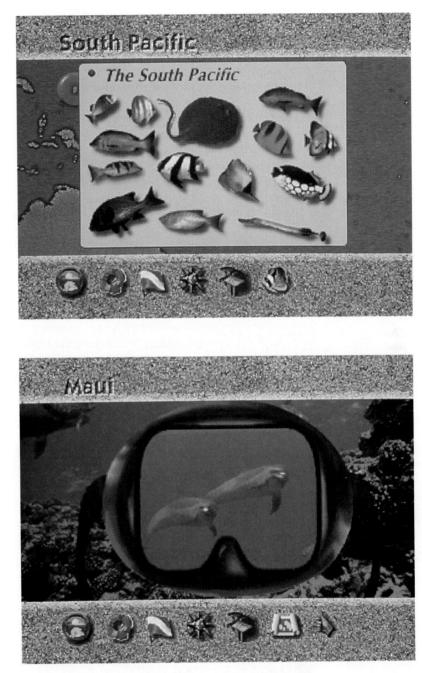

4-8

Full-motion videos play inside the frame of a face mask in *Oceans Below*.

Chemistry

Illman (1994) reviews the work of several chemistry teachers who are using multimedia tools to make presentations in classrooms, publish electronic journals, illustrate the periodic table, develop animations of ions and molecules, and make multimedia chemistry instruction available on the Information Superhighway. He predicts that multimedia PCs will become widespread in teaching chemistry due to the wide range of problems MPCs solve.

For example, one of the most perplexing problems in teaching chemistry is that students do not get enough time in the laboratory to conduct experiments. Many schools cannot provide the quantity or quality of lab experience needed for a good education in chemistry. Students are no longer permitted to handle some important chemicals that been found to cause cancer. Other experiments are too dangerous, expensive, or time-consuming. Enter the multimedia CD-ROM *Exploring Chemistry*. Published by Falcon Software, it is a comprehensive introductory chemistry course covering both inorganic and organic topics. Its 150 lessons provide 180 hours of instruction. The interactive lab design by Professors Stanley G. Smith and Loretta L. Jones (1993) uses full-motion video to let students conduct lab experiments repeatedly until they have mastered the material. Two of the experiments are on the *Multiliteracy CD* enclosed with this book. One is of a grain dust explosion, and the other is of an equilibrium experiment.

To try the grain dust explosion, go to the Demonstrations section, select Applications, and click the Exploring Chemistry: Dust Explosion button. As you can see, this is much too dangerous to let students try in class. Figure 4-9 shows how the step frame option lets you view the explosion as it develops; each frame represents a thirtieth of a second.

The equilibrium experiment can also be found by going to the Demonstrations section, selecting Applications, and clicking the Exploring Chemistry: Equilibrium

4-9

The grain dust explosion lasts only a quarter of a second; students view it in stages by stepping through each frame of video.

4-10

Students mix chemicals to find the one that changes potassium chromate into dichromate.

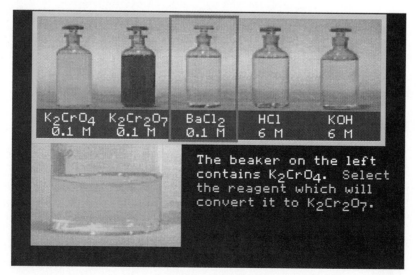

4-11

The result of entering a wrong answer in the equilibrium experiment.

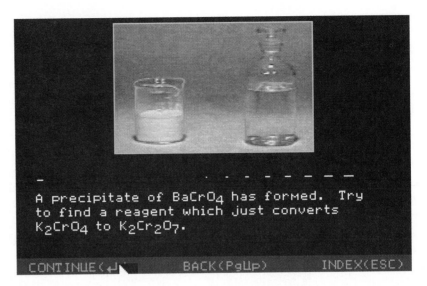

A precipitate of BaCrO4 has formed. Try to find a reagent which just converts K2CrO4 to K2Cr2O7.

CONTINUE(↵)   BACK(PgUp)   INDEX(ESC)

button. Figures 4-10 and 4-11 demonstrate how you mix a variety of chemicals, observe the reactions, and learn from the results. The two chemicals used in the experiment, potassium chromate and potassium dichromate, have been widely used in chemistry education. Recently, they have been found to be carcinogens, so the only safe way to teach about them is through simulations like this. The simulations are so realistic that when you click a chemical with your mouse and see a hand pour the chemical into the beaker, it is as if your own hand poured it in.

Civics

Instead of teaching civics with textbooks that only talk about it, multimedia lets teachers bring civics to life with multimedia CD-ROMs, live video feeds from congress, and online access to government agencies and offices, including the White House.

Capitol Hill is a CD-ROM from The Software Toolworks that provides a behind-the-scenes look at the inner workings of congress. It explains the origins of the two-party system and what the various congressional committees do. There is even a capitol tour conducted by C-SPAN commentator Mike Michaelson. After finding out who's who in government, a multiple-choice game tests what you have learned.

To provide more of a historical perspective, Compton's NewMedia publishes *U.S. Civics*, a guide to U.S. history from the 1700's to the present. Biographies, government structure, reference manuals, and sample tests round out this educational database.

A highly motivating teaching resource is *The '92 Vote* by ABC News Interactive. This CD-ROM is presented in the form of a multimedia news magazine. It contains one hour of ABC News video, another hour of supplemental audio, dozens of full-color pictures, and text from ABC News journalists. Students use hypermedia tools to research the people and events of the 1992 campaign from the primaries through Inauguration Day. Resources include biographies of the major personalities and news stories on the convention, debates, election night, and inauguration.

Foreign Languages

When abroad, try conversing in a foreign language you supposedly learned in school, and you will quickly grasp the importance of multimedia in foreign language instruction. While books can teach grammar and vocabulary, they cannot interact with you the way people do when they converse. Enter multimedia.

Multimedia computers are a natural for teaching language. Digital audio gives them pronunciation capabilities, and full motion video can put students in real-life situations. Exploiting these factors, Syracuse Language Systems has published the award-winning *Playing with Language* series on CD-ROM. Available in Spanish, French, German, Japanese, and English, the titles include *Introductory Games*, *Goldilocks & the Three Bears*, and *TriplePlay*. In Figure 4-12 you can see how

An interactive comic strip in *TriplePlay Spanish.*

TriplePlay Spanish uses interactive comic strips depicting everyday situations to build comprehension and conversation skills at a slow or natural rate of speech. Players advance at their own pace from words to phrases, and ultimately to conversations. In Figure 4-13, the user clicks icons to control story narration and hear characters speak in *Goldilocks & the Three Bears* in Spanish.

Just as this book went to press, Syracuse Language Systems was about to release *TriplePlay Plus!*, which uses speech recognition software licensed from Dragon Systems. A pre-release version won a *NewMedia* INVISION 1994 medal of merit, and an INNOVATIONS 1994 Software Honors Award at the Consumer Electronics Show. According to Syracuse president Martin Rothenberg, "Using the Automatic Speech Recognition games in *TriplePlay Plus!*, language learners can develop a natural-sounding accent and confidence in their speaking skills. Learners will immediately know if they are saying words and phrases correctly, and will be able to practice and improve as they play. The games are also designed so that a native-speaker's voice is always available as a pronunciation model." Except for the specially designed dynamic microphone packaged with the software, no additional hardware is required.

Goldilocks & the Three Bears has buttons that let the user control narration and dialog or move to one of 27 challenging games.

Heinle & Heinle publishes *Nouvelles Dimensions,* an instructional program for listening comprehension in French developed by linguist Dr. James Noblitt. It is based on video materials produced by Bernard Petit, a professor of French at SUNY Brockport. Petit uses a hand-held video camera to get authentic samples of French as it is spoken by French people in everyday life. He focuses on situations and speech samples that are useful for the learner. On the computer screen, students can view scenes of French daily life: greetings, ordering food, statements of personal preferences, and introduction of family members. Since what is seen and heard can be controlled through the computer keyboard and mouse, viewers interact with the program, proceeding at their own pace as they practice, take tests, and complete writing exercises. Figure 4-14 shows an example of how the student learns to hear key words in a conversational context. The user may click the Show Text button to see the script, or call up a map, or use the accompanying word processor and dictionary. The interactive format provides user control of instructional support.

In *Nouvelles Dimensions* the student learns to hear key words in a conversational context.

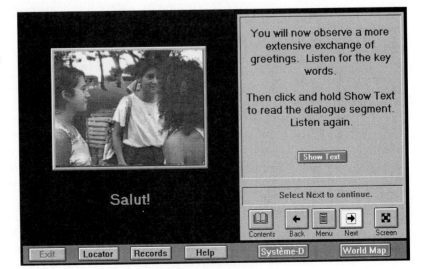

Nouvelles Dimensions offers several advantages over simply viewing a videotape. Students may control the pace of instruction, repeating at will any segment that is not clear. Comprehension aids, such as pop-up help screens, may be used for guidance in the analysis of unfamiliar vocabulary or grammar. Maps and a learner's dictionary are available for more extended exploration. An online word processor that permits direct access to the reference materials provides a means for using what has been learned. Students enjoy the authentic feel of the material and the interactive control. The computer permits an analysis of gestures and facial expressions, on a frame-by-frame basis if necessary, that enhance the understanding of communicative intent. By adding visual context and reference material to language study, the program can help the learner master techniques for aural comprehension, such as listening for key words. Figure 4-15 shows one

4-15

Nouvelles Dimensions facilitates learning by doing.

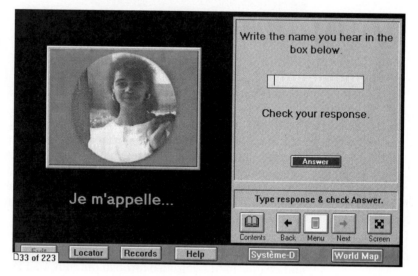

example of how *Nouvelles Dimensions* facilitates learning by doing. The learner listens for the person's name, writes it in the response box, then clicks the Answer button to confirm the entry. Samples from speakers of all ages and backgrounds assist in ear training. According to Dr. Noblitt, instructors like having an enriched environment for learning essential skills outside the classroom. There is a demonstration of *Nouvelles Dimensions* in the Demonstrations section of the *Multiliteracy CD*. To view it, select Applications, then click the Nouvelles Dimensions button.

Geography

The highly visual nature of geography makes it a natural for multimedia. *Picture Atlas of the World* is a CD-ROM from the National Geographic Society. Covering both physical and cultural geography, it includes world, continental, and regional maps, in addition to high-resolution interactive political and topographical maps. More than 1,200 captioned full-screen photographs, 50 video clips, and dozens of vocal and musical audio clips bring human and cultural geography to life. Essays give detailed information about each country along with screens showing vital statistics. Animations, illustrations, and diagrams enliven map projections and show the earth's rotation.

The Software Toolworks publishes the CD-ROMs *U.S. Atlas* and *World Atlas*. They use multimedia to play state songs and national anthems, display flags, and show topographical and statistical maps. An important feature is the way you can add to the database, make personal notes, mark maps, and print stunning graphic reports.

One cleverly designed CD is Brøderbund Software's *Where in the World Is Carmen Sandiego?* Carmen and her gang of villains are stealing the treasures of the world. Sixty countries are involved, with hundreds of animations and thousands of audio clues, including 500 digitized in foreign languages. The student uses Funk & Wagnall's *World Almanac* to help solve the crime, doing research to find out where to go next to find the criminal and the loot. Figure 4-16 shows the high-tech on-screen tools. Clues include languages spoken, landmarks, and cultural sites. As you can see in Figure 4-17, places are illustrated with pictures from *National*

On-screen tools in *Where in the World Is Carmen Sandiego?* include the videophone (left), Dataminder (bottom center), and Note Pad (bottom right).

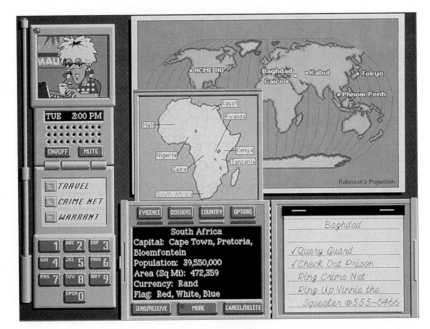

Dramatic photographs place players in 45 countries around the world.

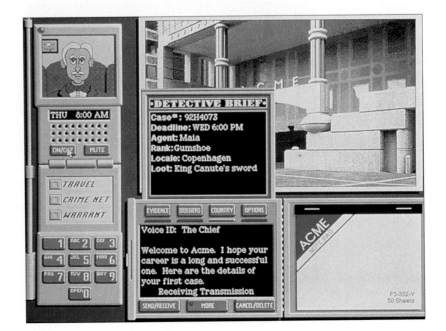

Geographic and accompanied by songs from the Smithsonian. Thus, *Carmen* teaches geography in the context of world culture.

While *Carmen* is so popular that hundreds of middle schools have held Carmen Sandiego Geography Days, some teachers have trouble figuring out how to integrate programs like *Carmen* into teaching because it shifts the focus from teacher-centered to student-centered instruction. As Neuwirth (1994) explains, "… this game cannot be used in a classroom setting. It is not a very didactic tool as the teacher is not given any time for talking to the student during the game."

National Parks of America by Multicom is more utilitarian. Figures 4-18 through 4-20 show how this multimedia CD uses the metaphor of a map to let you

This map appears when you start the *National Parks of America* CD-ROM. Clicking the buttons lets you navigate down through Regional and State menus to individual parks.

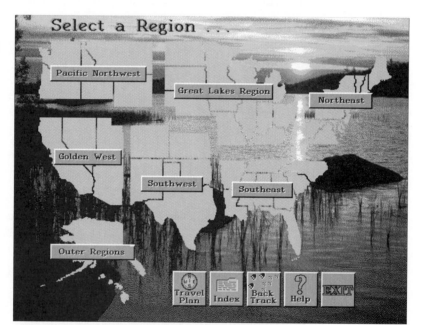

At the state level, *National Parks of America* lets you view a map that locates each park in the state.

4-20

At the park level, *National Parks of America* lets you access detailed information about each park and view spectacular photos.

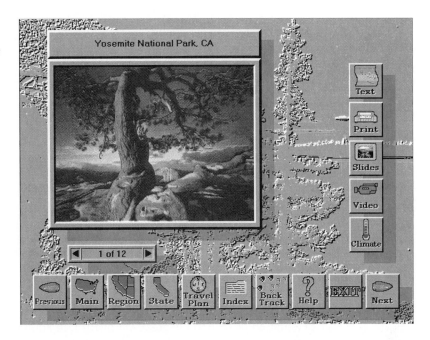

navigate to any park in the country and tour it virtually before deciding whether to plan an actual trip there. There are more than 900 photographs by renowned nature photographer David Muench. The CD lets you locate and select any one of 230 parks by name, geographic location, or by specific criteria such as camping or hiking. You can research park background information or just tour through dramatic videos and the magnificent beauty of David Muench's photographs, as shown in Figure 4-20.

History

There are many ways multimedia brings history to life. As you are about to see, almost all recorded video history of the twentieth century is available on interactive videodiscs; history textbooks on CD-ROMs have video and audio clips with full-text search; multimedia has inspired the creation of new history resources on CD-ROM for which no prior book exists; and the Information Superhighway provides online access to source documents, newsletters, and discussion groups.

Videodisc

Instead of attending a traditional lecture in which the instructor occasionally scribbles something on a blackboard for students to take note, imagine a classroom in which the teacher has access to every major video clip of recorded history. Thanks to a monumental effort by CEL, the most extensive indexed video archive is now available in the form of *The Video Encyclopedia of the 20th Century*. It contains 83 hours of full motion video on 42 laserdiscs. There are 2,338 video chapters, each supported with historical text. Students can compare and link people, events, and time periods. Companion software facilitates the search for subject matter. With a multimedia authoring tool, students can assemble and edit video clips, add narration, and create their own video documentaries.

CEL also publishes a single videodisc version of the series. It allows teachers to access a summary of the materials without having to keep track of 42 videodiscs. One of the great hopes for the Information Superhighway is to make all of this video available digitally on demand to every classroom, thereby avoiding the need to juggle videodiscs.

History Textbooks

D.C. Heath and the Voyager Company have developed multimedia CD-ROM versions of established history textbooks. D.C. Heath has published the American history text *The Enduring Vision, Interactive Edition.* In addition to the text and photographs of the printed version, the CD-ROM includes three thousand pages of historic documents, U.S. Census data from 1790 to 1990, and audio and video recordings that include footage of President Franklin D. Roosevelt's war message to congress.

Who Built America? is a CD-ROM by Voyager. Developed by history professor Roy Rosenzweig at George Mason University, it covers the period from the centennial celebration of 1876 to the great war of 1914. In addition to the text of the printed version, the CD contains historic documents, audio recordings, videos including *The Great Train Robbery,* and more than a thousand pictures.

Multimedia History Titles

Several history titles have been developed on CD-ROM without first appearing as a book. ABC News Interactive publishes an exciting series of interactive videodiscs that include *Communism and the Cold War, Martin Luther King Jr., In the Holy Land,* and *Powers of the U.S. Government.*

The National Geographic Society has published on CD-ROM *The Presidents: It All Started with George,* which describes the personal and political lives of U.S. leaders. This encyclopedic reference tool for home, library, and classroom features historic moments on video; famous speeches; a historical perspective and commentary on each president; more than a thousand captioned photographs; election maps and essays; a political party index; a multimedia timeline that gives a social and historical context for each president; and photo essays on the presidency. It also has a narrated tutorial, a pop-up glossary, a game, and the ability to print captions, essays, and speeches.

Wars

Quanta Press and Compton's NewMedia publish a series of war CD-ROMs. Titles include the *Civil War, World War II, Korea,* and *Vietnam.* In April of 1991, Time Warner Interactive released *Desert Storm: The War in the Persian Gulf,* advertising it as "the first electronic magazine with over 6,000 screens of selectable documentation covering the Gulf War." Users follow the evolution of a Gulf War story from its origins to the actual article as it eventually appeared in *TIME* magazine. The CD includes *TIME* correspondents' files, exclusive audio reports, 300 full-color photographs, and every story report in its original, unedited form, organized chronologically and indexed by subject. There is a glossary of high-tech weapons and a photo gallery, as well as exclusive audio reports, including "as-it's happening" correspondent analyses and interviews. An active timeline of the war lets the user see and hear a synopsis of each week's key events.

Compton's NewMedia offers a competing product, *Desert Storm with Coalition Command*, which comes with a game that lets you deploy ground forces from a sophisticated command post, set policies for providing information to the media, and get vital feedback through direct hotlines to the White House and Pentagon.

The Assassination of JFK

A CD-ROM that fosters debate is the award-winning *The JFK Assassination: A Visual Investigation*. Published by Medio, it includes more than twenty minutes of narrated overview, video clips from five films documenting the assassination, and computer animations showing conflicting bullet angles. Also included is the complete text of the *Warren Commission Report*, Jim Marrs' best-selling book *Crossfire*, and *The J.F.K. Assassination: A Complete Book of Facts*. Figures 4-21

The main menu in *The JFK Assassination* introduces you to the background leading up to the assassination, lets you visit the scene in Dealey Plaza, and presents Text, Analysis, Films & Photos buttons to help you determine whether there was a conspiracy.

The Films & Photos screen from *The JFK Assassination* lets you view the Nix, Hughes, Zapruder, and Muchmore films.

Autopsy photo from *The JFK Assassination* refuting the *Warren Commission Report.*

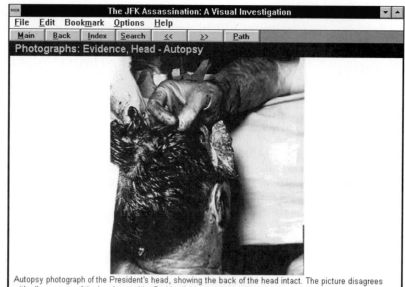

Autopsy photograph of the President's head, showing the back of the head intact. The picture disagrees with all accounts of the head wound by Parkland doctors and staff.

Evidence of forgery on the *The JFK Assassination* CD-ROM.

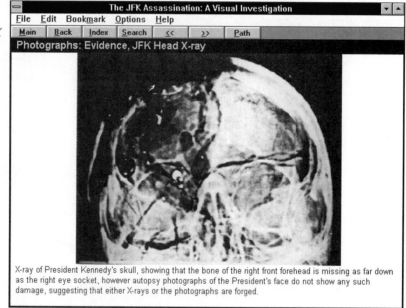

X-ray of President Kennedy's skull, showing that the bone of the right front forehead is missing as far down as the right eye socket, however autopsy photographs of the President's face do not show any such damage, suggesting that either X-rays or the photographs are forged.

through 4-24 show how you review the evidence and decide whether there was a conspiracy and who was involved in it. There is a demo of *The JFK Assassination* on the *Multiliteracy CD.* To try it, go to the Demonstrations section, select Applications, and click the Assassination of JFK button.

Internet Resources for Historians

DeLoughry (1994) tells how the H-Net (history network) project at the University of Illinois at Chicago has set up twenty Internet mailing lists that have attracted more than 4,500 subscribers in 47 countries. HNSOURCE at the University of Kansas provides historians easy access to historical texts and data located all over the network. The *Historical Text Archives* at Mississippi State University provide

Internet users with such historical documents as the *Instruments of Surrender* signed by Japanese leaders at the end of World War II, and *Up From Slavery*, the autobiography of Booker T. Washington.

Music

The music industry has been so totally transformed by multimedia technology that the America 2000 accreditation guidelines require that every music student learn about computer music applications, including music recording, editing, arranging, and printing. MidiSoft's *Music Mentor with Recording Session* is an example of the powerful new learning environment multimedia provides. Instead of studying static musical examples printed on staff paper in textbooks, students learn about musical style from the interactive tutorials in *Music Mentor*, as shown in Figure 4-25. At any time, students can switch to *Recording Session*, which copies the musical example being studied in *Music Mentor* to the dynamically active computer screen shown in Figure 4-26. Students can experiment by varying the melody, rhythm, orchestration, tempo, and accompaniment. For example, while using *Music Mentor* to study the variations in the second movement of Haydn's Surprise Symphony, students can switch to *Recording Session* and create a variation of their own.

MidiSoft also publishes *Studio for Windows,* which is very easy to use because of its graphical tape recorder controls. Anyone who knows how to work a tape recorder can use this program to record and play MIDI sequences. It even notates anything you play automatically. *Studio for Windows* is great for teaching class piano; music teachers can record each one of their students on a different track, complete with orchestral accompaniment, which is highly motivating for students when they rehearse.

There is a demonstration copy of *Studio for Windows* on the *Multiliteracy CD.* To try it, go to the Demonstrations section, select Applications, and click the Studio for Windows button.

4-25

Music Mentor with Recording Session delivers tutorials in a wide range of musical styles.

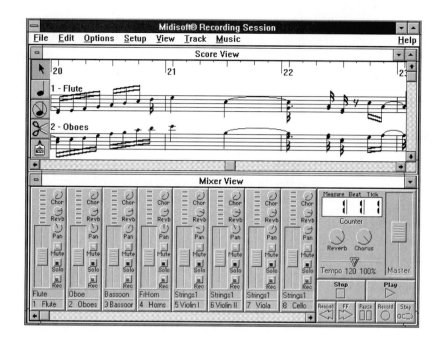

4-26

Graphical tape recorder
controls make MidiSoft's
*Music Mentor with Recording
Session* easy to use.

Composer Quest is a multimedia CD from Dr. T's Music Software. It lets the user explore music, history, arts, and sociological change from the year 1600 to the present. It was conceived and developed to provide a general, yet thoroughly researched and technically accurate overview of musical developments over the years, as well as provide a synopsis of trends in the visual arts and general world history. *Composer Quest* features two modes of operation: the learn mode lets the user investigate freely any musical period or style of music, and the play mode offers a fun and challenging adventure game. In learn mode, a timeline screen lets students take a tour through time to investigate the greatest composers in classical and jazz music. In play mode, the game Face the Challenge plays a melody and requires that students board the Time Machine and travel back in time to find the composer who wrote the music. The CD includes more than 60 musical performances, composer biographies, news events from 1600 to the present, major visual art styles and artists, music trivia questions, a quiz to test student knowledge during the program, online help, hotword definitions of musical terminology, and a quick index to search for any composer. *Composer Quest* adheres to the curriculum guidelines outlined in *The California Framework for the Visual and Performing Arts*.

The success of the hit CD title *Multimedia Beethoven* from Microsoft has led to more interactive music titles, including *Multimedia Mozart, Multimedia Stravinsky,* and *Multimedia Vivaldi.* These CDs let you interact with musical scores through annotated program notes, learn about musical style, review historical notes, see musical notation, and learn about musical instruments. For example, *Multimedia Beethoven* contains pages from Beethoven's sketch books, which show how Beethoven would rewrite a melody dozens of times until he got it right.

Microsoft also publishes *Musical Instruments,* a CD-ROM based on the Eyewitness book by Dorling Kindersley. It includes more than 200 articles, 500 photos, and 1,500 audio recordings. There are four pathways through the material: Families of Instruments, Musical Ensembles (focusing on musical styles ranging from chamber music to rock & roll), Instruments of the World (including rare and exotic instruments and plenty of musical samples), and the A-Z of Instruments (an alphabetical index).

Jazz: A Multimedia History.

Music education titles include jazz as well as classical music. Compton's NewMedia publishes the CD-ROM title *Jazz, A Multimedia History*, shown in Figure 4-27. It takes users on a musical journey from the origins of jazz to the vibrant, electric sounds of today. Students learn about the fathers of jazz, including Duke Ellington, Charlie Parker, and Louis Armstrong, as well as modern jazz innovators, such as Miles Davis, Herbie Hancock, and Weather Report. The CD explains how early jazz was formulated and how it has evolved through the ages, teaching the user how to appreciate and interpret the nuances of jazz.

Music resources are also coming to the Information Superhighway. Leonard Bernstein's vast collection of correspondence, scores, recordings, and photos has been donated to the Library of Congress, which is creating a multimedia archive that will be accessible from any Internet node in the world.

Physics

The Video Encyclopedia of Physics Demonstrations shown in Figure 4-28 is published by The Education Group. It consists of 25 videodiscs that present 600 demonstrations of basic physical principles. Most segments have narration (written scripts are included), and many segments feature slow motion photography or computer animations. Topics include mechanics, waves, sound, fluid dynamics,

4-28

The Video Encyclopedia of
Physics Demonstrations.

heat, thermodynamics, electricity, magnetism, optics, and modern physics. An extensive 1,500-page companion explains how to use the videos. In his very positive review of this package, Beichner (1993) describes how the series can be used to assign homework in which students use data from the videos: "For example, a series of balls of varying diameters and masses are dropped from nearly 4 meters. By stepping through the video a frame at a time, position measurements can be made as the balls fall. Time is included on each frame." The series is also available in middle school and primary school versions.

There is a video clip on the *Multiliteracy CD* that shows examples from the *The Video Encyclopedia of Physics Demonstrations*. To view it, go to the Demonstrations section, select Applications, and click the Video Encyclopedia of Physics Demonstrations button.

The *Multiliteracy CD* also includes a lesson plan for *The Puzzle of the Tacoma Narrows Bridge Collapse*, published by Wiley Educational Software. Developed by Professors Robert Fuller, Dean Zollman, and Thomas Campbell under an NSF grant, this videodisc is one of the best examples of how effectively multimedia can help students visualize complex phenomena. To access the lesson plan, which teaches the physics of sympathetic vibration, go to the Demonstrations section of the *Multiliteracy CD*, select Applications, and click the Tacoma Narrows Bridge Collapse button. You must have a videodisc player attached to your multimedia PC with the *Tacoma Narrows* videodisc in order to see the video in this lesson plan.

Science

Science 2000 is a comprehensive seventh-grade science curriculum published on interactive videodisc by Decision Development Corporation. Consistent with the

4-29

Carbon dioxide turns the earth into a giant greenhouse by absorbing heat and trapping it inside the atmosphere. From *Science Forums*, Volume I, "Fossil fuel & the Greenhouse Effect".

most advanced science frameworks and employing the latest in educational technology, Science 2000 takes an activity-based, thematic approach to teaching science. Within its flexible and open-ended structure, students actively investigate and explore science. They gain a better understanding of a world increasingly shaped by science and technology, plus an insight into the importance of science in solving some of today's critical environmental and health issues. Organized into four units, each of which takes approximately nine weeks to complete, the curriculum in Science 2000 is connected by central themes and is oriented toward solving problems. Multiple disciplines—life, health, social, earth, physical and environmental sciences, math, anthropology, and language arts—are brought into play as students research real-life situations.

Videodiscovery publishes a series of innovative videodiscs for teaching science. There are two volumes of *Science Forums* that challenge students in sixth through ninth grades to grapple with real world problems. Using a town meeting format, the forums present role-playing scenarios that focus on science, technology, and societal problems. For example, Figure 4-29 is from a forum on fossil fuel and the greenhouse effect. Students consider whether fossil fuel users should be taxed according to the amount of carbon dioxide that the fuels release into the atmosphere, with the tax revenue used to pay for the greenhouse effects of global warming.

Also from Videodiscovery is the videodisc *Science Sleuths*, in which students solve wacky dilemmas using the research methods and tools of actual scientists. There are 24 open-ended mysteries, ranging from exploding grain silos to crashing computers. Through careful observation and research, students must develop a rational explanation and report their findings. For example, Figure 4-30 is from Chapter B3, "The Misplaced Fossil." An amateur paleontologist found a dinosaur bone from the Cretaceous Age (65-140 million years ago) in a Tertiary Stratum dating back to only 10 million years ago, and the student must explain the mystery of how it got there. Beautifully produced student manuals and instructor guides accompany the Videodiscovery discs, which can be controlled either by multimedia computers or laser bar code readers.

MECC adds a new dimension to reading by making it possible for kids to write their own stories. MECC's best-selling *Story Book Weaver* lets kids choose from hundreds of scenes, add characters, and weave stories accompanied by sounds and music. Another MECC product, *My Own Stories*, lets kids write, illustrate, and publish stories about themselves and their friends. Both of these MECC products can be downloaded from the *Club KidSoft* CD-ROM discussed in the section on elementary education.

Preschool

Computers are used in preschool as objects of study and to help youngsters developmentally. If children have a positive experience with computers at an early age, the computer phobia older students experience can be diminished or avoided altogether.

Cartoon characters are often used to make computers attractive to children. For example, *Our House* is a CD-ROM from Context that features characters from the Family Circus comic strip. It offers children a fascinating view into a typical American home by showing them how everyday objects in each room are used, and comparing modern conveniences to the home life of generations gone by.

Mixed-Up Mother Goose is a CD-ROM from Sierra Online. Winner of the 1990 Software Publishers Award for Best Early Education Program, it presents 16 Mother Goose rhymes with certain pieces missing. Kids learn logic and problem-solving skills while having fun finding the missing pieces.

Figure 4-37 shows *Tuneland*, a CD-ROM by 7th Level. Created with financial backing from Wall Street investor Michael Milken, it is a fully animated cartoon with singing, dancing characters, and voice-over narration by comedian Howie Mandel. Kids explore the beautifully animated barnyard fantasy screens while interacting with dozens of characters, including Mandel, who plays the part of a teddy bear that tells jokes and performs hilarious comedy gags. Songs include *Three Blind Mice*, *This Old Man*, and *The Itsy Bitsy Spider*. The goal is to get kids interacting inside a cartoon, get them involved with the story and the singing, and make them comfortable with their computer. The CD comes with a *Tuneland* coloring book that contains the words to all the songs.

4-37

An animated barnyard scene from the *Tuneland* CD. Almost every object in the scene is active. For example, you click on the rope to see the monkey swing; the bucket to see the frog do a swan dive; the pig to make him sing Oh, Susanna; or the hen to see the whole gang do a square dance.

Word Tales is a CD-ROM from Time Warner Interactive that uses animated activities to teach young children word recognition and initial letter sounds. Figure 4-38 shows how the CD features an animated character named Milo, who teaches children the sounds of letters and how the letters combine to form words. In the first part of the game, children match the correct initial letter to a word as

4-38

The cartoon character Milo stars in *Word Tales*.

Government

O B J E C T I V E S

After completing this chapter, you will be able to:

■ Realize how multimedia can be used to improve access to state and local government.

■ Assess how your state is using multimedia, and determine whether the way it is using multimedia is good or bad for its citizens.

■ Understand how the city of Atlanta used multimedia to win its bid to host the 1996 Olympic Games.

■ Question whether multimedia makes too much information available too quickly to the public during wartime.

Government officials have turned increasingly to multimedia for solutions to problems inherent in governance. Multimedia kiosks make services more widely available and enable municipalities to respond more quickly to emergencies and disasters. Video conferencing and electronic town meetings provide ways for politicians to reach, canvass, and broaden their constituencies. Countries that want to be competitive in the new global economy are quickening the pace of the development of their national information superhighways. Governments are using the superhighways to find out more about what is happening around the world and to document it for the United Nations. Since human nature unfortunately dictates that peace keeping will inevitably break down, the military uses multimedia to wage war effectively.

Public Service Kiosks

CITY-INFO kiosks have been installed throughout Vienna, Austria, to offer citizens and travelers the ability to find information on addresses, points of interest, shops, restaurants, public transportation, opening hours, guided tours, and the cost and location of tickets, buses, museums, and events. Set up in public areas like train stations, monuments, and other frequently visited places, the kiosks were designed to be easily recognizable yet blend in with their surroundings. They are connected to a network that updates them simultaneously. Figure 6-1 shows a traveler using the CITY-INFO kiosk, and Figure 6-2 shows its main menu. In their careful analysis of user reaction to the CITY-INFO kiosks, Professors Hitz and Werthner (1993) from the University of Vienna reported these results:

> It can be stated that the system is judged extremely positive (93%)... Typical users are young (43% under the age of 25), male (70%), tourists (55%) and well educated (32% high school, 34% university). They strongly recommend the usage of such a system (62% very much)... It is interesting that more than half would like to access such information via their [own] equipment and also 52% are willing to pay for such a service.

The states of California and Oregon are using multimedia kiosks to provide a wide range of government services. For example, California uses multimedia kiosks for driver license renewal. Multimedia computers test the driver, score results, collect

6-1

An indoor designer model of the CITY-INFO kiosk. There is also an outdoor vandal-proof model.

6-5

Oregon kiosk users can select the cities in which they are interested in finding jobs.

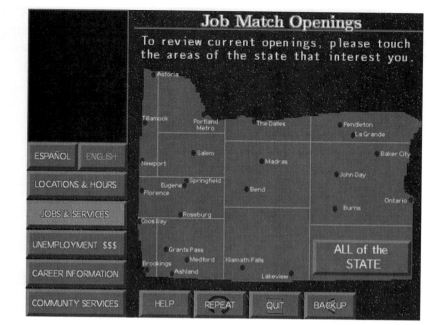

Electronic Town Meetings

Larry King and Ross Perot are champions of electronic town meetings, in which telephones are used to provide interactivity during television broadcasts from government officials to their constituents. Since the number of people who can phone in is limited by the length of the broadcast, interactive discussion groups on the Internet are being used to provide more people an opportunity to discuss their views. The Internet makes the meetings virtual, since they are no longer bounded by time or place.

The Internet is also becoming popular as a polling device on commercial television networks. Polls are traditionally taken by asking viewers to dial different phone numbers to register their response to a given question. Pollsters now advertise Internet addresses, which enable viewers to respond over the Information Superhighway. Many television shows are followed up by discussion sessions on computer networks, where the issues can be debated in more depth.

Internet and the National Information Superhighway

Governments are spending billions of dollars to hasten the construction of their nations' Information Superhighways. The global connection of these highways into a worldwide network is referred to as the Internet. When this book went to press, more than seventy countries were already connected, with more than a million local networks online on the Internet.

For the reasons mentioned in the first two parts of this book, any country that does not go online and become proficient in using the Internet will become disenfranchised and seriously impede its ability to compete in the global economy.

The Internet tutorial in Part Seven of this book will show you how widespread government use of the Internet has already become. Having access to the Internet will enable you to go online to the White House, retrieve a wealth of information about the government, and contribute your own views.

Safeguarding National Interests

As President of the United States, George Bush criticized the CIA for being so slow to issue reports that the White House learned more about world developments by watching commercial TV. The government now uses multimedia computers to provide officials with live TV feeds from news channels such as CNN, which appear in windows on the screen alongside other applications. In Part Seven of this book, you will learn how to get live TV feeds on your computer screen.

The government is also using the Internet to solve crimes. For example, the FBI posted a message on the Internet asking for help in solving the Unabom case, which involves a series of bombings targeting the computer industry, universities, and the aircraft and airline industries. A million dollar reward is offered for information leading to the conviction of the perpetrator. The FBI used a NASA computer to post the documents, which are accessible at naic.nasa.gov. In Part Seven of this book you will learn how to access this information (*Wall Street Journal* 12/31/93: 10).

Warfare

The Gulf War demonstrated how effectively multimedia can wage war. Imagine yourself in control of a smart bomb. You are seated at a multimedia computer aiming a laser that steers the bomb. In a window you view a live video feed from a camera in the smart bomb showing precisely where it is headed. Your multimedia computer provides such fine control that you can fly the bomb into an air duct to penetrate an otherwise highly fortified building.

While the accuracy of aerial multimedia weaponry lessens the need for ground forces, army combat is still a reality. When casualties occur, multimedia medicine steps in. For example, consider a group of army doctors at an EVAC hospital facing a tough decision. Shrapnel has mutilated an artery and a vein in a soldier's leg. Conventional field medicine recommends amputation. Instead, doctors photograph the wound with a Kodak DCS 200 digital camera, which has a SCSI port for plug-and-play capability. The images and patient history are uploaded via satellite to the Walter Reed Army Medical Center in Bethesda, Maryland, where specialists guide the field doctors through delicate reconstructive surgery that saves the leg.

Olympic Bidding

A big problem faced by the city of Atlanta in bidding for the 1996 Summer Olympics was that only about 15 of the 90 voting members of the International Olympics Committee had ever been to Atlanta, which was known more for *Gone With the*

Wind and similar visions of the Old South. Based on recommendations by Dr. Pat Crecine, President of Georgia Tech, Atlanta used a multimedia campaign to promote a modern image of the city and project through realistic computer graphics what the planned stadium and other proposed facilities would be like. For example, Figure 6-6 shows the proposed Olympic dormitory complex, and Figure 6-7 shows

A computer graphics rendering of the proposed Olympic dormitory.

6-7

The computer-generated "Golden Athlete" carries the Olympic torch.

the computer-generated "Golden Athlete" who carries the Olympic torch into the proposed Olympic stadium. As Gamble-Risley (1992) described the experience:

> Just sit down and prepare yourself to take a magnificent journey as you rush from space toward the Earth, plunge past fluffy clouds and down over snow-capped mountains, rivers and forest until you soar over Georgia and come to the city of Atlanta. After you've flown into the city, you'll come to a futuristic-looking stadium where you'll glide down corridors into an office, and exit out a window where you'll view the future site of the Olympic village... From there, the tour is literally placed in the hands of the user who uses a trackball to take control over the adventure and can essentially go sight seeing around the city.

A more complex system was developed for the final vote in Tokyo. It used multimedia techniques to depict what life would be like in the proposed Olympic village. According to Frederick B. Dyer, Associate Director of the Georgia Center for Advanced Telecommunications Technology, "The systems were unique in many ways and clearly helped with the winning bid, among other things demonstrating Atlanta's ability to handle the very complex process of managing the 1996 Centennial Games, which are likely to be the largest media event of the century, with as many as 4 billion people watching portions of the events!"

Since winning the bid, Atlanta's multimedia presentation has evolved into a system called Atlanta Vision. Figure 6-8 shows how the presentation begins with a view of the world highlighting previous Olympic host cities, and then moves to a panoramic view of the Atlanta skyline. By selecting one of the five colored Olympic rings that float above the city, users can explore various topics. For example, there is a tour of Stone Mountain with an explanation of plans for the equestrian and bicycling events to be held there. Other options let users access information on the history of the Olympics, study how Atlanta won the 1996 Summer Olympics bid, and inspect facilities for more than thirty games. In addition, the system allows the observer to tour all of Georgia via a GIS (Geographical Information System) database system showcasing economic development opportunities and other highlights of the state.

6-8

The Atlanta Vision kiosk uses a multiscreen panoramic presentation system.

Video Conferencing Network

Klinck (1993) describes how the Voluntary Hospitals of America (VHA), the nation's largest alliance of hospitals, is building a video conferencing network to connect its 900 nonprofit hospitals. Based on VTEL Corporation's PC-based video conferencing technology, the system will enable health care professionals at different hospitals to use video conferencing for patient diagnosis and treatment. The equipment can capture videotape transmissions of medical images and clinical procedures, which is ideal for providing continuing medical education to physicians and other health care professionals. Doctors can annotate test results, allowing a more personal and immediate diagnosis. The system also permits the use of stethoscopes, EKG units, X-rays, teleradiology systems, sonograms, and other medical devices. In time-sensitive cases, VTEL's system can allow for quick decisions vital to saving a patient's life.

Life Support Skills

The best way to avoid medical problems is to stay healthy; that is the goal of the *HeartBeat Personal Trainer* by HeartBeat. Built around the Sega Genesis video game machine shown in Figure 7-7, it lets you upgrade an old piece of exercise equipment into an interactive aerobic training system. Sensors keep track of your speed and heart rate and enable the video games to keep your heart rate within the target zone. Figure 7-8 shows the *HeartBeat Personal Trainer* used with an exercise bicycle, and Figure 7-9 shows the *Trainer* connected to a stepper. It will also work with a ski machine or a treadmill. You can also purchase the sensors and game cartridges separately if you already own a Sega game machine.

7-7

The *HeartBeat Personal Trainer* adds speed and heart-rate sensors to a Sega Genesis video game machine.

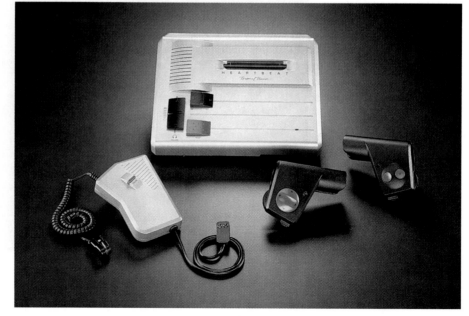

The Sound Blaster 16-bit waveform audio board.

Yamaha MS202 powered speakers provide excellent sound reinforcement for a multimedia computer.

Video Overlay

A video overlay card allows your computer to display common video sources including video cameras, VCRs, and videodiscs while simultaneously displaying computer graphics. The overlay card makes one of the colors in your computer graphics transparent; when that color appears on your screen with the video overlay card activated, the video source shows through.

You must exercise caution when purchasing a video overlay card. There are a lot of competing brands, and they do not all provide the features you may need. You should consider the following features when making a purchase:

Multiple Inputs

Many cards only let you connect a single video source at a time; if you need to switch among multiple devices, such as a camera, a VCR, and a TV tuner, you will need an overlay card with multiple inputs.

Frame Grab

Some cards cannot grab still images and save them as bitmaps; this is a nice feature to have when you are creating a multimedia application.

TV Tuner

Some cards have a TV tuner on board. If you know in advance that you want a TV tuner in your computer, getting it on your video overlay card can save you the slot you will use if you add the tuner later.

Video for Windows

Overlay cards do not necessarily enable you to record full-motion video; if you want to make Video for Windows recordings, you need an overlay board that can capture moving video.

Memory Conflicts

Many overlay cards will not work if your computer has more than 14 MB of RAM. Check this out before you buy.

Video Adapter Compatibility

Some overlay cards may not be compatible with your computer's video adapter, especially if you have one of the latest adapters.

Figure 11-5 shows the Super VideoWindows video overlay board used by the author. Manufactured by New Media Graphics, it has three video inputs and functions as both an overlay board and a digital video recorder.

The Super VideoWindows board.

Digital Video

When you purchase a digital video board to make Video for Windows recordings, make sure you get one that comes with a Microsoft MCI overlay driver. You can use it to make Video for Windows recordings and also take advantage of the video overlay features just discussed. Be aware that not all digital video boards provide support for MCI video overlay.

TV Tuner

TV tuner cards give your multimedia computer the ability to tune into both broadcast and cable television channels. Some have video overlay capability on board, while others require that you have a video overlay board to which you can connect the video output of your tuner card. If you know in advance that you will want a TV tuner, purchase an overlay card that has a TV tuner built in. Figure 11-6 shows the TV tuner used by the author.

The Super TV tuner board.

MIDI

MIDI is the Musical Instrument Digital Interface. Because MIDI is a required part of the MPC specification, you do not have a multimedia computer if you do not have MIDI. However, the kind of MIDI required by the MPC is not what musicians would refer to as the "real" MIDI. MIDI was invented to provide a means for music keyboards, synthesizers, and computers to communicate with each other. Playing a key on a music keyboard can cause any number of events to happen on other external devices to which it is MIDI'd. The MPC standard does not require that your computer have MIDI jacks into which you can plug music keyboards and synthesizers. Instead, it requires a driver that plays MIDI sequences through your computer's waveform audio board. Musicians criticize this because it almost always sounds worse than it would if you had an external MIDI device attached.

If you are serious about MIDI, get a multimedia computer that has MIDI IN and OUT jacks that you can connect to keyboards and synthesizers that sound good, such as the Roland Sound Canvas. You may need to devote a slot to your MIDI interface unless you get a waveform audio board that also has MIDI IN and OUT jacks. This is an option on the popular Sound Blaster waveform audio board from Creative Labs. Make sure any MIDI synthesizer or keyboard you purchase follows the General MIDI specification, which standardizes the set of instrumental sounds MIDI devices produce.

Videodisc

Because it requires the installation of a Windows MCI driver and a serial connection to your computer in addition to video and audio cabling, videodisc is always a challenge to install and get working, but it remains the best way to provide access to full-motion video. Eventually videodisc will surely be replaced by digital video, which eliminates the need for a videodisc player by allowing the video to play back from hard disk drives, CD-ROMs, and networks. The problem is that at present, digital video requires too much storage to record and requires special hardware to play back with the beautiful full-screen, full-motion capability of videodisc.

When you buy a videodisc player, make sure it has a serial port that can be connected to your computer, and make sure there is a Windows MCI driver for it. Some players have a longer seek time than others; the longer the seek time, the longer you will wait to see the video when your application tells it to play. Select a player with a seek time no greater than two seconds, or one second if you can afford the additional expense of the faster player.

As noted earlier, most videodisc players cannot show still frames from CLV videodiscs. If you need that capability, you must purchase a high-end player that can. When this book went to press, the only player able to still-frame CLV discs was the Pioneer LD-V 8000.

Most videodiscs are pressed in the NTSC video format used in the U.S. and Japan. Users from countries that follow the PAL video format will probably want to purchase videodisc players that can play both NTSC and PAL formatted videodiscs. The author sympathizes with people who have to deal with this problem in standards, especially since the NTSC video standard is inferior to PAL.

Multimedia Read/Write Storage

Multimedia requires a lot of storage if you are into digital audio and video. The storage alternatives are discussed here.

Hard Disk

When you purchase a multimedia computer, you should get as much hard disk built into it as you can afford. No matter how much capacity you get, you will eventually run out as your library of multimedia software grows. Hard disk size is measured in megabytes. The 30 MB requirement in the original MPC standard would not even get you started today. Even the 160 MB requirement of the MPC2 is minimal. Hard drive capacities of 400 MB and higher begin to look credible for serious users of multimedia.

SCSI

SCSI stands for Small Computer System Interface. It lets you daisychain up to eight mass storage devices. While many CD-ROM drives use SCSI, most MPCs do not provide an external SCSI connector to which you can attach additional SCSI devices. If your computer does not come with a SCSI connector, you will probably need to devote a slot to installing a SCSI board. A wide array of SCSI devices are available, including external hard drives, CD-ROM drives, and read-write optical drives, which are discussed next.

Read-Write Optical Disk

A read-write optical disk is an attractive storage medium for multimedia because the disks are removable. After you fill one up, you can take the disk out and insert another, providing access to more storage. However, read-write optical drives are usually slower than hard disks; their slower seek times tend to slow down multimedia applications.

The author uses the 3.5-inch read-write optical disks shown in Figure 11-7 to back up his hard drives. Each 3.5-inch optical disk holds 128 MB. You can get larger size disks that hold even more.

It takes nine boxes full of high-density diskettes to equal the storage capacity of one 3.5-inch read/write optical disk.

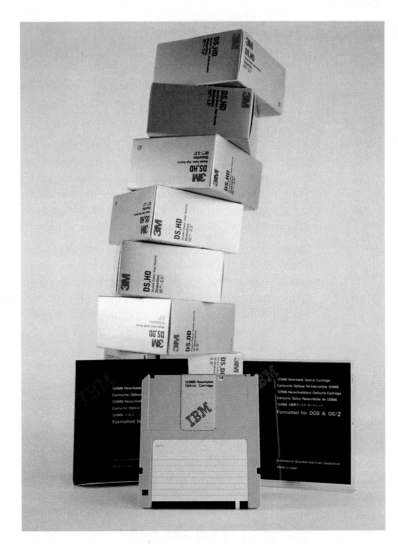

Writable CD-ROM

Writable CD-ROM is called CD-R; the *R* stands for Recordable, indicating that you can record on the CD. Each CD-ROM can store about 650 MB.

If you purchase a CD-R drive, you should also purchase a hard disk drive large enough to hold twice the amount of data stored on the largest CD-ROM you expect to make. You may also need a separate SCSI board for each of these drives; check with a knowledgeable vendor for advice.

PCMCIA Cards

PCMCIA stands for Personal Computer Memory Card International Association, the name of a standards group, which creates specifications for credit-card sized peripherals for personal computers. The group got its name because the first PCMCIA cards were for memory, but PCMCIA is now branching out into modems, network cards, and even multimedia cards. At present PCMCIA memory cards are expensive when compared to other forms of storage, but as the technology progresses, you can expect prices to drop while memory sizes increase.

Communication Options

If your multimedia computer is connected to the Information Superhighway, you have access to millions upon millions of hard drives from all over the world.

Modems

The least expensive way to connect to the Information Superhighway is by way of a modem, which can be either internal or external. Internal modems often take up a slot, while external modems connect to your computer's serial port. If you plan to have more than one serial device in use at a time, such as a modem and a videodisc player, you will need a computer with two serial ports.

The faster your modem, the less time it will take to download files to your computer. If long distance telephone charges are involved, higher speed modems can save cost as well as time. Modem speeds are measured as a **baud rate**, which tells how many bits per second can be transmitted. Modems slower than 2,400 baud are hardly useful anymore, and modems with speeds as high as 28,800 baud are becoming common.

Networks

Network cards provide even faster ways to access multimedia files. The most popular network topologies are Ethernet and Token Ring. Ethernet cards provide access at speeds up to 10 MB per second, depending on how many users are connected to the network. Token Ring networks are less prone to slow down as the number of users increases; they run at 4 MB or 16 MB per second. The faster the connection, the higher the cost.

Internet Connections

A connection to the Internet by modem is much slower than a "real" Internet connection, which connects you to the Information Superhighway via a network card at high speed. The datacommunication protocol used on the Information Superhighway is called TCP/IP, which stands for Transmission Control Protocol/Internet Protocol. Several vendors sell TCP/IP drivers for Windows which add to your computer's system software a *winsock.dll* and related system software. The *winsock.dll* allows applications like PODIUM to open a socket on the Information Superhighway and let you communicate through it. "Winsock" stands for Windows socket, and "dll" stands for dynamic link library, the expandable software technology that enables vendors to add features easily to your Windows environment.

In order for your multimedia computer to have a real Internet connection, it must have the following components:

- network card
- LAN or broadband wiring to the Internet
- TCP/IP network connection
- *winsock.dll* installed under Windows

Your local network administrator can recommend specific brands that will work best in your area.

Auxiliary Input

The auxiliary input devices described here provide convenient ways to digitize pre-existing texts and pictures for use with your multimedia computer. The program that converts scanned text into machine-readable characters is known as Optical Character Recognition (OCR) software. OCR software does not necessarily ship with scanners, so if you plan to scan printed text into machine readable form, make sure you have the necessary OCR software.

Hand-Held Scanners

Hand-held scanners have fallen in cost while increasing in reliability. The author used Caere Corporation's The Typist hand-held scanner extensively to scan the quotations that appear in this book. If you are an educator, be sure to ask the vendor if there is an educational discount; most scanner manufacturers have special discounts for educators.

While personal opinions may vary, the author does not believe you need a color hand-held scanner. To scan text, all you need is a monochrome scanner, which will cost less than a color scanner. For scanning pictures, color hand-held scanners cost as much as Camcorders; if you have a video overlay card capable of grabbing frames into bitmaps, you are much better off using a camera to grab the frame instead of hand-scanning it; the hand-scanning software takes much longer to render the image than the frame grab.

Flatbed Scanners

Flatbed scanners do a nice job of scanning both text and graphics, and the price of color scanners has fallen steadily. If your budget permits, a flatbed scanner is a good addition for producing multimedia text and graphics objects.

Slide Scanners

Slide scanners have a slot into which you insert a 35mm slide; their purpose is to scan the slide and produce a bitmap image of it. However, the term **slide scanner** gets used loosely. Some slide scanners do the complete job of scanning the slide and producing the bitmap, while others merely output a video signal that you still need to digitize.

If you have a video overlay card that can grab frames into bitmaps, the most cost effective way to scan slides is to purchase the RasterOps Expresso slide scanner. It is the type of "scanner" that produces a video image you still need to digitize. But if you have a video overlay card, you can plug the video output of the Expresso into your overlay card and grab the resulting video frame into a bitmap. Figure 11-8 shows the Expresso in use.

The RasterOps Expresso being used to digitize a slide.

Digital Cameras

Like slide scanners, the term **digital camera** also gets used loosely. Sometimes it refers to cameras that snap pictures by producing a real digital bitmap that you can read directly into your application, but most often it refers to cameras that output a video still frame that you need to digitize with a video capture board.

If the camera is not really digital you are better off buying a Hi8 Camcorder. The Hi8 Camcorder will cost about the same or less than the so-called "digital" camera, but you can also shoot full-motion video with it and use it with a video capture board.

Recently a low-cost, truly digital camera has come to market. Apple's QuickTake 100 can snap 32 standard-resolution (320x240) or 8 high-resolution (640x480) images, which it stores on its internal megabyte memory chip. To download the images, you connect the camera to your Macintosh or IBM-compatible serial port. Windows file formats that the camera supports include TIFF, BMP, PCX, and JPEG. For more information contact Apple Computer.

Printers

No list of computer accessories would be complete without mentioning printers. Since color is important in multimedia applications, you would ideally like to have a color printer. Happily the cost of color printers has been declining steadily. If you do not have a color printer, the Windows device drivers automatically convert color bitmaps to grey-scale images that look surprisingly good when printed on a black-and-white printer.

The quality of a print is largely determined by how many dots-per-inch (DPI) your printer can print. Printers that print at 300 DPI produce acceptable graphics, but 600 DPI looks a lot better. This book was printed on a printer that produces 2,400 DPI.

Laser printers produce the best and fastest prints, but they also cost the most. Inkjet printers are an alternative that costs less yet looks almost as good as long as you don't smear the ink before it dries. Some inks run when you get them wet, which is another reason why laser printers are preferred over inkjets.

E X E R C I S E S

1. Define the following terms and explain the role they play in a multimedia computer:
   - Central processor
   - RAM
   - Hard disk
   - Modem

2. Run through the multimedia components discussed in this chapter and make a list of which ones your computer has, which ones it does not have, and of the latter, which ones you would like it to have.

3. Have you ever used a trackball? If not, go to your local video arcade and play a game that uses one. What advantages does the trackball have over a mouse? What are the disadvantages? Which do you prefer?

4. Does your multimedia PC have MIDI connections (MIDI IN and MIDI OUT), or does it merely do an internal software emulation of MIDI? Have you ever used an application that would have benefitted from MIDI IN or MIDI OUT connections? If so, name the application and describe how MIDI connections would have helped.

5. Do you believe PCMCIA cards will become important in multimedia? Why or why not? Does your computer have PCMCIA slots?

Multimedia Computer Buyer's Checklists

OBJECTIVES

After completing this chapter, you will be able to:

☐ **Use multimedia computer buyer checklists that clarify what you need to buy and why.**

☐ **Assess the multimedia PC you are using now and decide what upgrade(s) it needs next.**

This chapter contains three checklists. The first one lists the equipment in an affordable, low-budget system that will get you started without a large cash outlay. The second describes a mid-range system that is the most strategic buy if you can afford it. The third list is for a multimedia dream machine with all the bells and whistles. While few readers will ever buy all the components that this chaper enumerates, a checklist is useful because it shows you all the options and lets you consider which items you really need.

The annual *NewMedia Magazine Multimedia Buyers Guide* is very helpful when it actually comes time for you to buy multimedia equipment. Chapter 17 tells you how to apply for a free subscription to *NewMedia*.

Low-Budget System

System Unit
☐ 486SX 33Mhz central processor _____

☐ 8 MB RAM _____

☐ SVGA color display _____

☐ Mouse or other pointing device _____

Multimedia Accessories
☐ CD-ROM double speed _____

☐ 16-bit waveform digital audio _____

☐ Audio speakers (self-powered or with external amp) _____

Multimedia Read/Write Storage
☐ 160 MB hard disk _____

Communication Options
☐ 9,600 baud modem _____

Printer
☐ Inkjet printer _____

Mid-Range System

System Unit
☐ 486 DX/2 66Mhz central processor _____

☐ 8 MB RAM _____

☐ SVGA color display _____

☐ Mouse or other pointing device _____

Multimedia Accessories
☐ CD-ROM double speed _____

☐ 16-bit waveform digital audio _____

☐ Audio speakers (self-powered or with external amp) _____

☐ Video overlay with: _____

    ☐ Multiple inputs _____

    ☐ Frame capture _____

    ☐ Video for Windows capture _____

☐ Videodisc with 2 second maximum seek time _____

Multimedia Read/Write Storage

☐ 400 MB hard disk   _____

☐ External SCSI connector   _____

☐ Read-write optical disk   _____

Communication Options

☐ Network card   _____

☐ TCP/IP network connection   _____

☐ *winsock.dll* installed under Windows   _____

Auxiliary Input

☐ Hand-held scanner   _____

☐ Hi8 camcorder   _____

Printer

☐ 300 DPI laser printer   _____

High-End System

System Unit

☐ Pentium 90 Mhz central processor   _____

☐ 16 MB RAM   _____

☐ SVGA color display   _____

☐ Mouse or other pointing device   _____

Multimedia Accessories

☐ CD-ROM triple speed   _____

☐ 16-bit waveform digital audio   _____

☐ Audio speakers (self-powered or with external amp) _____

☐ Video overlay with: _____

    ☐ Multiple inputs   _____

    ☐ Frame capture   _____

    ☐ TV tuner   _____

    ☐ Video for Windows capture   _____

☐ MIDI IN and OUT   _____

☐ MIDI keyboard   _____

☐ General MIDI external synthesizer   _____

☐ Videodisc, high-end with CLV still framing   _____

Multimedia Read/Write Storage

☐ 800 MB hard disk _____

☐ External SCSI connector _____

☐ Read-write optical disk _____

☐ Writable CD-ROM (CD-R) _____

☐ PCMCIA cards _____

Communication Options

☐ 14,400 baud modem _____

☐ Network card _____

☐ TCP/IP network connection _____

☐ *winsock.dll* installed under Windows _____

Auxiliary Input

☐ Hand-held scanner _____

☐ Flatbed scanner _____

☐ Slide scanner _____

☐ Digital camera _____

☐ Hi8 camcorder _____

Printer

☐ 600 DPI color laser printer _____

E X E R C I S E S

1. Which one of the three checklists provided in this chapter most closely matches your multimedia PC? What features does your MPC have in addition to those listed? What features does it lack?

2. Do you think any of the items listed in the high-end checklist are not needed in a multimedia computer? If so, list the items and explain why they are unnecessary.

3. Take the three checklists to your local computer store and price the equipment. Create an itemized list that shows what each component costs, and compute the total cost of each system.

4. Does your local computer store sell any multimedia peripherals not listed in the high-end checklist? If so, what are they? Do you feel they should be added to the checklist? Why or why not?

Configuring a Multimedia Computer

OBJECTIVES

After completing this chapter, you will be able to:

■ Connect the audio and video components of a multimedia computer in order to optimize its functionality and minimize wiring difficulty.

■ Use the multimedia hardware preferences of the author as a benchmark against which to compare and contrast other choices.

■ Save slots by combining multiple features on a single circuit board.

■ Use a low-cost audio/video switch that can increase the number of device connections to your computer.

When the author makes multimedia presentations around the world, his hosts often express amazement at the simplicity of the setup requirements. They expect that it will be complicated to connect all of the video and audio sources to their video projector and sound system, but it is actually quite simple. A clever configuration of multimedia features mixes and switches all of the video and audio sources inside the computer and limits the number of wires emerging from the computer to three: one for SVGA video, and one pair for stereo audio. This chapter shares with you the design that makes this possible.

Feature Cards

The author's multimedia computer has a built-in CD-ROM drive and the following three circuit cards:

- Creative Labs Sound Blaster 16 ASP digital audio board with Musical Instrument Digital Interface (MIDI)
- New Media Graphics Super VideoWindows video overlay and capture board
- New Media Graphics Super TV Tuner

Sometimes multimedia computers contain a separate MIDI board that occupies an additional slot; the author saves a slot by getting the MIDI option on the Sound Blaster card.

Audio Connections

Figure 13-1 shows how some users run their audio outputs into an external mixer, which is in turn connected to loudspeakers. While this configuration is very straightforward and easy to set up, it has three disadvantages. First, you lose the capability of the computer to switch audio sources on and off. For example, when your multimedia software turns off the sound to a TV channel, you will keep hearing the sound because you wired the audio directly to the mixer. Second, external mixers inevitably introduce noise into the signal, some more than others. Third, it costs more to wire your multimedia computer in this way, because you have to buy an external mixer you do not need. Why spend the extra money?

Audio Wiring

Figure 13-2 shows you how to wire your multimedia PC so the audio mixing is done internally. There are four sets of connections in this diagram:

1. Connect the audio outputs of your peripherals (videodisc, camcorder, and TV tuner) to the audio inputs of your video overlay card. Always connect your videodisc to the first set of inputs on your overlay card. Put your camcorder on the second set, and your TV tuner on the third. *Note:* Overlay cards that come with a TV tuner on board already have this third connection made internally.

2. Connect the left and right audio outputs of your overlay card to the external input of your waveform audio board.

3. Connect the audio output of your CD-ROM drive to the *internal* input of your waveform audio board. If your computer came with a CD-ROM drive installed, this connection was probably already made. If you try to make this connection yourself, you will need to open up your computer. Make sure your computer and all devices attached to it are *disconnected* from any power sources, and read the sound card and CD-ROM manuals carefully to make sure you connect it right.

13-1

Using an external mixer for multimedia sound connections.

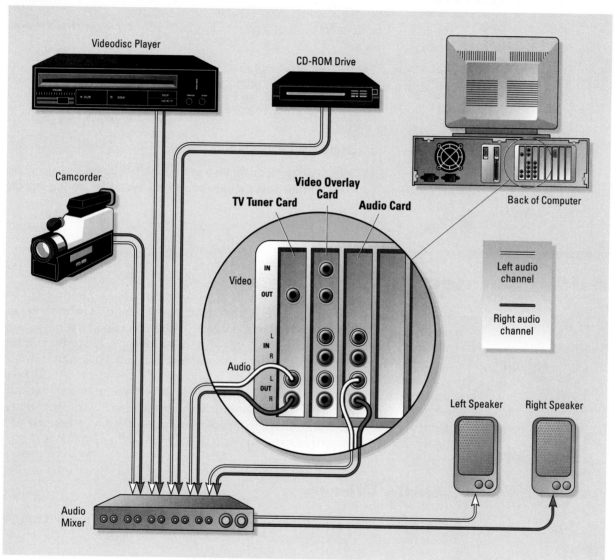

4. Connect the stereo output of your waveform audio board to the left and right line inputs of an audio amplifier and speaker system, or to powered speakers that have an audio amplifier built in; Yamaha's MS202 powered speakers do a very nice job at an affordable price.

Audio Mixing

Now you may ask: since you have eliminated the external mixer, how can you adjust and balance the volume levels of your audio sources? Through software! Figures 13-3 and 13-4 show the mixer programs that come with the Sound Blaster and Turtle Beach audio boards, respectively. The mixer programs let you adjust the relative volumes of each audio input by clicking and dragging on-screen audio controls. The resulting sound is cleaner than when you use an external mixer, and since all of the sound is under the control of the Microsoft MCI, your multimedia software can turn the sound on and off as needed.

13-2

Internal audio mixing.

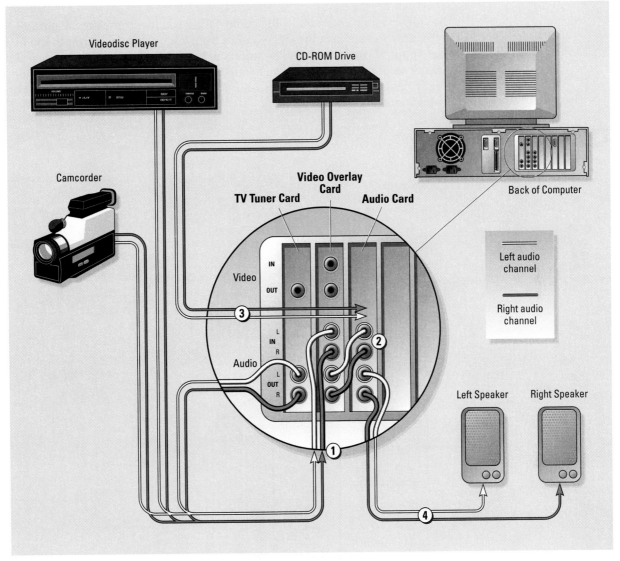

13-3

The Sound Blaster mixer screen.

13-4

The Turtle Beach mixer screen.

Video Connections

The video connections parallel the audio wiring you just completed. Figure 13-5 shows how you connect the video output from your videodisc player to the first video input of your video overlay card. Plug the video output of your camcorder into the second input, and connect your TV tuner to the third input. *Note:* Video overlay cards that have TV tuners on board already have this third connection made internally.

13-5

Connecting video sources.

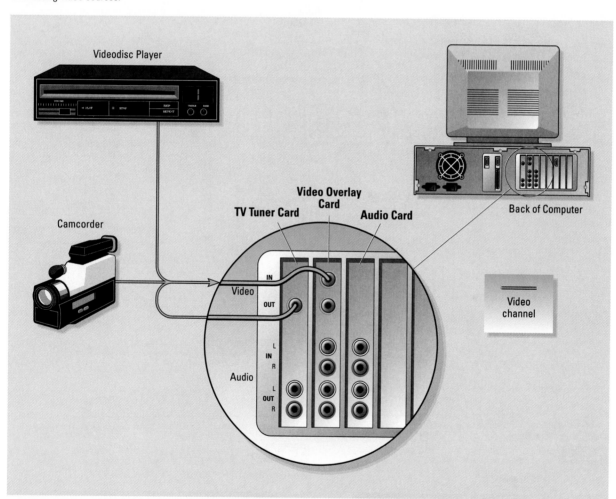

A Low-Cost Audio/Video Switch

Radio Shack makes a low-cost but highly useful switch that comes in handy in the following two situations. First, if your overlay card lacks multiple inputs, but you need to connect more than one video source to it; second, when your overlay card has multiple inputs, but you have a greater number of video sources to connect.

13-6

Radio Shack's Stereo Audio/Video Selector Switch lets you connect up to four devices and select any one of them by simply pressing a button.

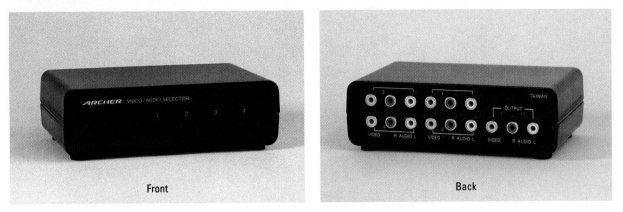

Front   Back

Figure 13-6 shows the Radio Shack switch, which costs less then $20. (Its catalog number is 15-1956.) You can connect up to four devices to it, including their video and stereo left and right audio outputs. Then you connect the video and stereo outputs of the switch to the corresponding inputs of your overlay card. To change sources, you simply press one of the four buttons on the switch.

E X E R C I S E S

1. Draw a wiring diagram that shows how the multimedia components in your computer are connected. Compare your diagram to the ones in this chapter. How are they alike? How do they differ?

2. Can you improve upon the suggestions made in this chapter? If so, how?

3. How does the mixing screen for your digital audio board compare to the ones illustrated in this chapter? Can you control the volume of your microphone input? Of your CD-Audio playback? Of your external line input? Do you have separate left and right volume controls?

Training on an exercise bicycle with the *HeartBeat Personal Trainer.*

Training on a stepper with the *HeartBeat Personal Trainer.*

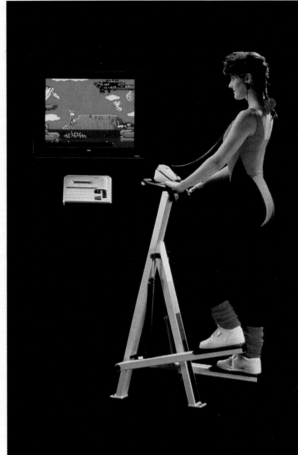

Online Resources

To allow physicians speedy access to the latest clinical research, the American Association for the Advancement of Science publishes the electronic *Online Journal of Current Clinical Trials.* The Library of Medicine has blessed this new online journal by including it in its MEDLINE data base and its *Index Medicus.*

The Nursing Network offers nationwide job and educational opportunities, clinical information, sources for nursing equipment and literature, and live conferences with experts.

National Health Insurance

The Clinton Health Security Plan: What It Costs and What It Means to You is available on CD-ROM or floppy disk from Allegro New Media. It includes the full text of the plan, plus an analysis by business, health, insurance, and political commentators.

E X E R C I S E S

1. Your life or that of a loved one could depend on the extent to which your local health care provider uses multimedia in preparing its staff to handle medical situations correctly. Find out whether your local health care facility knows about Stewart's *Interactive Healthcare Directories*, and ask how many of the interactive video training programs are in place and how many staff members have completed the training.

2. Does your local school of nursing belong to the HESC? Does it have enough multimedia computers to train all of its nursing students on the HESC materials? If your nursing school does not know what HESC is, you've got problems.

3. Is your doctor connected to the Internet? Ask about this during your next appointment. Find out how he or she uses the network to stay current and learn about new procedures, such as by reading the *Online Journal of Clinical Trials*.

4. List three ways multimedia computers can help you maintain your personal health today. What other ways do you foresee technology being able to help improve your health in the future?

Encyclopedic Resources

After completing this chapter, you will be able to:

- **Take advantage of the encyclopedic resources already on CD-ROM and the Information Superhighway.**

- **Appreciate the power of online searching as a research tool.**

- **Understand how the Smithsonian, the Library of Congress, and museums and libraries all over the country are going online.**

- **Realize why the *Encyclopedia Britannica* is finally online.**

A wealth of encyclopedic resources are available on multimedia CD-ROMs and online via networks on the Information Superhighway. CD-ROMs provide the convenience of owning the resource and being able to use it on any multimedia PC. Networks provide access to much more information which, depending on how recently the CD-ROM was pressed, is probably the most up-to-date information available.

Multimedia CD-ROMs

Anyone who has used a printed encyclopedia will appreciate the convenience of multimedia CD-ROMs. Not only does it seem to take forever to find the information you want in a printed encyclopedia, but you also have to check all of the annual updates, which are printed in separate volumes. CD-ROMs not only solve this problem by providing rapid full-text searching, but they also cost less. Thanks to the MPC price wars, the entire multimedia PC costs less than the printed *Encyclopedia Britannica.*

In 1985, Grolier became the first company to publish its printed encyclopedia in a multimedia CD-ROM version. Now *The New Grolier Multimedia Encyclopedia* has been supplemented with additional text, expanded audio capabilities, enhanced video clips, narrated animations, and a wider variety of pictures, photographs, and maps. It won a *Home Office Computing* "Editors' Pick" award and was named "Best Multimedia CD-ROM Title" by *Multimedia World.* It was also named one of the 27 good reasons to buy a CD-ROM player by *PC Magazine.*

Figure 8-1 shows Grolier's main menu. It provides many ways to access the 33,000 articles in the encyclopedia. For example, the Knowledge Tree lets you find articles using a topic hierarchy. The Timeline accesses a database of more than five thousand historical events. Figure 8-2 shows one of the Multimedia Maps, a new feature of the revised encyclopedia in which narrated animations let you sail around the world with Magellan, march through Civil War battlefields with Generals Grant and Lee, study U.S. territorial growth, and learn about the Gulf War. Figure 8-3 shows another new feature that Grolier calls a Knowledge Explorer audio visual essay. Combining photographs, music, and voice narration, there are Knowledge Explorer essays about Africa, the human body, space exploration, music, the animal world, and architecture. While each essay is fully narrated and self-contained, there are links to the many relevant text articles within the encyclopedia.

The main menu of *The New Grolier Multimedia Encyclopedia.*

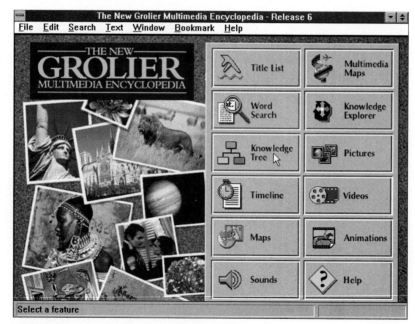

Grolier's new Multimedia Maps feature lets you travel through time using maps that chart journeys accompanied with sights, sounds, and motion.

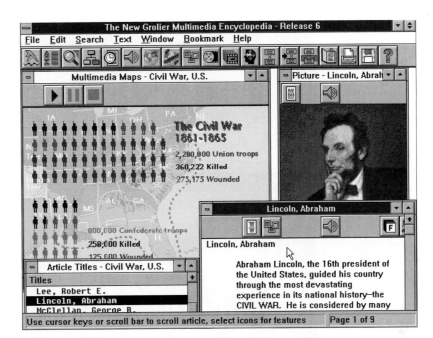

Grolier's Knowledge Explorer essays combine photographs, music, and voice narration to make learning a multisensory experience.

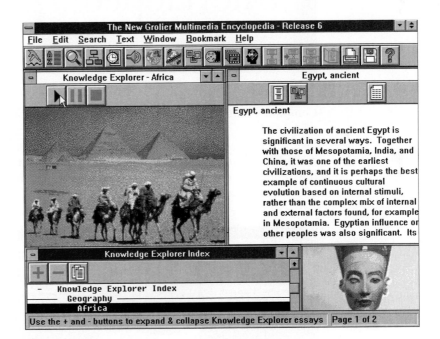

Compton's also publishes a multimedia version of its printed encyclopedia. Shown in Figure 8-4, *Compton's Interactive Encyclopedia* contains the full text and graphics of the 26-volume *Compton's Encyclopedia*; thousands of pictures, drawings, and photos; easy-to-use research paths to retrieve information; an interactive world atlas with links to 121,000 related pictures and articles; enhanced sound and full-motion Video for Windows; the complete *Merriam-Webster OnLine Dictionary and Thesaurus*; and Compton's Virtual Workspace interface, which lets users open multiple windows into the encyclopedia and move them around the screen much like you spread books out on a conventional desktop.

8-4

*Compton's Interactive
Encyclopedia.*

Compton's thought hard about what tools would make the encyclopedia most useful and provided a rich set of options for browsing and searching. For example, Figure 8-5 shows the InfoPilot, which generates a network of secondary topics related to a main topic. Making one of the secondary topics the main topic causes the InfoPilot to create a new network for that topic. This provides a powerful way of brainstorming ideas.

8-5

The InfoPilot in *Compton's Interactive Encyclopedia* automatically finds articles related to the main topic.

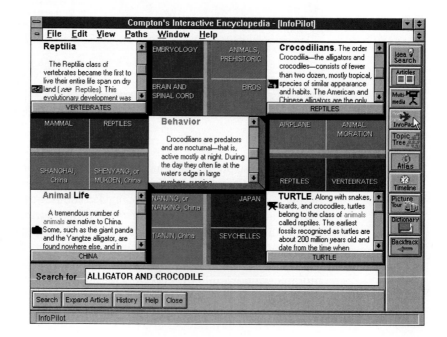

Figure 8-6 shows how the Timeline tool lets you access information on important people and events in U.S. and world history. It has an Outline view that displays a general outline of history, and a Detail view that offers detailed accounts of specific events. While researching a topic, you can end up with many windows open at once, showing different articles, photographs, maps, topic trees, and the dictionary. To help you manage multiple windows, Compton's developed the Virtual Workspace shown in Figure 8-7. The Virtual Workspace is the user's view of a "virtual desktop," a large surface you can fill with the tools and

8-6

The Timeline tool in *Compton's Interactive Encyclopedia.*

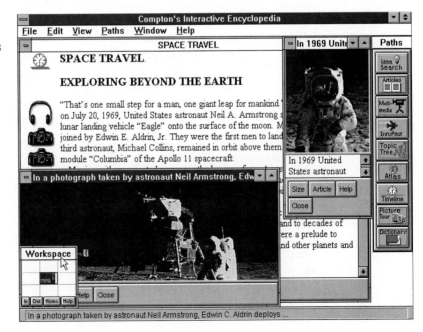

8-7

The Virtual Workspace lets users open multiple windows into *Compton's Interactive Encyclopedia.*

8-8

The McGraw-Hill Multimedia Encyclopedia of Science and Technology.

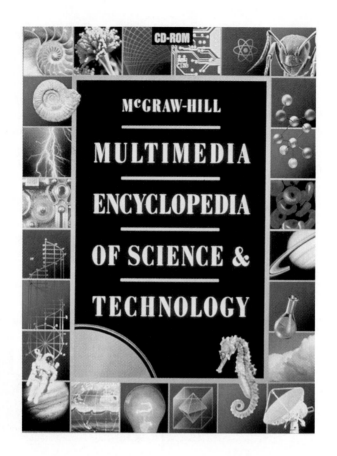

information you need. To move your view of the workspace, you click and drag the whole screen.

Encarta is a multimedia encyclopedia by Microsoft that includes more than 25,000 articles in 93 categories, a gallery with more than 7,000 photographic images and animations, and seven hours of audio. Users access this information in several ways. First, there is an alphabetical index; second, a category browser lets you narrow down topics by category and subcategory; third, a timeline puts events in chronological order; fourth, an atlas lets you select places by zooming in on a map; and finally, you can use the Boolean operators (AND, OR, NOT) to search for specific words or phrases within any article. *Encarta* also lets you set bookmarks, take notes, and copy both textual and multimedia material into personalized files.

Figure 8-8 shows the *McGraw-Hill Multimedia Encyclopedia of Science and Technology* by McGraw-Hill. It contains the updated text and graphics of the 20-volume printed version of the encyclopedia, and the new fifth edition of the *McGraw-Hill Dictionary of Scientific and Technical Terms*, enhanced by narrated animations to illustrate scientific concepts. There are more than seven thousand articles, one hundred thousand terms and definitions, three dozen animation sequences, forty minutes of audio, and five hundred color photos, drawings, and maps. To locate an item in the encyclopedia, you click the Search button and key in your search terms, as shown in Figure 8-9. From the list of relevant articles shown in Figure 8-10, you select the one you would like to view, and its full text appears with your search term highlighted, as shown in Figure 8-11. Clicking the Camera button and the Tile button lets you view the article and a photograph side-by-side, as you can see in Figure 8-12.

Locating an item in the *McGraw-Hill Multimedia Encyclopedia of Science and Technology.*

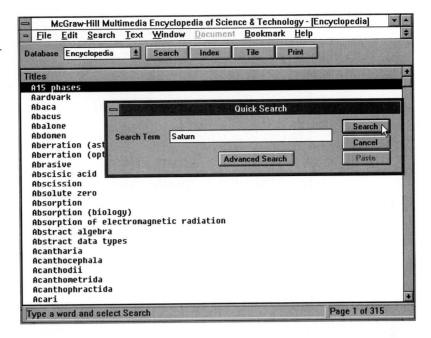

8-10

The *McGraw-Hill Multimedia Encyclopedia of Science and Technology* presents a list of relevant articles along with the number of times the search term appears in each article.

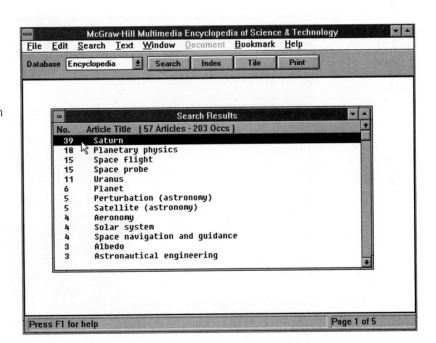

The *1993 TIME Almanac* by Compact Publishing is a complete current events and news reference program on CD-ROM. Working directly with Time and CNN, Compact Publishing included on this CD-ROM back issues of *TIME* magazine (the full text of every issue of *TIME* from 1989 through January 4, 1993); *TIME Highlights/Decades* (all of the important articles and coverage from 1923 to 1988); *TIME Highlights/Elections* (a complete news coverage of all presidential campaigns since 1924 including Clinton's election); *TIME Portraits* (in-depth articles, cover stories, videos and photo essays); Newsquest (a quiz that challenges the user's knowledge of the news); United States (a news directory of the 103rd Congress, complete profiles on the people, government, economy and

8-11

The search terms are highlighted in the full text of the article.

McGraw-Hill Multimedia Encyclopedia of Science & Technology - [Saturn]

File   Edit   Search   Text   Window   Document   Bookmark   Help

Database Encyclopedia   Search   Index   Tile   Print

Saturn

The second-largest planet in the solar system and the sixth in order of distance to the Sun. The outermost planet known prior to 1781, Saturn is surrounded by a beautiful system of rings. Despite the planet's huge size, its mean density is so low it could float in water. Saturn is also the only planet that has a satellite (Titan) with a dense atmosphere. This distant planetary system has been visited by three NASA spacecraft: a preliminary survey by *Pioneer 11* in September 1979, and a more sophisticated reconnaissance by *Voyager 1* in November 1980 and *Voyager 2* in August 1981.

Orbit and physical elements

Use cursor keys or scroll bar to scroll article, select icons for features   1 of 21513

8-12

The Tile button in the *McGraw-Hill Multimedia Encyclopedia of Science and Technology* lets you view text and graphics side-by-side.

McGraw-Hill Multimedia Encyclopedia of Science & Technology

File   Edit   Search   Text   Window   Document   Bookmark   Help

Database Encyclopedia   Search   Index   Tile   Print

Saturn

Picture - Saturn

CAPTION

Saturn

The second-largest planet in the solar system and the sixth in order of distance to the Sun. The outermost planet known prior to 1781, Saturn is surrounded by a beautiful system of rings. Despite the planet's huge size, its mean density is so low it could float in water. Saturn is also the only planet that has a satellite (Titan) with

Press F1 for help   1 of 21513

environment of each state, with full-color maps); and World (the complete *1992 CIA World Fact Book,* plus U.S. State Department notes on more than 200 countries, with full-color maps).

In the *20th Century Almanac* by The Software Toolworks, users can land on the moon, attend Woodstock, listen to President Kennedy's inaugural address, or join the crowd for the 1916 World Series. This multimedia reference work uses an extensive archive of motion videos to produce a visual encyclopedia of the century, including audio, photos, and text. Also by The Software Toolworks, *The 1993 Guinness Disc Of Records* lets the user relive fantastic feats and unbelievable facts from one of the world's best-selling books. The CD-ROM includes more than 2,000 new and updated records, a virtual library of video clips with audio, 300 all-new color photographs, as well as reproductions of *The 1993 Guinness Book of Records.*

Finally, National Geographic Society publishes a CD-ROM version of the *Picture Atlas of the World,* which provides full-color maps.

Internet Resources

Someday the Information Superhighway may eliminate the need for CD-ROMs by making available all of the necessary databases and programs in the form of a worldwide network, which will function as a public utility that will be as widespread as telephones and televisions are now. As you will learn in Part Seven of this book, you can already get on the Internet (the worldwide connection of more than a million networks) and visit the Library of Congress, the Smithsonian, and many museums. Even the *Encyclopedia Britannica* is finally coming online, having had sales diminish due to competition from CD-ROM encyclopedias by Compton's, Grolier, and Microsoft (*Forbes,* 2/28/94: 42).

Library of Congress

The Library of Congress operates a multimedia online service called LC MARVEL. MARVEL is an acronym for Machine-Assisted Realization of the Virtual Electronic Library. Online exhibits include Soviet government documents such as the directive from Lenin ordering the death of anti-Communist farmers; fifteenth-century manuscripts from the Vatican library; sections of the Dead Sea Scrolls along with maps and other images related to the scrolls; and an image bank that chronicles Christopher Columbus' 1492 trip to the Americas.

LC MARVEL also provides information about copyrights, access to the library's online catalog system, and full-text searching of federal legislation. Access to LC MARVEL is free; Chapter 36 will show you how to connect to it and take advantage of these MARVELous services.

Smithsonian

The Smithsonian Institution sponsors many Internet services that provide access to materials from its various museums and research arms. For example, the National Air and Space Museum, the National Museum of American Art, and the National Museum of Natural History are all online. If you have an Internet connection, the tutorial in Part Seven will show you how to access these and other fascinating resources on the Information Superhighway.

Museums

Gaffin (1994) tells how you can get on the Information Superhighway and visit many interesting museums, including the University of California at Berkeley's Museum of Paleontology, where the Remote Nature exhibit lets you download images of plants, birds, and other animals, including photos taken of a great white shark near the Farallon Islands off San Francisco. The Hull-House, a

Chicago settlement house that became world-famous in the late 1800's, is online; you can connect to it through Northwestern University, browse the museum, and learn about its famous founder, Jane Addams. The California Museum of Photography has online pictures that portray life in California from the mid-1800's to the early 1900's.

Several museums at Harvard University are online. For example, you can use the Information Superhighway to plan your visit to the Arnold Arboretum by looking up the locations of specific trees so you will know where to look for them. The famous Bishop Museum in Honolulu is online, as is the Royal British Columbia Museum. Part Seven will show you how to connect to all of these exciting places on the Information Superhighway.

Encyclopedia Britannica

Encyclopedia Britannica Inc. has been slow to offer an electronic version of its flagship *Encyclopedia Britannica*. It has been frustrating to have such wonderful tools for searching encyclopedic resources but not have the world's finest encyclopedia available online. The desire for online searching led many people to purchase lesser encyclopedias that used these new tools, and this led to the loss of market share for the *Britannica*.

Finally, the *Britannica* is going online. According to the *New York Times* (2/8/94 C1), it will be offered initially over the Internet to universities and some public libraries. The online version will use the *Mosaic* hypertext software, which makes it possible for an article to link to related articles and illustrations, including audio and video clips. *Mosaic* is discussed below in the section on the Information Superhighway.

NOTE: Just as this book went to press, the *Encyclopedia Britannica* and the *World Book Encyclopedia* were published in CD-ROM versions. Now the finest encyclopedias are finally available on CD.

E X E R C I S E S

1. Name three CD-ROM encyclopedias and find out whether you can get access to one or more of them at home, work, or school.

2. Select a topic, such as the role Amelia Earhart played in aviation history. Then time how long it takes you to find out information about her and construct an appropriate bibliography from a printed encyclopedia. Now try one of the CD-ROM encyclopedias mentioned in this chapter. How much time did the CD-ROM search save?

3. New technology has benefited researchers considerably. For example, the Xerox machine was invented while the author was a student. No longer did we have to write out by hand the materials we wanted to excerpt from books and magazines in the library; for ten cents per page, we could make Xerox copies, thereby saving many hours of handwriting time. Today, multimedia CD-ROMs and the Information Superhighway provide much more powerful tools. How do you see multimedia computers helping you conduct research? (If you have never used the Information Superhighway, completing the tutorial in Part Seven of this book will help you answer this question.)

Application Development Packages

After completing this chapter, you will be able to:

■ **Define the categories of application development packages and recognize the names of the major packages in each category.**

■ **Know when to use a presentation package, a hypermedia program, or a full-fledged authoring tool.**

■ **Experience what the different packages are like by running product demonstrations on the *Multiliteracy CD*.**

There are three kinds of development software for creating multimedia applications: presentation packages, hypermedia programs, and authoring systems. This chapter defines each kind, identifies available products, and provides demonstrations on the *Multiliteracy CD*.

As with most categorizations, there is an overlap among the classifications defined here. For example, some presentation packages provide a limited hypermedia capability; hypermedia programs can create presentations; and full-fledged authoring systems can do just about anything. However, just as you would not normally use a sledgehammer to pound a finishing nail, so also do multimedia tools have their appropriate uses, according to which you will find them classified in this chapter.

Presentation Packages

Presentation packages try to make it easy for you to produce convincing multimedia shows consisting of slides, audio clips, animations, and full-motion sequences. Vendors often select product titles that imply how their packages can influence an audience; for example, consider the titles Compel from Asymmetrix, PowerPoint by Microsoft, and Persuasion from Aldus.

Several graphics packages also have presentation capabilities. Lotus Freelance and Harvard Graphics are high-powered graphics packages with presentation capabilities. More recently, word processing giant WordPerfect has entered the multimedia market with WordPerfect Presentations.

PowerPoint

According to Microsoft, there are more than two million users of PowerPoint. It addresses the needs of business professionals who need to create compelling graphics and present them effectively. Based on the slide-show metaphor shown in Figure 9-1, PowerPoint has a slide sorter that lets you drag slides and position them in the order you want to present them. You can drag and drop slides from one presentation to another, and import charts and spreadsheet data from Microsoft Excel. An AutoContent Wizard helps you figure out what to say, and an Outliner helps organize and reorder thoughts by letting you selectively collapse and expand outline headings.

PowerPoint has a clip art library of more than 1,100 business graphics, a graphing feature to create your own figures, an organization chart creator, and an equation editor to create and display scientific and mathematical equations. A rehearsal feature helps you practice and learn how long a presentation will take, showing how much time you spent on each slide. You can print speaker's notes, audience handouts, and outline pages. There is also a GraphicsLink communications package to send presentations to Genigraphics for next-day delivery of 35mm slides.

9-1

The slide sorter in PowerPoint.

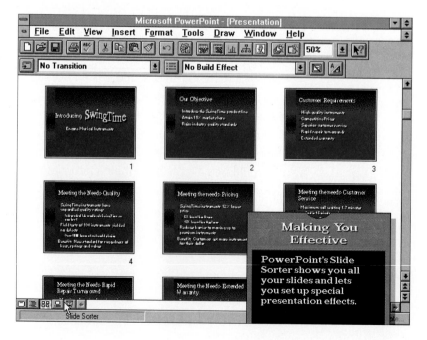

You can drag and drop charts from Excel into PowerPoint presentations and documents created in Word.

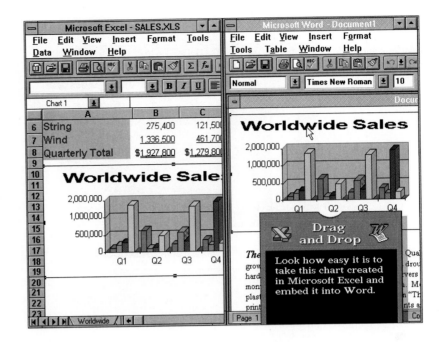

According to Microsoft research, only 8% of presenters use multimedia computers to deliver presentations; the rest use slides and overhead projections. Therefore, PowerPoint's ability to print to film is key to its market penetration. Indeed, PowerPoint swept all the categories in *CIO* magazine's Readers Choice Awards for presentation graphics.

PowerPoint is one of five programs you can purchase bundled together as Microsoft Office Professional. The other four programs include Microsoft's Excel spreadsheet, Access database, Word text processor, and Mail communications package. All five programs look alike and work together. For example, Figure 9-2 shows how you can drag and drop a chart from Excel into a document in Word. When you work on the document in Word and click the chart to edit it, the Excel menu bar appears automatically, without requiring you to switch programs. The Present It button in Word flows text from your word processed documents into PowerPoint templates.

The *Multiliteracy CD* contains an entertaining demonstration of Microsoft's PowerPoint. To run it, go to the Demonstrations section, select Software, and click the PowerPoint button. Be sure to run the part of the demo that shows how PowerPoint functions as part of Microsoft Office.

Harvard Graphics

Harvard Graphics competes with PowerPoint for market share and claims to have as many users. Published by Software Publishing Corporation, its 5-Minute Coach helps users get started right away with a tutorial that covers creating, enhancing, and managing a presentation. You can view your presentation in outline format with the Outliner, or as a slide show in the Slide Sorter. The QuickLooks feature lets you try different colors, fonts, and perspectives to see how your slides look before you commit to any change. Figure 9-3 shows how the Advisor offers suggestions on layout, color, and fonts.

A chart gallery contains preformatted title, bullet, table, data, and organizational charts. There are 31 professionally designed presentation styles selected after extensive user input. Each style specifies the charting options, color palette,

The Harvard Graphics Advisor is always ready to provide tips as you create your presentation.

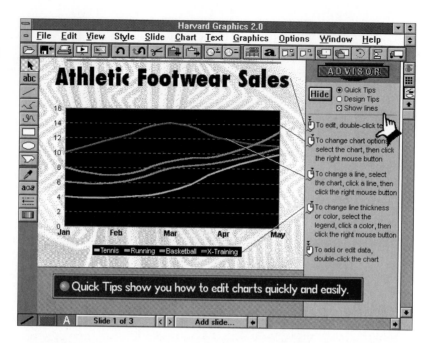

How a slide looks in different styles in Harvard Graphics.

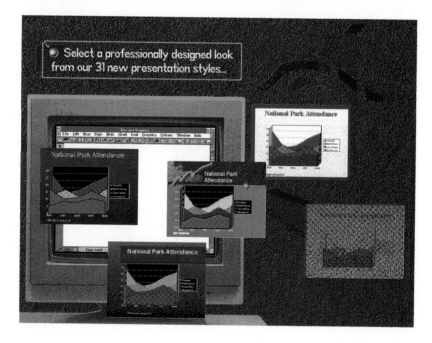

background design, and type font for a presentation. By editing a presentation's master template, you can change the appearance of every slide automatically. Figure 9-4 shows how a slide looks in different styles.

Harvard F/X lets you add special effects to text or drawings, and multimedia capabilities let you add music, video, and animation. Its print options enable you to create speaker notes, handouts, transparencies, and slides on your laser printer, plotter, color printer, or film recorder.

Like PowerPoint, Harvard Graphics has OLE (object linking and embedding) support that lets users drag and drop objects from other applications into a slide.

There is also a conferencing capability that lets network users display presentations on up to 64 other computers simultaneously.

The *Multiliteracy CD* contains a demonstration of Harvard Graphics. To run it, go to the Demonstrations section, select Applications, and click the Harvard Graphics button.

Hypermedia Programs

Hypermedia programs go beyond the linear slide-show metaphor used in presentation packages to provide an infinite capability to link objects and enable users to navigate among them. The most well-known hypermedia programs are HyperCard for the Macintosh, and ToolBook for Windows. HyperCard uses the metaphor of a stack of cards. Each screen is thought of as a card you can place anywhere in a stack and link to any other card. ToolBook works the same way, except that stacks of cards are thought of as books containing pages. A program from Heizer Software called ConvertIt! can translate HyperCard stacks into ToolBook books.

ToolBook

ToolBook is published by Asymmetrix. Its purpose is to reduce the amount of time and effort required to create Windows applications. You develop applications by creating books full of pages, which can contain text, graphics, and buttons that enable user interaction. Toolbook has a scripting language called OpenScript in which you program interactive and navigational commands that define what the buttons do. You can also attach scripts to hot words in text fields. Particularly useful is a script recorder that will automatically create a script for actions you perform on the screen, such as navigating to a page in a book or creating an animation by moving an object around the screen. ToolBook comes with more than 270 prescripted multimedia objects called widgets that you can copy and paste into your application.

The French language software *Nouvelles Dimensions* discussed in Chapter 4 is a ToolBook application. There is a demonstration of it on your *Multiliteracy CD*. To sample the kind of application you can create with ToolBook, go to the Demonstrations section, select Applications, and click the Nouvelles Dimensions button.

PODIUM

PODIUM is a hypermedia product invented at the University of Delaware in 1988. Its goal is to make it quick and easy to create multimedia applications. Since the hands-on section of this book contains beginning and advanced tutorials in PODIUM application creation, PODIUM will not be discussed further here. However, it should be noted that the *Multiliteracy CD* that comes with this book was authored in PODIUM. By completing the tutorials in the hands-on section, you can learn how to create multimedia applications like the *Multiliteracy CD*.

Authoring Systems

Full-fledged application development tools that let you present material, ask questions about it, evaluate user input, and branch accordingly are called authoring systems. In the past, before graphical user interfaces became popular, authoring was a tedious and time-consuming process, often requiring hundreds of hours of work to create one hour of completed material. Recently, windowed environments have led to the creation of graphically based authoring systems that have reduced considerably the time needed to create a sophisticated application.

Authorware Professional

Macromedia markets Authorware Professional for Windows as "the premier multimedia authoring tool for interactive learning." An advantage Authorware has over most other packages is that it can be used to create applications for both Windows and Macintosh users. This cross-platform capability has given Macromedia a competitive edge in the publishing industry, which wants to create products that will run not only under Windows, but on the installed base of Macintoshes as well.

Authorware is rooted in some pretty powerful technology. Its sophisticated judging, sequencing, and instructional management facility builds upon two decades of work by Authorware founder Mike Allen on a computer-assisted instruction (CAI) system called PLATO. Its multimedia engine comes from a Macromind product called Director, which is the most sophisticated and complete multimedia sequencer available. For example, Drew Pictures' *Iron Helix* and the Brøderbund titles *Just Grandma and Me* and *Arthur's Teacher Trouble* were created with Director. For a demo, go to the Demonstrations section, select Applications, and click the Just Grandma and Me button or the Arthur's Teacher Trouble button.

When Macromind and Authorware merged to create Macromedia in 1992, they set the stage for creating a blockbuster authoring system. Already, they have won multimedia publishing contracts with Paramount Publishing, Jostens Learning, HyperMedia Communications, and McGraw-Hill, and they have signed strategic alliances with Apple Computer, 3DO, Bell Labs, Bell Atlantic, Brøderbund, Kaleida, and others.

Figure 9-5 shows how Authorware Professional uses a flowline metaphor to create logic structures from 11 design icons. The author creates an application by selecting icons and dragging them onto the flowline. Double-clicking an icon opens it, allowing the author to add content. As icons accumulate on the screen, the author can click the Map icon to group related icons together. Thus, the author can view the application from a top-down approach, maintaining perspective on how the various program modules interrelate.

Icons control everything from user interactions to the decisions they trigger. For example, Figure 9-6 shows how the Decision icon opens a dialog that lets the author choose a sequential presentation of the attached icons, a selection of random icons, or the selection of a calculated path based on the value of a variable.

There is a demonstration of Authorware Professional on the *Multiliteracy CD*. It will introduce you to Authorware Professional, show you how Authorware works, and let you run a sample application about a 35mm camera. To try the Authorware demo, go to the Demonstrations section, select Software, and click the Authorware Professional button.

The flowline metaphor in *Authorware Professional.*

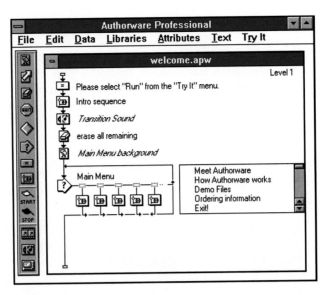

The Decision icon options dialog in *Authorware Professional.*

IconAuthor

Macromedia considers IconAuthor from AimTech to be the primary competition for Authorware Professional. Like Authorware, IconAuthor has a visual programming environment in which you create applications by moving icons into a flowchart that depicts the structure of your project. Then you add content by providing text, graphics, animation, and/or full-motion video to the screens in your application.

Macromedia has created a detailed side-by-side comparison of the two products. Before deciding which package to purchase, developers should have a look at this comparison. Contact Macromedia for their *Authorware Professional for Windows Reviewer's Guide.*

Quest

Macromedia may be getting some serious Windows competition. Allen Communication has recently created a Windows version of its award-winning Quest Multimedia Authoring System, which corporations and educational institutions have used to create thousands of hours of courseware during the past decade. Shown in Figure 9-7, the new Quest 5.0 for Windows is an object-oriented authoring tool. It lets you work at one of two levels: design or frame. At the design level, shown in Figure 9-8, you can experiment and map out the overall structure of your application. The postage-stamp representation of full frames gives the developer an overview of how the screens look and link together. At the frame

The Quest for Windows title page.

9-8

At the design level, Quest authors think of the big picture and chart their applications with postage-stamp representations of actual frames.

level, shown in Figure 9-9, you work on the individual frames that comprise the application, seeing exactly what the user will see on the screen.

The FastTrack feature shown in Figure 9-10 lets Quest authors use prebuilt buttons, interactions, screen layouts, and borders. You select a prebuilt object and then add your content, thereby saving the time it would have taken to create the object from scratch. Floating toolbars let you assemble graphics, text, audio, full-motion video, animations, and branching. Every object in Quest is a so-called "smart" object. A smart object has a life of its own, defined by the actions and conditions set for it by the developer, who can request data from it and even let the end-user manipulate it.

9-9

At the frame level, Quest authors work inside the frame, seeing exactly what the user will see.

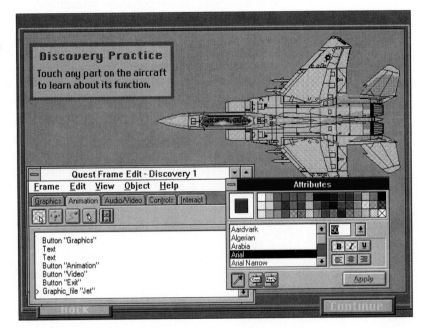

9-10

Quest's FastTrack feature lets authors add their own content to prebuilt screen layouts, menus, templates, borders, buttons, question/answer frames, and interactions.

There is a demonstration of Quest 5.0 for Windows on the *Multiliteracy CD.* To take it for a test drive, go to the Demonstrations section, select Software, and click the Quest button.

E X E R C I S E S

1. What presentation packages does your school or business own? What are the primary reasons for their selection over competing brands?

2. What percentage of the teachers at your school or the executives in your business use multimedia presentation packages? How many use the computer to make a presentation, as opposed to just printing slides or transparencies for noncomputer projection?

3. Does your school or business own an authoring system? If so, which one? Why was it selected?

4. What software would you personally use to create a presentation? Why do you prefer it over other brands? What improvements would you like to see the vendor make in its product's capabilities?

5. Given the features of the presentation packages, hypermedia programs, and authoring systems presented in this chapter, what is your overall impression of the state of the art of multimedia application development? What additional capabilities would you like these tools to have?

Part Three

Selecting Multimedia Hardware

C O N T E N T S

Chapter 10
Competing Multimedia Standards

Chapter 11
Multimedia Computer Components

Chapter 12
Multimedia Computer Buyer's Checklists

Chapter 13
Configuring a Multimedia Computer

Buying a multimedia computer may be the most complicated shopping you ever do. Four factors make it difficult. First, because there is no industry-wide standard for multimedia, each vendor creates its own brand and produces multimedia applications that work with only its brand. Potential buyers hesitate because they know that getting Brand X will prevent them from running applications made for Brand Y. Second, there are so many options you can add on to a multimedia computer that once you decide which brand to buy, you might still find it confusing to choose multimedia peripherals. Third, it is hard to get a list of all the options that are available, because vendors are only interested in showing those they sell. Finally, once you buy your computer and select the options you want, installing and getting them to work can be a nightmarish experience.

The next four chapters in this book will help you overcome these four dilemmas. The good news is that once you finally do get your multimedia computer up and running, you should not have many (hopefully not any) problems. In other words, most of the difficulty will happen right at the beginning, and if you can persevere through the startup problems, your time and effort will be repaid by the many benefits you will reap from your multimedia computing.

10

Competing Multimedia Standards

OBJECTIVES

After completing this chapter, you will be able to:

■ Understand the competing standards of multimedia and comprehend what is meant by the phrase "multi multimedia."

■ Realize how lack of standardization retards the progress of multimedia development.

■ Consider the level at which standardization would be appropriate.

■ Know which multimedia formats will have the most longevity.

■ Understand the basic architecture of the Microsoft MCI (Media Control Interface).

The multimedia computer industry is beset by an unfortunate lack of standardization. Instead of uniting the nation's best minds toward creating a compatible cross-platform system for multimedia, the computer industry is hard at work creating multiple standards and competing products. If this were happening accidentally, one might be more willing to tolerate the situation. Instead, vendors deliberately create disparity to differentiate their products from the competition and to make past purchases obsolete so customers will buy more hardware. In the area of graphics alone, there are more than 30 so-called "standards" for storing pictures in computer files. When an industry provides 30 different ways of doing something, there is no standard.

Computer industry leaders fail to recognize how self-defeating this lack of standardization is. They should learn a lesson from the musicians. During the early 1980's, the National Association of Music Merchants and the Audio Engineering Society began to discuss how a lack of standards was retarding the market for music synthesizers. Consumers were afraid to buy a keyboard because there was no guarantee that it would be compatible with later models in the same product line, much less with synthesizers made by other vendors. In 1983, the Musical Instrument Digital Interface (MIDI) standard was released, and all of the music merchants endorsed it. Consumers were no longer afraid of obsolescence, and music synthesizer sales mushroomed. Vendors made more money not so much because their market share increased, but because the entire market grew exponentially as a result of standardization.

Multi Multimedia

Instead of having one multimedia standard, consumers are faced with a complicated array of competing software and hardware platforms that the author (Hofstetter 1993) describes as "multi multimedia." When you create an application, you must be careful to store your objects in formats that will have the most longevity and compatibility. Otherwise the time and effort you spend will have to be reinvested when the so-called "standards" change.

Microsoft's MCI

Microsoft's MCI provides Windows users with a strategic approach to coping with this lack of standardization. MCI stands for Media Control Interface. The purpose of the MCI is to provide a device-independent means of developing multimedia software. The idea is that vendors who make multimedia hardware supply an MCI translation table for each device. Instead of hard-coding applications to specific devices, developers use MCI commands that get converted automatically by the translation table into the specific instructions needed to control the device. The MCI commands consist of generic multimedia instructions like PLAY, RECORD, PAUSE, SEEK, SAVE, and STOP.

For example, consider the industry-wide problem posed by the differences among videodisc players. Not only do videodisc command sets vary between vendors, but even within a product line manufacturers change the commands on different models. For example, to display a videodisc frame, developers must write different code for each individual brand of videodisc player. If MCI were adopted as an industry-wide standard, instead of hard-coding the commands needed to display the videodisc frame on every specific player, developers could simply send the MCI command SEEK TO the frame number. If every videodisc manufacturer provided a device driver with an MCI translation table, the user could use any videodisc player, just as MIDI lets musicians use any keyboard.

Adopting Microsoft's MCI as an industry-wide standard would significantly reduce the amount of time lost due to the lack of standardization. However, until vendors unite behind a common strategy, the multitude of multimedia will increase, making multimedia more "multi" in the wrong sense of the word. While multimedia has the potential to improve education and communication tremendously, "multi multimedia" retards its development and hinders its widespread adoption.

As this book goes to press, the author believes that Microsoft's MCI is the best solution, which is why Windows was chosen as the multimedia platform for this book. Nevertheless, since a multiliterate person should know about the alternatives, the competing standards will be discussed.

Apple's QuickTime

Apple's QuickTime is to the Macintosh what the MCI is to Windows. Like the MCI, it supports digital audio, MIDI, compact disc, and digital video. Apple's latest release contains many improvements over the original QuickTime. A faster data rate plays digital video more smoothly. Audio compression reduces the amount of storage required to hold digital audio recordings. And like Windows, QuickTime now supports MPEG (Motion Pictures Experts Group), which may emerge as an industry-wide standard for digital video.

QuickTime is a very good platform for multimedia. The reason it was not chosen for this book is because there are more than ten times as many Windows users as there are QuickTime users. The larger number of developers producing MCI devices will bring more innovations to Windows faster than to the Mac.

IBM Ultimedia

Ultimedia is not a typographical error; it is IBM's trademark for multimedia. It is meant to imply that IBM has the ultimate in multimedia. At first, the ultimedia trademark referred to a fairly well-defined product set, but then IBM began using the term to market a more loosely defined "Ultimedia Tools Series." This can be confusing because some of the titles run only under DOS, others under Windows, and still others under OS/2, and the types of files some of these products create are often not compatible with other tools in the series.

IBM has spent a tremendous amount of money trying to establish itself in the field of multimedia, but as the lack of standardization across the Ultimedia tools demonstrates, IBM has not adopted a consistent strategy for multimedia as have Apple and Microsoft. Instead of setting a company-wide standard, IBM has invested in multiple standards, probably hoping that one of them will become the mass market blockbuster.

Once known as the standard setter, IBM has encountered such intense competition that new directions it announces one year turn out to be dead ends a year later. A very good example is the Digital Video Interactive (DVI) technology, which will be discussed next.

Intel's Digital Video Interactive (DVI)

Digital Video Interactive (DVI) won "Best of Show" at Fall Comdex, 1992. Co-developed by Intel and IBM, it uses Intel's i750 chip to record and play back digital audio and video full-screen at 30 frames per second. The compression algorithm lets a single CD-ROM hold 72 minutes of video. Initially requiring users to purchase a DVI circuit board called ActionMedia, IBM had plans to integrate the i750 technology onto the motherboard so that all PC buyers would automatically have this capability, and DVI would become ubiquitous.

Then Microsoft announced Video for Windows, which required special hardware only to record the video; any computer with Windows could play it back. Although

Video for Windows did not perform as well as DVI, Intel quickly realized that by not requiring playback hardware, Video for Windows would become much more pervasive. So Intel jumped on the Video for Windows bandwagon by creating a Windows MCI driver called Indeo, which stands for Intel Video. The Indeo driver lets you record digital video with Intel's hardware, but then on playback, if the user does not have the Intel board, the video will still play back, albeit with lesser quality, through Video for Windows.

Meanwhile the beautiful full-screen, full-motion DVI technology that won at Comdex became a dead end. Developers like the author, who spent many months creating native DVI applications, became disenchanted and will be more wary the next time IBM and Intel announce a new "standard."

Philips' CD-I

Imagine a home CD player you can hook up to your television set and with which you can use a mouse or a joystick to control interactive software with audio and video coming from the CD. Such was the dream for Compact Disc-Interactive (CD-I). Philips and Sony invented it in 1986, and it came on the market in 1991. There are now more than 150 CD-I titles, ranging from interactive games like *Mad Dog McCree* and the *7th Guest* to a tour of the Louvre and an interactive encyclopedia. You can purchase a CD-I player at your local electronics store for about $400. For another $250, you can get a full-motion digital video add-on adapter that lets you view more than 80 conventional movies now available on CD-I, including *Top Gun* and *Star Trek VI*.

Pearson (1993) tells how CD-I has become portable with the Sony CD-I Viewer and the Philips' CDI350 portable players. "Both come with full-color active matrix LCD screens, built-in sound and the ability to operate from battery power, making them complete self-contained presentation systems... Both models play CD-I, CD-Bridge discs, Photo CDs and audio CDs."

However, many CD-I titles do not make good use of its interactive capabilities. For example, in his review of Dave Grusin's *The Gershwin Connection*, Rahlmann concludes, "Most of the additional information could have been put on an enhanced audio CD or in liner notes." He recommends you ignore the visuals and program the CD audio clips like a normal CD player. (*NewMedia* February, 1994: 56).

With multimedia computers offering so much more capability, will CD-I really take off? Forecasters remain skeptical.

Coping with Multi Multimedia

In hopes of encouraging industry-wide standards for multimedia systems, more than 200 multimedia vendors and end-user organizations created the Interactive Multimedia Association (IMA) in 1988. However, it did not take them long to realize they are going to have to cope with multi multimedia for a long time. So they changed their focus from hardware to software and are now encouraging software producers to create applications that will run on all the different hardware. This is time consuming, wasteful, and ultimately self-defeating for the multimedia industry. Developers do not have time to keep rewriting their applications for every new hardware platform. Since time is limited, they must be cautious. This wait-and-see attitude causes lost opportunities. For example, a company called TCI had to postpone its plans to purchase a million TV set-top converters because of the lack of industry standards for digital compression. Skeptics point to the year-long delay as evidence that the Information Superhighway will take much longer, cost much more, and have far fewer viewers than is generally believed (*Wall Street Journal* 1/21/94: B8).

You have no choice other than to learn to live with the uncertainty. Because of the fast pace of change you have to jump in quick and get to market fast, before the technology base shifts out from under you. The author recommends that your best strategy right now is to adopt the Windows MCI. Maybe if everyone refuses to purchase multimedia products that are not MCI compliant, we can send the industry the message that multimedia users simply will not tolerate multi multimedia.

E X E R C I S E S

1. Visit your local computer store and find out what multimedia brands it carries. Does it sell Microsoft MCI-based multimedia PCs? Does it carry Apple QuickTime-based Macintoshes? Philips CD-I? IBM Ultimedia? Intel DVI? What other brands does it have? Ask which brand sells best in your local community, and why.

2. Find out whether your local computer store owner believes in the recommendation this book makes, namely, that the Microsoft Windows MCI standard is the best one to follow, with Apple's QuickTime as the next best choice.

3. To standardize everything about multimedia today would be a mistake. The field is still too young for that, and there must be room for experimentation. On the other hand, certain objects could be standardized now. For example, there are more than 30 "standard" ways of storing bitmaps. The time and effort spent converting images from one format to another could be saved by an industry-wide standard for storing bitmaps. Are there other multimedia objects that should be standardized now? List them and state why.

4. Explain how Microsoft's MCI helps developers cope with the dilemma called *multi multimedia*.

5. Visit your local consumer electronics store and ask for a demonstration of CD-I. Do you believe this technology will take off? Why or why not?

Multimedia Computer Components

OBJECTIVES

After completing this chapter, you will be able to:

■ **Recognize the components of a multimedia PC.**

■ **Understand the shopping terminology necessary to make intelligent choices when purchasing a multimedia computer.**

■ **Know the difference between a mouse and a trackball, 8-bit and 16-bit audio, analog and digital video, CD-ROM I and II, modems and network cards, flatbed and hand-held scanners, inkjet and laser printers.**

■ **Understand the datacommunication terminology needed to procure equipment for connecting your multimedia PC to the Internet.**

There are five categories of components in a multimedia computer: the system unit, multimedia accessories, read/write storage, auxiliary input devices, and communication options. Understanding these components will enable you to follow the multimedia computer checklists provided in the next chapter.

System Unit

At the heart of every computer is the central processor, which is the "brain" in which computations are performed. The system unit includes the central processor and the electronics required to support it. System units normally ship with a color monitor and a pointing device.

Central Processor

The central processor has a numerical name that indicates the basic type and speed of the processor. Processors in MPC-compatible multimedia computers have the numbers 286, 386, 486, and Pentium, which would have been called 586 had the patent office not ruled that the number could not be trademarked. Figure 1-8 in Chapter 1 (page 7) compares the speed of the most popular central processors. A few of the processor names are followed by the letters *SX*, while others have the letters *DX*. SX processors are not rated as fast as DX models.

RAM

RAM stands for Random Access Memory; it is the main memory at the heart of your computer in which multimedia programs execute. RAM is measured in megabytes (**MB**). Mega means a million, and byte is the unit of measure for computer memory. A byte can hold a single character, and a megabyte can hold a million characters. **Meg** is another abbreviation for megabyte.

Since multimedia objects are big, you need a large amount of RAM to make a multimedia computer work well. 4 MB is the minimum required, but many applications need eight to run well. Large programs like Windows NT need 16 MB to run well.

Color Display

Color displays are also referred to as color monitors. Measured along the diagonal, they come in screen sizes ranging from 8 to 37 inches or more. The most typical sizes range from 12 to 19 inches. Larger monitors are very expensive and normally are purchased for classrooms or boardrooms where many people need to be able to see the display.

Independent of the number of inches is the number of pixels your computer can display on the monitor. The minimum number for multimedia is 640 pixels across by 480 pixels down the screen. On computer spec sheets, this is expressed as 640x480 (the number across is always printed first, followed by the number down). Other common pixel grids are 800x600, 1024x768, and 1360x1024; these **high resolution** monitors can also display the more common 640x480 graphics.

Your needs will most probably be met well by a 640x480 monitor. Equally important is the number of colors your system unit can display. Older computers with VGA (video graphics array) can only display 16 colors on a 640x480 pixel grid. For multimedia, you need SVGA (super VGA), which can display 256 simultaneous colors chosen from a palette of more than 16 million colors. By the end of the decade computers with 24-bit color, which can display all 16 million colors simultaneously, will predominate.

Pointing Device

The mouse is the most common pointing device on multimedia computers today. In the Windows world, mice have two or three buttons; for most applications, a two-button mouse works fine. Alternatives to mice include mouse pens, which let you write with a stylus instead of dragging a mouse; trackballs, which let you spin a ball instead; and the innovative TrackPoint, which is a tiny joystick mounted in the center of the keyboard on IBM ThinkPad notebook computers. As shown in Figures 11-1 and 11-2, you work the TrackPoint with the tip of your index finger, eliminating the need for a surface to run a mouse on.

11-1

The tiny joystick in the center of this IBM ThinkPad's computer keyboard substitutes for a mouse.

11-2

A user positions the mouse cursor on the screen with the IBM TrackPoint device.

Multimedia Accessories

Multimedia accessories give your computer the ability to make sound, play music, and record movies.

CD-ROM

By definition, multimedia personal computers (MPCs) have a CD-ROM drive. If you do not have a CD-ROM drive, you do not have an MPC. CD-ROMs can contain computer data as well as audio sound tracks. Some early CD-ROM drives could read computer data but did not have the audio circuitry needed to make sound. Make sure the CD-ROM you get can play audio as well as read data.

CD-ROM is an evolving technology that keeps improving. The original CD-ROM drives read computer data at a speed of 150 KB per second. Second generation drives are twice as fast, reading data at 300 KB per second. Called "double-speed" drives, they can also read multi-session CDs, which are discs that have had additional data written onto them in subsequent recording sessions.

Triple and quadruple speed CD-ROM drives are also becoming available. When you purchase a multimedia computer, you should get the latest in CD-ROM technology.

Digital Audio

By definition, MPCs have the ability to record and play back waveform digital audio files. If your system does not have waveform audio, it is not a multimedia computer.

The original MPC standard called for 8-bit sound, which produces a dynamic range of 50dB. The MPC2 standard uses 16-bit sound, which increases the dynamic range to 98dB. The greater the dynamic range, the more faithful the sound reproduction. Any new system you buy should have 16-bit waveform audio. Figure 11-3 shows the Sound Blaster 16-bit audio board used by the author; it is manufactured by Creative Labs.

Audio Speakers

You will need a pair of audio speakers to listen to the sound produced by your multimedia PC. If you get powered speakers with amplifiers built in, you will not need a separate amplifier. Otherwise, you will need an amplifier as well. If your home stereo system amplifier has auxiliary line inputs, you may be able to plug your MPC into them, depending on competition for use of the stereo by other family members.

The author uses the pair of Yamaha MS202 powered speakers shown in Figure 11-4. They sound so good you would swear they were two or three times larger than they really are.

Part Four

Looking into the Future of Multimedia

CONTENTS

Chapter 14
Multimedia Frontiers

Chapter 15
Emerging Technology

Chapter 16
Societal Issues

Chapter 17
How to Keep Up

We must make sure the Information Superhighway is not a toll road for the rich.

—Linda Roberts, Clinton White House Education Adviser, STATE keynote address, 3/19/94

Technology is one of the most difficult areas in which to make predictions because new inventions occur at such a fast pace that the future changes before it gets here. How can the future change before it gets here? Big companies invest millions of dollars promoting new products, leading consumers to believe that their products will be in the mainstream in the future, but shortly after coming to market, the products get abandoned because the vendors pursue newer technologies that promise bigger profits. This has happened so often during the past decade that almost anyone involved with multimedia has been frustrated by purchasing so-called "mainstream" technologies that quickly go out-of-date and are abandoned by their manufacturers.

Knowledge is the best strategy for coping with fast-paced change. The more you know about the issues and technologies, the better prepared you will be to make strategic choices. Specifically, you can

- Identify the frontiers that multimedia researchers are investigating

- Study technologies that are emerging

- Identify societal issues raised by the manner in which multimedia technologies are used

- Find out about and even contribute to new knowledge in this exciting field

The next four chapters will consider these topics.

CHAPTER

14

Multimedia Frontiers

OBJECTIVES

After completing this chapter, you will be able to:

☐ **Understand how researchers invent new uses for multimedia and use multimedia to find new methods for solving problems.**

☐ **Consider what kinds of books can be or should be replaced by CD-ROMs.**

☐ **Know what is meant by the term "rural datafication."**

☐ **Explore how virtual reality will improve the multimedia user interface.**

☐ **Consider whether there are other frontiers of multimedia that ought to be explored.**

☐ **Join and participate in the Electronic Frontier Foundation.**

A multimedia frontier is a field of technological research and development in which investigators invent new uses for multimedia or determine the extent to which multimedia can solve problems by finding better ways of doing old things. This chapter discusses how multimedia is being used to improve and transform publishing, provide better access to networked information, enhance rural communication, and simplify the user interface.

Electronic Publishing

How much longer will books, magazines, and newspapers continue to be printed on paper? Anyone who has used hypertext knows how printed manuscripts pale by comparison. Printed manuscripts do not contain links that let you expand the text and navigate to related information; hot words that let you trigger explanatory sound tracks, videos, or animations; or full-text Boolean (AND, OR, NOT) searching that lets you locate quickly the material you need. Printed music does not let you scroll the score back and forth to locate and hear precisely the theme you want to study. Math textbooks do not allow you to manipulate formulas and visualize your changes through dynamic real-time graphs.

The publishing industry knows this very well. They realize their entire way of doing business is undergoing rapid and fundamental change, but they are not sure how it will emerge. Take this book for example. It includes a CD-ROM. How much of the text in this book would you have preferred to have on the CD-ROM instead?

Due to the prohibitive costs of producing and printing books, few authors could afford their own four-color separation equipment and printing presses. But what about electronic media? As Chapter 40 will demonstrate, you can produce a CD-ROM for much less than a book, and you do not need a publisher to do it. For example, Coupland (1993) discusses eight independent multimedia developers who produced and published their own lucrative CDs.

The Information Superhighway

In 1993 Vice President Gore issued a report entitled *The National Information Infrastructure: Agenda for Action.* The full text of this report is on the *Multiliteracy CD;* you can access it by going to the Demonstrations section, selecting Textbook Examples, and clicking the NII-Agenda for Action button. It describes how the private sector will build, operate, and maintain the Information Superhighway, while the government will develop policies to ensure that all Americans have access to it, encourage private sector investment in building the network, and create a competitive market for telecommunications and information services.

The Electronic Frontier Foundation is concerned about how these policies will control what happens on the network. As Farber (1993) explains:

> In July 1990, the Electronic Frontier Foundation (EFF) was founded by John Perry Barlow and Mitch Kapor (who also founded Lotus Development Corporation) to help civilize the frontier more rapidly. It has the aim of trying to assure freedom of expression in digital media with emphasis on applying the principles embodied in the Constitution and the Bill of Rights to computer-based communication. From the beginning, EFF was determined to become an organization that would combine technical, legal, and public policy expertise. It would then apply these skills to the large number of complex issues and concerns that arise whenever a new communications medium is born. To paraphrase John Perry Barlow, it will take years to civilize the electronic frontier and bring law and order to it. And to quote Mitch Kapor, "There's a new world coming. Let's make sure it has rules we can live with."

You can participate by joining the EFF; send e-mail to eff-request@eff.org containing the one-line message **Please add me to the mailing list.** Then add a line providing your real name, and one more line stating your e-mail address.

Rural Datafication

Rural America has traditionally lagged behind the rest of the country in gaining access to technological innovations. Telephones, radio, and television came first to big cities. To provide access to the rest of the country, the Department of Commerce made capital funding available through its Public Telecommunications Facilities Program for rural communities to install modern telecommunications equipment. These funds are still available and have recently been used to provide rural communities access to satellites.

Thanks to the efforts of Dr. Michael Staman and his associates, rural America will not experience a delayed access to the Information Superhighway. As president of CICNet, a nonprofit regional computer network founded by the schools of the Big Ten, he has received funding from the National Science Foundation to extend Internet connectivity to typically underserved and underutilized communities. Dr. Staman refers to this process of extending the Information Superhighway to rural America as **rural datafication**. Rural datafication is a service mark of CICNet. For more information, send e-mail to info@cic.net.

Virtual Reality

As you are aware from using this book and its CD, multimedia computers can show any picture, play any sound, and link any word of any document or any part of any picture to any object on your computer. What's missing? A better human interface. We need better ways for users to communicate with multimedia computers. As you learned in Chapter 5, researchers in virtual reality have made this an important part of their business, and as they invent new input and output devices, multimedia computers will benefit.

EXERCISES

1. Consider the text of this book and the CD-ROM that accompanies it. What is the role of the book, and what role does the CD play? If you could redesign either the book or the CD or both, how would you present the material they cover? Is either the book or the CD unnecessary?

2. Do you think CDs will ever replace books? Are some kinds of books more likely to be replaced by CDs than others? Give an example of a kind of book that should be replaced by CD and explain why. Then give an example of a book that should not be so replaced and explain why not.

3. To what extent has your local community become "datafied"? Are your schools connected to the Information Superhighway? Do teachers have access to it, or just the administrators? How about students? Is your local library connected? What about homes: does a cable TV, telephone, or Internet company make Information Superhighway connections available to homes? If so, at what speeds? What online services are provided?

4. View the movie *Lawnmower Man*. Do you believe multimedia PCs will ever enable users to experience VR immersion to the extent Jobe Smith (Jeff Fahey) did in the movie?

5. If you could invent anything you could think of, what kind of devices would you create for improving your computer's user interface? How would the devices help you communicate with your computer better than you can now? How would they make it easier to use? How would they make the simulated environments you experience seem more real? How would they get you more involved in the interaction?

15

Emerging Technology

After completing this chapter, you will be able to:

- ◻ **Recognize emerging multimedia technologies.**

- ◻ **Understand the role that MPEG, HDTV, and video dial tone technologies will play in the future of digital video.**

- ◻ **Realize what ISDN is and how much of the United States has access to it.**

- ◻ **Consider the challenge of pen computing and the promise of voice recognition.**

- ◻ **Understand what knowbots can do for you on the Information Superhighway.**

- ◻ **Recognize the extent to which multimedia is an emerging technology, and question whether its use is just a fad or an important life skill.**

New technologies follow a cycle that includes invention, prototyping, proof of concept, productizing, and manufacture. Throughout this process, they are called emerging technologies. It often takes many years for an emerging technology to achieve widespread use in the marketplace.

An excellent example of an emerging technology in multimedia is the laser videodisc. Introduced by Pioneer in 1980, videodisc showed great promise. A laser beam would provide split-second access to movies with stereo sound tracks, and still frame capability would enable you to access any one of 54,000 slides within a second. RCA slowed things down somewhat by confusing and disillusioning the public enormously with a stylus-based system that played video off vinyl discs that worked like phonograph records. The stylus negated the random access and still frame capability of the laserdisc. RCA's product fizzled and disappeared from retail stores, while laserdisc emerged as a powerful way to deliver education and training in schools, business, and industry. There is a growing home market as well, witnessed by the large collection of laserdiscs for sale in Sam Goody stores.

Fad or Future Trend?

This chapter discusses multimedia technologies that are in the process of emerging. Some of them could get cancelled prior to manufacture, and others may fail in the marketplace. Only those that succeed really belong here, because the ones that fail to emerge are by definition not emerging.

Digital Video

There is little doubt that digital video will emerge as the primary way in which movies will be recorded and transmitted in the twenty-first century. The question is, what standard will be followed? Doyle (1994) discusses 15 different algorithms that are in use today. None of them is ideal, and there is still room for someone to invent and patent a better digital video recording algorithm and make a fortune from it.

As this book goes to press, MPEG appears to be the most likely standard to emerge. MPEG stands for Motion Picture Experts Group, the name of the ISO standards committee that created it. Endorsed by more than 70 companies including IBM, Apple, JVC, Philips, Sony, and Matsushita, MPEG compresses video by using a discrete cosine transform algorithm to eliminate redundant data in blocks of pixels on the screen. MPEG compresses the video further by recording only changes from frame to frame; this is known as **delta-frame encoding**. MPEG is expected to become the digital video standard for compact discs, cable TV, direct satellite broadcast, and high-definition television. Bell Atlantic is already using MPEG in its Stargazer service.

HDTV

HDTV stands for High Definition Television. It is being developed to replace NTSC as the television standard for the United States. HDTV is based on four technologies:

- MPEG digital video compression
- Transmission in packets that will permit any combination of video, audio, and data
- Progressive scanning for computer interoperability up to 60 frames per second at 1920x1080 pixels
- Compact-disc quality digital surround sound using Dolby AC-3 audio technology

Even though the broadcast standard is still NTSC, television studios are already recording shows in HDTV so reruns can be broadcast in HDTV when the standard changes. The first HDTV sets, which will have ten times as many pixels as appear on a standard TV set, are expected to be on the market in the second half of 1996 (*Wall Street Journal* 2/17/94: B6). They will be demonstrated during the 1996 Olympics and will cost about $4,000 (*Atlanta Journal-Constitution* 2/27/94: R1).

ISDN

ISDN stands for Integrated Services Digital Network. It is a digital telephone system being installed by regional Bell companies in most of the United States; when this book went to press, about 60% of the country could get ISDN. As Fox (1993) reports, "The first national ISDN call was made in November of 1992, connecting 22 sites nationwide, from Reston, Virginia to Los Angeles, California." ISDN services include voice conferencing, voice mail, caller ID, e-mail, fax, shared printers and databases, remote file access and data transfer, and video conferencing.

ISDN signals are carried over two or more 64 Kbps (64,000 bits per second) circuit-switched channels to carry voice and data, and a lower speed packet-switched channel that carries control signals. The Basic Rate Interface (BRI) service of ISDN is 144 Kbps, made up of two 64 Kbps data channels and one 16 Kbps control channel. This basic service can carry about 15 times as much information as conventional telephone lines. The Primary Rate Interface (PRI) service uses 23 data channels and a 64 Kbps control channel to boost the data rate to 1.544 Kbps. A second-generation standard, known as **broadband ISDN**, is under development; it uses fiber optic cables and ATM (Asynchronous Transfer Mode) technology to provide speeds of 155 Mbps and higher.

When this book went to press, there were 125,000 ISDN lines in service. That number is expected to grow to a million by the end of 1997 (*Telecommunications* 5/94: 18).

Video Dial Tones

In 1992 the FCC legalized a new way of delivering TV signals. Called **video dial tone**, it allows TV signals to travel over telephone lines. This technology has spurred a furious round of mergers and alliances among phone companies, cable TV operators, and filmmakers wanting to capitalize on it. For example, Baby Bell company US West purchased 25% of Time Warner (a major owner of cable TV systems around the country), Warner Brothers film studio, and HBO (a pay TV channel).

Many more channels will be available via video dial tone than over cable or broadcast. As Lerner (1993) explains, "With current analog technology, in which signals are sent as continuously varying waves, only about 50 channels can be provided. But by digitizing the signal and eliminating redundant bits, 500 channels are possible." Digital transmission also permits a return signal, creating the possibility of two-way interactive TV.

Rosenthal (1993) predicts that by 2008, "Personalized cable systems will offer virtual channels in which video servers furnish material to individual users on a personalized basis." Instead of needing to decide which one of 500 channels to watch, you will only get one channel, but since it will be personalized and interactive, it will always be showing what you want.

Holography

Most people think of holograms as 3-D photographs. Popularized by their use on credit cards to prevent counterfeiting, holograms are also being printed on U.S. passports to prevent forgeries. But holograms can also store huge amounts of data. For example, IBM scientists predict that holographic technology will make it possible to store the entire *Encyclopedia Britannica* in a space the size and thickness of a penny. Holographic memory systems can stack data 40 layers deep, as opposed to computer disk and magnetic tape, which line up data on flat, single-layer tracks. The deeper layers can be read by tilting the angle of the laser beam that reads the data (*Investor's Business Daily* 1/20/94: 4).

Pen Computing

Pen computing is an emerging technology that Apple's hand-held Newton computer brought to public attention. Referred to as a Personal Digital Assistant (PDA), Newton was supposed to revolutionize business by providing a powerful communication device small enough to put in your pocket. By using a pen to input characters by writing on the screen, the need for a bulky keyboard was avoided.

However, consumers quickly found that pen computing has a long way to go before it will work well enough for everyday use. Apple claimed that Newton was trainable, that it could learn to recognize your handwriting. But in practice, Newton trained the user, who ended up learning how to write in a format Newton could understand.

Lee and Francis (1994) report how Newton had such a negative impact on the market that "The market for all personal digital assistants (PDAs) has fallen to a level that equals slightly more than half the number of Newton MessagePads that Apple alone sold during a two-month period last year following the Newton's introduction." During those two months, Apple sold 50,000 Newtons.

Voice Recognition

With pen computers crying out for a better handwriting algorithm, voice recognition is fast emerging. At present it takes more RAM than most people will want to devote to it, but impressive progress is being made. Already physically challenged people who cannot type are using voice recognition to create and edit documents with word processors.

Telecomputing

Withrow (1993) credits George Gilder with coining the phrase **telecomputer** to describe the merging of the telephone, television set, and computer into a single utility device. It will be interesting to watch as these technologies merge and the physical form of the telecomputer takes shape. What do you think it will look like? A black box? A TV? According to *Business Week*, AT&T is betting that the telephone will emerge as the gizmo of choice for accessing the Information Superhighway. AT&T's Project Sage is working on a phone that can be the central controller for routing information to and from household electronic gadgets such as TVs, VCRs, PCs, fax machines, and video cameras (*Business Week* 1/24/94: 37).

Wireless Communications

Wireless communication technologies are enabling users to access telecommunication systems from almost anywhere. No longer must your computer be tethered to the nearest telephone line.

Developing nations are using wireless technologies to avoid the high cost of wiring their countries physically. Cellular networks in Malaysia, Thailand, and the Philippines are expanding so fast that they may leapfrog traditional networks to become the most common form of telephone service. In South America, so many Venezuelans are carrying cellular phones that some restaurants require customers to check them at the door to control the noise level (*St. Petersburg Times* 5/16/94, Business: 2). In Brazil, cellular phones have become such a highway safety hazard that it is illegal to talk on a hand-held cellular phone and drive at the same time (*Miami Herald* 5/18/94: C1).

Technology prophet George Gilder envisions wireless systems that will eventually offer worldwide bandwidth on demand, buffering and transmitting information whenever there is room (*Forbes ASAP* 4/11/94: 98). Microsoft chairman Bill Gates is teaming up with Craig McCaw of McCaw Cellular Communications to create such a network, a $9 billion wireless "global Internet." Known as Teledesic, it will use low earth orbit satellites to provide wireless interactive voice, data, and video services. The system will have 840 refrigerator-sized satellites to connect hand-held phones and other electronic devices to telephone networks all over the world (*Wall Street Journal* 3/21/94: A3).

Knowbots

Knowbots are software applications programmed to act as intelligent agents that go out on the network and find things for you. You tell a knowbot what you want, and it worms its way through the Internet finding all the relevant information, digesting it, and reporting it to you succinctly.

Likening them to robotic librarians, Krol (1992: 259) refers to knowbots as "... software worms that crawl from source to source looking for answers to your questions. As a knowbot looks, it may discover more sources. If it does, it checks the new sources, too. When it has exhausted all sources, it comes crawling home with whatever it found."

Multimedia

In what sense is multimedia itself an emerging technology? Will the craze fade or evolve into something else, like when the term "multimedia" was invented and people began using it to describe preexisting technology?

The author believes that the ability to use multimedia will emerge as a life skill in the twenty-first century. Citizens who do not know how to use multimedia will become disenfranchised. Cut off from the Information Superhighway, they will end up watching life go by instead of living it fully.

E X E R C I S E S

1. It seems like it is taking forever for HDTV to come on the market. Did you know about HDTV before you read this book? If so, how did you first find out about it? Have you ever seen an HDTV demonstration? If so, what was your impression of it? If you have not seen one, contact your local video store and ask where you can see an HDTV demo in your area.

2. Is there a video dial tone service available to homes in your neighborhood? If so, which service? What percentage of homes in your community would you say subscribe to it? What does it cost? What impact has it had on the video stores in your community; are they still in business? Do you think video stores will ultimately go out of business because of video dial tone technology, or will people still prefer to go to the store to pick out videos?

3. Contact your local telephone company and find out whether ISDN services are available to homes in your neighborhood. Find out how much it costs to get an ISDN connection. Make sure you ask about ongoing as well as one-time costs. What services are available via ISDN in your neighborhood? Can you get video conferencing? Does it cost more than lower bandwidth services?

4. Ask around and find out what percentage of your friends' homes have ISDN installed. Do you think this percentage will increase? Why or why not?

5. If you could program a knowbot to go out on the Information Superhighway and do your bidding for you, what all would you want the knowbot to do? If you have never been on the Information Superhighway, completing the tutorial in Part Seven of this book will provide the background information that can help you answer this question.

6. Do you believe multimedia is just a fad, or is its use emerging as a life skill for the twenty-first century? Give reasons for your belief.

Societal Issues

After completing this chapter, you will be able to:

■ Question the potentially negative impact of multimedia on violence, game addiction, sexual exploitation, pornography, and obscenity.

■ Understand the regulatory nightmare facing lawmakers on issues of privacy, encryption, censorship, and protectionism.

■ Realize how fortune seekers have tried to profit from the legal system's lack of experience by patenting basic multimedia technologies that were already widely used.

■ Consider the copyright law and a teacher's right to fair use of multimedia, and the need to call upon campus copyright officials to get organized, take the lead, and revise their faculty copyright guidelines to permit these fair uses of multimedia.

■ Understand the issues of entitlement, equity, cost, usability, and universal access, and then question whether the building of the Information Superhighway will create a technological underclass in our society.

Until now this book has touted the great advantages of multimedia. But will its true potential be reached? Who will control access? Almost any good thing can be misused; how can multimedia harm society?

Human Impact

A lot of people worry about graphic violence in video games. Is it right to have laser shooting games in video arcades, which can train young people how to aim and fire weapons at people, when the leading cause of death among urban youth is gunshot wounds? Sex CDs let men exploit women severely. With more than 60% of families reporting problems of marital violence, should CD-ROMs in which men can torture women virtually be legal? Research shows that virtual reality is even more addictive than conventional video games. What effect will this have on humankind?

Violence and Game Addiction

In her review of violence in video games, Stefanac (1994) mentions that there were more than 10,000 murders involving handguns in the United States in 1990. During the same year, only 10 such murders occurred in Australia, 13 in Sweden, 22 in Great Britain, and 87 in Japan. In 1991, 55% of those arrested for murder in the United States were under the age of 25. According to federal crime reports, the number of children arrested for murder during the past decade has risen by 55%.

The author suggests you visit your local arcade and try one of the video games that has laser targeting firearms attached. As you hold the weapon, people appear on the screen in front of you. They are not mere "pixellated" computer graphics that only suggest human forms, but real live video recordings of street scenes. You must aim accurately and fire quickly to avoid being shot. Now go outside and walk down the street. Someone appears from around the corner in front of you. What is your basic instinct after playing the game?

The Mad Dog McCree Shooting Game will help you sharpen your skills to do battle with him and rescue the town's mayor and his daughter.

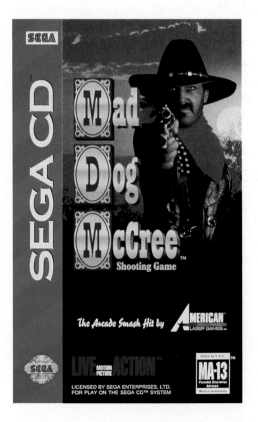

Not everyone agrees that video game violence provokes street crime. According to popular culture Professor Christopher Geist (Stefanac 1994):

> People often assume that findings for one medium apply necessarily to the next. Some people are saying that interactive games will have more impact. That's a guess. It could turn out that the interactivity in some of these combat games actually lessens the negative impact; it could serve a cathartic effect. Much more research needs to be done before we start drawing absolute conclusions.

Sex

Sex is very important to most people. Traffic on the Internet reflects this: the newsgroup *alt.sex.stories* is the second most popular group on the net with 330,000 readers when this book went to press, and 10 MB of new messages per month (that's the equivalent of three bibles). *alt.sex* is the third most popular news group with the same number of readers and 7 MB of new messages per month. *alt.binaries.pictures.erotica* is the fifth most popular news group; 280,000 readers download 23.9 MB of erotic images per month.

But multimedia is being used for more than just distributing erotic stories and pictures. Interactivity is letting users live out their fantasies virtually. For example, *NightWatch* allows the voyeur/player to snoop around a plush singles resort via a bank of security monitors. *Virtual Valerie*, which had already sold more than 100,000 copies when this book went to press, lets you roam about and explore Valerie's apartment and have sex with her in the bedroom. Commenting on this controversial form of interactivity, Newson (1992) states "Yes, there is pornographic sex on the disc. Is this animated pornography wrong and/or degrading to women? That's something you'll have to decide for yourself. Personally, I wasn't offended."

For users who want physical contact with their virtual partner during sex, Thinking Software Inc. (TSI) markets The Cybersex Machine, which they advertise as "A virtual world of pleasure for the open-minded adult without a companion." For $25,900 it includes a 486 PC, Super VGA monitor, joystick controller, PC controlled genitals, easy to use menu system to select your VR companion, and a medical certificate of safety and effectiveness. It should be noted that The Cybersex Machine was not tested by the author!

Linea Jacobson, editor of *CyberArts* (Miller Freeman 1992), has a warning about the dangers of these applications (Stefanac 1994):

> What's wonderful about interactive media is also what's reprehensible about this kind of application: the idea of handing control over to the user. Smut on paper or video is much more benign than interactive stroke books. These products show men that they can have control over women. You can force them to do your bidding and they do it willingly. I am absolutely opposed to censorship, but I think men have to be made aware that this kind of thing can make women feel very uncomfortable.

Pornography and Obscenity

Mike Godwin (1994), online counsel for the Electronic Frontier Foundation, also has concerns about the risks of putting graphic sexual materials on the Internet. The GIF file format is capable of reproducing over the net full-color photos of explicit "hardcore" pornography and child pornography. The federal government has been searching and seizing servers that contain such material. These are so popular that Delft University in the Netherlands has had to limit each user to eight downloads per day from its erotic image file server.

The Supreme Court's 1973 *Miller* ruling gave communities the right to legislate obscenity. To help interpret the laws, Godwin (1994: 58) developed the following four-part test for obscenity:

1. Is the work designed to be sexually arousing?

2. Is it arousing in a way that one's local community would consider unhealthy or immoral?

3. Does it picture acts whose depictions are specifically prohibited by state law?

4. Does the work, when taken as a whole, lack sufficient literary, artistic, scientific, or social value?

Distributing such materials over the Internet raises some interesting issues. For example, while an erotic picture might not be immoral in the community where it was uploaded, it may very well be considered obscene in the place it gets downloaded. Internet tools like the Gopher make it very easy to take things out of context; who can prevent users from circulating an image devoid of the supplementary material that made it legitimate? Moreover, children can easily access materials over the Internet that were intended for adults.

The U.S. child protection laws forbid any pornographic images that use children, whether or not they meet Godwin's obscenity test. Individuals convicted can be fined up to $100,000 and imprisoned up to ten years.

Internet providers are beginning to take action. For example, Canada's best-known computer science school, the University of Waterloo, banned from its campus five Internet bulletin boards dealing with violent sex out of concern that their contents break laws on pornography and obscenity (*Toronto Globe & Mail* 02/05/94: A1).

Meanwhile, the soft porn industry plans to capitalize on the "boom" that multimedia can bring to erotic sales. *Playboy's* CEO Christie Hefner sees the electronic marketplace as the sexy business to be in these days; she views the merging of computers, televisions, electronic publishing, and telephones as opening new ways of using *Playboy* magazine's back issues (*New York Times* 12/21/93: C1).

Regulation

With the broadcast television, cable TV, telephone, and computer network industries all jockeying for position, the Information Superhighway presents a regulatory nightmare. Television broadcasters have requested congressional permission to use some of their allocated spectrum to offer advanced telecommunication services, including sending data to laptops, fax machines, and pagers. TV station owners claim they just want to stay competitive with cable and telephone companies, but opponents say they should have equal opportunity to any extra spectrum (*Wall Street Journal* 2/2/94: B1).

When Senator Hollings introduced a bill that would open up the local telephone market to competition by lifting the remaining line-of-business restrictions on the seven RBOCs (Regional Bell Operating Companies), long-distance carriers expressed concern over letting RBOCs into the long-distance service area. Spokespersons from AT&T and Sprint testified against the proposed change (*BNA Daily Report for Executives* 2/3/94: A21).

The Clinton administration has realized it could get hopelessly tangled in a long series of debates and filibusters with long-distance phone carriers battling to put limits on House and Senate bills that would let the regional Bell telephone companies compete in the long-distance marketplace, cable companies hoping both to offer local phone service and keep local phone companies from providing video services, and TV broadcasters demanding the right to provide data services along with their regular programming (*New York Times* 2/4/94: C1). To prevent this legislative quagmire from holding up progress on the Information Superhighway, Vice President Al Gore announced the Clinton administration's intent to deregulate the telecommunications industry to a point where any company can offer any services to any set of consumers (*Atlanta Constitution* 12/21/93: C9). According to a recent survey by the National Consumers League, the public sides with the administration on this issue by a two thirds majority (*BNA Daily Report for Executives* 2/1/94: A12).

Privacy

Do you realize that many employers claim the legal right to read all of the e-mail and other electronic correspondence that flows through their computer network? While the Federal Electronic Communications Privacy Act of 1986 protects the privacy of messages sent over public networks like MCI Mail and Compuserve, it does not cover a company's internal e-mail (*New York Times* 12/6/93: A8). The author believes this infringes upon freedom of speech and should be changed. Even though your employer pays for the telephone line in your office, your employer cannot listen in on your telephone conversations without having a court order. How then can it be legal to eavesdrop on your electronic conversations? Beware of this and do not ever communicate anything electronically that you would not want read by your employer or network administrators.

You should also be aware that when you send e-mail on the Information Superhighway, it passes through one or more **gateways**. Each gateway is a computer that can (and often does for backup and reliability purposes) retain a copy of your communications. Any computer systems analyst with access to that network can read your messages. It is also possible to write sophisticated snooper software that can monitor all of your electronic communications and alert the eavesdropper when they contain certain key words or phrases. The Canadian Security Intelligence Service has awarded three contracts to a Montreal firm for a system that can quickly isolate key words and phrases from millions of airborne phone, fax, radio signals and other transmissions (*CTV National News* 01/31/94 11:00 pm).

Encryption and the Clipper Chip

To prevent people from reading electronic correspondence, many firms encrypt their messages. The government is concerned that this prevents law enforcement agencies (who have court orders) from eavesdropping on digital communications. The Clinton administration wants to control the encryption process by requiring that every government computer contain a **Clipper Chip**, which is an encryption device with a "back door" that allows detectives with the proper access to decipher the messages. The Clipper Chip has been denounced by industry groups as well as civil liberties groups concerned about privacy (*New York Times* 2/5/94: A1). The CPSR (Computer Professionals for Social Responsibility) has organized a protest; for more information, gopher to cpsr.org. The Electronic Frontier Foundation is also fighting the Clinton administration's plans for the

Clipper Chip, and is asking for supporters to send e-mail to Congresswoman Maria Cantwell (cantwell@eff.org) to show support of H.R. 3627, her bill to liberalize export controls on encryption software.

InfoWorld publisher Bob Metcalfe opposes Clipper Chip technology for different reasons than those cited by the CPSR and the Electronic Frontier Foundation: "I am against Clipper simply because it will not work, and it will cost an unnecessary amount of tax money to outfit government computers with the chips... Smart criminals can easily get around Clipper by using additional encryption. Stupid criminals will continue to do stupid things and get caught." (*Wall Street Journal* 3/22/94: A14). In support of the notion that smart criminals can circumvent Clipper, an AT&T computer scientist at Bell Labs has found a flaw in the chip that would allow expert computer users to defeat the government's ability to decode messages (*New York Times* 6/2/94: A1).

Censorship

Many people are concerned that in addition to being able to read electronic communications, network administrators also have the ability to censor them. To what extent and under what circumstances should the government act as a censor on the Information Superhighway?

Few would argue that the University of Waterloo erred in banning obscene bulletin boards from its network. But what prevents users from avoiding the ban by distributing the material through e-mail?

In a well-publicized criminal trial in Toronto, the Canadian government exercised its right to ban any publicity about the case, lest prospective jurors become biased and the hearings end in mistrial. So the University of Toronto stopped carrying an Internet bulletin board that disclosed banned information about the case. But that did not stop people from distributing the information through e-mail. It has become virtually impossible to intercept the electronic exchange of such information (*Toronto Globe & Mail* 12/02/93: A4).

Protectionism

Protectionists present the Information Superhighway with yet another stumbling block. Canadian phone company BCE Telecom ran into opposition over its proposed $275 million joint venture with Jones Intercable. Edward Markey, chair of the House Subcommittee on Telecommunications and Finance, said it "... raises serious policy issues regarding foreign investment in and control of the U.S. telecommunications infrastructure," and he advocated limiting foreign investment to noncontrolling stakes in American information highways (*Toronto Globe & Mail* 01/21/94: B1).

Nationalism poses yet another obstacle to connectivity. Perceiving the unification of Canada with an information highway as another threat to preserving its regional cultures, Quebec's Internal Department of Communications is considering imposing rules and restrictions on the content of information flowing on the superhighway to Quebec (*Ottawa Citizen* 01/31/94: A4). Saudi Arabia has banned satellite dishes in order to maintain control over the information its citizens can obtain (*St. Petersburg Times* 3/12/94: A8).

Multimedia and the Law

Multimedia is putting new pressures on the legal system, which has been slow to learn about new media. Embarrassing mistakes have been made in the patent office, and misunderstandings about copyrights are preventing fair use in multimedia. Law makers and enforcers need to be multiliterate so they can bolster the use of new media on the Information Superhighway instead of retarding its progress through lack of understanding.

Patents

Recently the U.S. Patent and Trademark Office granted two multimedia patents so broad in scope that the awardees blatantly announced all other vendors owed them royalties on all past, present, and future products. This created an industry-wide protest so severe that one of the vendors withdrew its claim, while the patent office overturned the other patent. In both cases there was so much prior art that for people in the industry these claims were likened to trying to patent sunlight (*Wall Street Journal* 3/25/94: B2).

The Optical Data Patent

The first case involved a patent awarded to Optical Data for the instructional methodology used in their *Windows on Science* program. Their syllabus-based curriculum outlining method is so basic to the teaching process that practically all other products already use it. Kinnaman (1993) describes how Videodiscovery filed a lawsuit seeking a declaratory judgment finding the patent invalid because of prior art and the obviousness of the claims. The Interactive Multimedia Association (IMA) supported the Videodiscovery complaint; as IMA president Philip Dodds politely stated, "Patents such as these, which require nearly every company involved in interactive multimedia and education to license an idea and application that have a long history and are widely known, are not in the best interest of the industry or educators." (Kinnaman 1993)

To stop the flow of negative publicity stemming from the patent, Optical Data Corporation dedicated the patent permanently to the public. According to Optical Data chair William Clark, "It was never our intent to use this patent to inhibit the development of multimedia based interactive teaching methods. A tremendous amount of concern—including a lawsuit by one of our competitors—arose from this patent award. We hope that by voluntarily dedicating this patent to the public, we will end any unfounded fears that Optical Data, or any other company, might try to limit the diversity of interactive, multimedia programs available to educators." (Kinnaman 1994)

But Foremski (1994) mentions another company attempting to do just that. Compton's caused an uproar by claiming at Fall Comdex, 1993, that they had been awarded a patent that would require all multimedia developers to pay them royalties. As Compton's CEO Stanley Frank said, "We helped kick start this industry. We now ask to be compensated for our investments. We will do whatever it takes to defend our patent."

The Compton's Patent

The Compton's patent is very broad. It covers any type of computer-controlled database system that allows a user to search for mixed media that includes text with graphics, sound, or animation. Compton's did not limit their claims to CD-ROM products; they also claimed rights to any type of database involving interactive TV or the Information Superhighway.

The title of the Compton's patent is *Multimedia search system using a plurality of entry path means which indicate interrelatedness of information*. It claims:

> A computer search system for retrieving information, comprising:
>
> means for storing interrelated textual information and graphical information;
>
> means for interrelating said textual and graphical information;
>
> a plurality of entry path means for searching said stored interrelated textual and graphical information, said entry path means comprising:
>
> textual search entry path means for searching said textual information and for retrieving interrelated graphical information to said searched text;
>
> graphics entry path means for searching said graphical information and for retrieving interrelated textual information to said searched graphical information;
>
> selecting means for providing a menu of said plurality of entry path means for selection;
>
> processing means for executing inquiries provided by a user in order to search said textual and graphical information through said selected entry path means;
>
> indicating means for indicating a pathway that accesses information related in one of said entry path means to information accessible in another one of said entry path means;
>
> accessing means for providing access to said related information in said another entry path means; and
>
> output means for receiving search results from said processing means and said related information from said accessing means and for providing said search results and received information to such user.

Compton's presented all multimedia developers with four patent royalty payment options. Kinnaman (1994) explains how they included "...entering into a joint venture with Compton's; distributing products through the company's *Affiliated Label Program*; licensing Compton's *SmarTrieve* technology; or paying royalties." Compton's had the audacity to require back royalties of 1% of net receipts from sales before June 30, 1994, and 3% thereafter.

To say the least, developers reacted negatively to Compton's demands. Some suggested that users should burn all Compton's CD-ROMs and refuse to purchase future titles from any company that would try to force such a Machiavellian proviso on the multimedia industry. As a result of public hearings held by the U.S. Patent and Trademark Office to review its handling of software patents, the Compton's patent was rescinded.

Hopefully the furor caused by the Optical Data and Compton's patents will cause the patent office to review more carefully such broad claims in the future. In fairness to the government, industry leaders like Optical Data and Compton's (who know better) should stop trying to profit from patenting prior art; instead, they should concentrate on improving their products and moving the industry forward.

Meanwhile, the U.S. Patent and Trademark Office has pledged to rework the software patent system. Reforms include publicizing patent applications, hiring seven software specialists as examiners, revamping the examiner bonus program so it does not encourage superficial review, and requiring more information about patent applications before decisions are made (*Wall Street Journal* 4/11/94: B6).

Copyright

All of the elements presented in Chapter 2 (Taxonomy of Multimedia Objects) of this book—including illustrations, text, movies, video clips, documentaries, music, and software—are protected by copyright. Whenever you plan to publish a multimedia work, whether on a CD-ROM, diskettes, or the Information Superhighway, you must make sure you have the right to use every object in it.

The National Music Publishers Association is suing Compuserve for allegedly distributing the song *Unchained Melody* without permission. They claim infringement at least 690 times by subscribers who downloaded the song onto their multimedia PCs (*Wall Street Journal* 12/16/93: B1). The Software Publishers Association took action in 1993 against 577 organizations for pirating commercial software, resulting in $3.6 million in fines (*Atlanta Journal-Constitution* 2/3/94: C2).

Even if you do not plan to publish the material, but just wish to present it, you may still have to seek permission. For example, Wertz (1993) describes how a University of South Carolina student preparing for a juried media festival called MediaFest included a song by The Doors without obtaining copyright permission to use it. South Carolina's attorneys ruled that the university's agreements with ASCAP, BMI, and SESAC do not cover dramatic uses of musical works, nor synchronization rights; moreover, they ruled that the MediaFest, which is open to the public, probably violated fair use. So the student sought permission. After a copyright search led the student to the copyright holder, it turned out to be a company that would not allow use of the song without a significant fee. As Wertz reports, "It mattered not to the company that the user was a student."

Fair Use

Fair Use is a section of the U.S. Copyright Law that allows the use of copyrighted works in reporting news, conducting research, and teaching. The law states:

> Notwithstanding the provisions of section 106 [which gives authors specific rights], the fair use of a copyrighted work, including such use by reproduction in copies or phonorecords or by any other means specified by that section, for purposes such as criticism, comment, news reporting, teaching (including multiple copies for classroom use), scholarship, or research, is not an infringement of copyright. In determining whether the use made of a work in any particular case is a fair use the factors to be considered shall include:
>
> 1. the purpose and character of the use, including whether such use is of a commercial nature or is for nonprofit educational purposes;
>
> 2. the nature of the copyrighted work;
>
> 3. the amount and substantiality of the portion used in relation to the copyrighted work as a whole; and
>
> 4. the effect of the use upon the potential market for or value of the copyrighted work.

Interpreting Fair Use for Teachers

To summarize the Fair Use law for teachers, one may paraphrase its first paragraph as follows: "... the fair use of a copyrighted work for... teaching (including multiple copies for classroom use)... is not an infringement of copyright." The difficulty arises from interpreting the four tests, which are intentionally left vague, as the law goes on to state that "Although the courts have considered and ruled upon the fair use doctrine over and over again, no real definition of the concept has ever emerged. Indeed, since the doctrine is an equitable rule of reason, no generally applicable definition is possible, and each case raising the question must be decided on its own facts."

The vagueness of the law and the fear of lawsuits has led school administrators to publish guidelines that are much more restrictive than the spirit of the law intends. Some of these guidelines are especially detrimental to the classroom use of multimedia, and it is important that lawmakers provide leadership in changing them.

For example, consider the following provisos in the Howard Community College *Faculty Copyright Manual*, which is typical of guidelines used throughout the country; phrases in the provisos that are problematic for multimedia appear in bold print.

New Medium Proviso

> An educator **may not convert** one media format into another (e.g., film to video, filmstrip to slide, etc.) without permission.

Using multimedia computers to present slides, pictures, videos, texts, and audio recordings requires that they be digitized, which changes the medium of the work. Declaring that it is not a fair use for teachers to change the medium of a work prevents their using multimedia computers to create classroom presentations and networked cooperative learning projects.

Frequency of Use Proviso

> Recorded commercial television programs may be retained for forty-five calendar days from date of recording. **After forty-five days they must be erased** or permission must be obtained for continued retention and use. Programs may be shown to a class once, **and repeated once for reinforcement**, during the first ten "teaching days" following a broadcast.

It takes a lot of time and effort to digitize a video clip. If its repeated showing in a class does not deprive the commercial television station of profit, which it rarely would, why require teachers to pursue the difficult permissions process or erase their digital video clips after forty-five days? Moreover, the limit of repeating the clip only once negates one of the most important educational principles of hypermedia, which permits access to a clip as often as needed to accomplish the instructional goal. Less able students may need to view it more than twice.

Electronic Editing Proviso

> Programs need not be used in their entirety but **may not be edited or electronically altered or combined.**

One of the most effective multimedia techniques is to cut, copy, and paste video clips, rearranging the material to juxtapose video sequences for teaching purposes. For example, consider the use of the Memorex commercial in the videodisc *The Puzzle of the Tacoma Narrows Bridge Collapse*. To help students understand the sympathetic vibration caused by the wind striking the bridge, a video clip of Ella Fitzgerald breaking a champagne glass by singing has been cut into the clip of the bridge collapse. Surely the fair use law never meant to prevent teachers from creating effective teaching materials like this.

Transmission of Audiovisual Works Proviso

> Cable "transmission" of copyrighted works is limited to non-dramatic literary works. Because audiovisual works are excluded from the definition of literary works, **audiovisual works may not be transmitted without a license.**

One of the most effective uses of multimedia technology is to provide students access to material via networks that permit review and study from locations as varied as computer labs, dorm rooms, and homes. Is it the intent of Fair Use to prevent students from reviewing the material presented in class? And what about classes conducted solely over networks; are they thereby denied fair use? Since networks can deny access to users who are not registered for a course, should not networked students have the same fair use as classroom students?

Fair Use for Multimedia

By including references to photocopiers and phonograph records in the Fair Use law, its authors clearly intended to permit the fair use of technology. Since the law was last revised in 1976, it predates the personal computer revolution.

Multimedia computers clearly require a fresh interpretation of fair use. It must be fair for teachers to change the medium of a work, electronically combine it with other works for didactic purposes, use it as frequently as needed for students to master the learning objective, and provide students registered in the class with access from locations as varied as computer labs, dorm rooms, and homes over the Information Superhighway. The author believes that all of these uses are within the spirit of the law and the four tests of infringement. Campus copyright officials need to take the lead and revise their faculty copyright guidelines to permit these fair uses of multimedia.

To quote Dr. Kenneth Crews (1992: 17), Professor of Business Law at San Jose State University, "The objective of an institutional copyright policy should be not merely to achieve compliance with the latest standards, but also to identify maximum opportunities for the institution to lawfully pursue its informational and academic objectives. Many standard form policies, particularly the Classroom Guidelines, are questionable responses to a flexible law that should address diverse circumstances."

In the words of American Library Association council member Nancy H. Marshall (1992: 243), "The fair use doctrine does have applicability to the products of the new technologies no matter whether groups, individuals, or copyright proprietors attempt to mislead by the publication of official-sounding documents to the contrary."

Equity, Cost, and Universal Access

The Clinton administration has promised the public that everyone will have equal access to the Information Superhighway. However, with estimated costs of building the network as high as $200 billion, critics are calling this yet another entitlement for the middle class.

Entitlement

Wall Street Journal writer Alan Murray warns that Vice President Gore's call for "universal service" on the "information superhighway" is just one more entitlement for the middle class. The current plan proposes expanding on subsidies already inherent in the phone system, but as Columbia Business School's Eli Noam warns, only a small portion (less than $1 billion) of the telephone benefits goes to the truly needy. The rest subsidizes monthly service for the middle class and the affluent (*Wall Street Journal* 1/31/94: A1).

Consumer groups are pressuring government officials to ensure protection from the high costs of the Information Superhighway for people who only want basic telephone service (*Toronto Globe & Mail* 01/07/94: B2).

Cost

The Clinton administration has estimated the cost of building the Information Superhighway at between $50 billion and $100 billion over the next 10 to 15 years. But industry analysts say that figure could double, up to $200 billion by the time the network is built (*BNA Special Report: Outlook '94* 1/28/94: S21).

A Yankee Group analyst has said that the up-front cost to a cable or phone company for providing a customer with video-on-demand will be $1,000 per household (*New York Times* 1/23/94, Sec. 3: 14). The extra channels available via video dial tones may be used mainly for pay-per-view. As Columbia University Communications Professor Eli Noam warns (Lerner 1993), "The good stuff will inevitably migrate to pay-per-view, so people with just the basics will inevitably get less than they do now. Within ten years, people will be paying cable bills of $100 to $200 a month because they'll be paying per view for things like baseball and football games that they get for free now."

Even the basic information services to be provided by the Continental Cablevision system will offer each subscriber an Ethernet-speed 10 megabit-per-second full Internet connection, including mail and real-time links such as Telnet and Internet Relay Chat (IRC). PSI officials have said that price estimates of under $100 per month when it launches in early 1994 are not unreasonable.

Fox (1993) estimates the cost of ISDN lines range from $93 to $440 to install and $14 to $45 per month. Voice conferencing will require an additional charge of $20 per month. Desktop conferencing with video requires two ISDN lines, ISDN interface equipment ($300), a personal computer ($2,000), and a video interface package ($4,000 to $10,000).

Will it ever really happen? Look at the proposed $33 billion merger of Bell Atlantic and Tele-Communications, Inc (TCI). They called it off because they said it would cost too much. But was it dollars or the other issues this chapter raises that made them back off? Even if they could afford it, they would still have had to contend with Attorney General Janet Reno's promise that the proposed merger would undergo antitrust review (*Atlanta Constitution* 10/22/93: H1).

Usability

Sprint CEO William Esrey questions the potential for consumer services on the Information Superhighway, claiming that the people touted as the prime market are the ones who cannot program a VCR (*Toronto Star* 02/02/94: B1). In 16% of American households, VCRs are permanently blinking 12:00 because no one knows how to set the digital clock, much less program the VCR (*Miami Herald* 2/2/94: C1). Can something as complex as the Information Superhighway be made easier to use than a VCR?

When networks get overloaded, they respond slowly, and if steps are not taken to upgrade them, users get frustrated very quickly. The Information Superhighway runs this risk. It is going to be a lot more difficult to size the resources needed to transmit simultaneous digital television channels over the Internet than it was to size the resources needed for analog cable TV.

E X E R C I S E S

1. If you have never played the *Mortal Kombat* video game, find a friend who has it, and give it a try. Set it for the highest level of violence; if you cannot figure out how to do this, ask the kids who play it. Do you believe that this kind of graphic violence in video games is good for children to experience? What do you think should be done about it?

2. Visit your local video arcade and try the latest laser shooting games. Notice how real video footage is used to put you in a situation in which you must kill or be killed. See how realistic the interaction is, and how well you can learn to aim and fire the weapons. Do you believe these games should be available to the kind of crowd attracted to video arcades, especially when gunshot wounds are the leading cause of death among teenagers in our cities? What do you think should be done about this?

3. How do you feel about the use of multimedia for sex? Does virtual sex serve any useful role in our society? How can it be misused? Could it help solve any societal problems?

4. Do you believe software that lets men force women to do their bidding encourages men to believe they can and should have control over women in real life? If so, what should be done about this?

5. As explained earlier in this chapter, a lot of traffic on the Information Superhighway deals with sex. Do you believe this large amount of sexual traffic detracts from the goals and objectives of the Internet? Do you object to the use of public funds to transmit such material? Why or why not?

6. Do you agree that the University of Waterloo was justified in banning obscene bulletin boards from its network? Should obscene bulletin boards be banned from the Information Superhighway as a whole? Are obscene bulletin boards accessible from your connection to the network?

7. Has a government regulation ever prevented you from accessing services you felt you had a right to? For example, when the FCC ruled that cable companies cannot rebroadcast FM signals, the author's community lost its cable access to National Public Radio and several other FM stations. Since we live in an area too remote for good FM reception, we became disconnected from these important stations. And without any warning! Have you had a similar experience? If our government cannot regulate access to a simple FM radio station, how will it ever manage an Information Superhighway?

8. How do you feel about encryption and the Clipper Chip? Since court-ordered wiretaps on the analog telephone lines of criminals will no longer be effective when all of the communication channels go digital, is the government justified in requiring that a "back door" be built into the system through which it can eavesdrop on digital communications? Why or why not?

9. The Clinton administration has promised the public that everyone will have equal access to the Information Superhighway. Do you believe this, or do you feel that its construction will create a technological underclass in our society? What do you see as the major obstacles that must be overcome to provide equal access for everyone?

CHAPTER

17

How to Keep Up

OBJECTIVES

After completing this chapter, you will be able to:

■ **Know what magazines you should read to keep up with the fast-paced field of multimedia.**

■ **Understand how multimedia CDs and networked resources can help you stay current with new technology.**

■ **Find out about conferences and exhibits where you can see the latest multimedia hardware and software products.**

There are many reasons why you need to keep up with what is happening in multimedia. Since the ability to use it is emerging as a life skill, you will continually need to develop your multimedia techniques to stay competitive in your profession and live life fully in the information society. As the technology changes and you upgrade your computer, you will need the latest information and advice on what to buy. By subscribing to the periodicals, joining the associations, and attending the conferences listed in this chapter, you will be able to remain current and even contribute your own opinions and ideas about multimedia access to the Information Superhighway.

Periodicals

NewMedia

NewMedia magazine is probably the best single source for keeping up with what's new in multimedia. It appears monthly and publishes an annual buyer's guide. *NewMedia* contains dozens of full-color pictures that illustrate the products it describes, and the layout is visually appealing.

To subscribe to *NewMedia*, write to P.O. Box 1771, Riverton, NJ 08077-7331. Phone (415) 573-5170. Fax (415) 573-5131. Be sure to ask about a free subscription, which is available to qualified readers.

Morph's Outpost

Morph's Outpost on the Digital Frontier admits to being on the far side, "… where the information superhighway runs into the jungle, and pioneers stop for supplies and sustenance before moving on to blaze new trails," but that makes it captivating to read. Loaded with information, *Morph's Outpost* contains new product announcements, buyers guides, marketing tips, new tools, CD-ROM reviews, news on alliances and mergers, and interviews with leading developers. You will surely enjoy the *Adventures of Morph* cartoon strip.

Morph's Outpost is published monthly by Morph's Outpost Inc., P.O. Box 578, Orinda, CA 94563. Phone (510) 238-4545. Fax (510) 238-9459.

Multimedia Today

Published by IBM, *Multimedia Today* contains guest editorials, feature articles on customer applications of IBM's multimedia technology, as well as announcements and sales promotions of multimedia production tools, peripherals, and CD-ROM titles.

Multimedia Today is free to qualified readers. To subscribe, send your name and address to IBM Multimedia Solutions, 4111 Northside Parkway, Atlanta, GA 30327. Fax (404) 238-4298.

Internet World

A good source for the latest news about the Information Superhighway, *Internet World* features articles about new trends on the network, advertises Internet addresses of new online resources, and reviews books about the Internet. Vendor advertising shows how entrepreneurial commercial users of the network have become.

Internet World is published monthly by Mecklermedia Corporation, 11 Ferry Lane West, Westport, CT 06880. Phone (203) 226-6967. Fax (203) 454-5840. E-mail meckler@jvnc.net.

T.H.E. Journal

T.H.E. stands for Technological Horizons in Education. *T.H.E. Journal* appears monthly; each issue contains application highlights and dozens of new product announcements. Each year, *T.H.E. Journal* publishes the *Multimedia Source Guide*, which lists hundreds of multimedia products and tells how to order them. Subscribers also receive special multimedia supplements from vendors like IBM, Apple, and Zenith.

T.H.E. Journal is free to qualified individuals in educational institutions and training departments in the United States and Canada. To subscribe, phone (714) 730-4011 or fax (714) 730-3739. The mailing address is 150 El Camino Real, Suite 112, Tustin, CA 92680.

Technology & Learning

Technology & Learning is published monthly, except in December and the summer months. Targeted primarily at pre-college educators, it reviews software, advertises grants and contests, contains vendor supplements, articulates classroom needs, reviews authoring tools, and has a Q&A section to answer questions about technology and learning. Plus it has great cartoons.

To subscribe, phone (513) 847-5900. The mailing address is Peter Li, Inc., 330 Progress Road, Dayton, OH 45449.

The Videodisc Compendium

The Videodisc Compendium is a great way to find out about new videodisc titles. It appears quarterly and catalogs more than 2,000 videodiscs that have been produced for use in education and training. To subscribe, contact Emerging Technology Consultants, 2819 Hamline Avenue North, St. Paul, MN 55113. Phone (612) 639-3973. Fax (612) 639-0110.

CD-ROM World

Published monthly, *CD-ROM World* is a good source of information on CD-ROM hardware and software. Each issue includes late-breaking news, editorial comment, product reviews, and articles on using CD-ROM at home, at the office, and in schools.

To subscribe, contact Mecklermedia Corporation, 11 Ferry Lane West, Westport, CT 06880. Phone (203) 226-6967. Fax (203) 454-5840. E-mail meckler@jvnc.net.

Virtual Reality World

Published bimonthly, *Virtual Reality World* features product news, entertainment, marketplace updates, and articles about the latest VR trends and techniques. Beautifully illustrated, it contains lots of advertisements marketing the newest VR products.

To subscribe, contact Mecklermedia Corporation, 11 Ferry Lane West, Westport, CT 06880. Phone (203) 226-6967. Fax (203) 454-5840. E-mail meckler@jvnc.net.

Whole Internet Catalog

Krol's (1992) *Whole Internet Catalog* lists Internet resources covering the broad range of topics listed in Table 17-1. For each topic, Krol tells you how to access the resources on the Internet and gives a sample entry.

Table 17-1 Topics in Krol's *Whole Internet Catalog*

Aeronautics and Astronautics	Government, U.S.	Oceanography
Agriculture	Health	Pets
Anthropology	History	Physics
Astronomy	Hobbies and Crafts	Political Activism
Aviation	Humanities	Popular Culture
Biology	Internet	Recreation, Games
Chemistry	Journalism	Recreation, Sports
Computer Science	Law	Reference Books
Computing	Libraries	Religion
Cooking	Library and Information Science	Resource Directories
Education	Literature	Science Fiction and Fantasy Literature
Electrical Engineering	Mathematics	Science
Engineering	Medicine	Society and Culture
Environment	Molecular Biology	Standards
Forestry	Music	Travel
Freenet	Network Information	Weather, Meteorology, and Climatology
Gardening and Horticulture	Network organizations	White Pages
Genealogy	Network Services	Zymurgy
Geography	News, Network	
Geology and Geophysics	Nutrition	

HOTT

HOTT, which stands for Hot Off The Tree, is a free monthly electronic newsletter featuring the latest advances in computers, communications, and electronics. Each issue provides article summaries on new and emerging technologies, including virtual reality, neural networks, personal digital assistants, graphical user interfaces, intelligent agents, ubiquitous computing, wireless networks, smart cards, video phones, set-top boxes, nanotechnology, massively parallel processing, and genetic and evolutionary programming.

Summaries are provided from the *Wall Street Journal, New York Times, Los Angeles Times, Washington Post, San Jose Mercury News, Boston Globe, Financial Times* (London), *Daily Telegraph* (U.K.), *Time, Newsweek, U.S. News & World Report, Business Week, Forbes, Fortune, The Economist* (London), *Nikkei Weekly* (Tokyo), *Asian Wall Street Journal* (Hong Kong), more than 50 trade magazines including

Computerworld, InfoWorld, Datamation, PC Week, Dr. Dobb's Journal, LAN Times, Communications Week, Electronic Engineering Times, NewMedia, VAR Business, Midrange Systems, Byte, and more than 50 research journals, including all publications of the IEEE Computer and Communications Societies, plus technical journals published by AT&T, IBM, Hewlett Packard, Fujitsu, Sharp, NTT, Siemens, Philips, and GEC. More than a hundred Internet mailing lists & USENET discussion groups are indexed, along with listings of forthcoming and recently published technical books, and upcoming trade shows and technical conferences.

Send subscription requests to listserv@ucsd.edu; leave the "Subject" line blank, and in the body of message enter **SUBSCRIBE HOTT-LIST** (do not include first or last names following "SUBSCRIBE HOTT-LIST").

Lucas Newsletter

Film maker George Lucas established the George Lucas Educational Foundation to help shape his vision for a technology-enriched educational system. To subscribe to an online newsletter on the subject, send e-mail to edutopia@kerner.com.

E X E R C I S E S

1. Visit your local library and find out whether it subscribes to the periodicals listed in the first part of this chapter. If it does not, ask why not, and then suggest or insist that it should.

2. Several multimedia periodicals offer free subscriptions. If you do not already subscribe to them, apply for your free subscription today, following the instructions provided in the "Periodicals" section in this chapter.

3. Are you aware of good sources for keeping up with multimedia that were not mentioned in this chapter? If so, what are they?

4. Phone (800) 448-2323 to get your free issue of the *Nautilus* magazine on CD-ROM. Use a multimedia PC to read the issue. What advantages do CD-ROM magazines have over conventional publications? Are there disadvantages?

5. Of the many conferences and exhibits listed in this chapter, find out which one will occur nearest you during the coming year, and make plans to attend it. Do you know of other multimedia conferences or exhibits not listed in this chapter?

6. If you ever plan to visit Washington, D.C., be sure to phone (202) 707-4157 in advance to make an appointment to visit the National Demonstration Laboratory. If you live within driving distance, ask your teacher to make arrangements to take your class there for a field trip.

Part Five

Multimedia Tools and Techniques

CONTENTS

Chapter 18
Text

Chapter 19
Graphics

Chapter 20
Triggering

Chapter 21
Waveform Audio Recording

Chapter 22
CD Audio Clipmaking

Chapter 23
MIDI Sequencing

Chapter 24
Digital Video Recording

Chapter 25
Videodisc Clipmaking

It should be as easy to author in a medium as it is to experience works created in it.

Ivan Illich, paraphrased by Brenda Laurel, *Edutopia* 1, no.1 (Winter 1993): 6

It is now time to begin the hands-on tutorial that will prepare you to create your own multimedia applications. In order to do this, you need to learn how to use a set of multimedia tools, and through practice, develop techniques that will make you proficient in their use.

This part of the book teaches you how to use the following tools: Paint Shop Pro to capture and format graphics; Video for Windows to record and edit movies and animations; Band-in-a-Box to generate MIDI sequences; and a suite of tools in PODIUM for Windows that lets you record and play back waveform digital audio, make CD audio and videodisc clips, snap still pictures from a live video source, cruise the Information Superhighway to locate and download files, and use a multimedia toolbox to link hypertext and hyperpicture triggers on the screen to multimedia objects. Thus, you will learn how to create multimedia applications.

PODIUM is just one of many software packages you can use to create multimedia applications. The many alternatives to PODIUM include presentation packages such as PowerPoint, Compel, Freelance, Harvard Graphics, Aldus Persuasion, or WordPerfect Presentations, and authoring systems such as Authorware Professional, ToolBook, Quest, TenCore, and Icon Author. Many of these packages were discussed in Chapter 9.

PODIUM was chosen for this book because it contains a multimedia toolbox that makes it easy for students to complete the tutorial exercises. Users who are familiar with other packages will realize that many of the PODIUM techniques taught in this book can be applied using other sets of tools. What is important here is not the choice of a specific tool, but rather the concepts that are being presented. Later on the student can apply these techniques using the tools available in different software packages.

18

Text

After completing this chapter, you will know how to:

■ **Use the Windows File Manager to create the directories that store multimedia applications on hard disk drives.**

■ **Create a new multimedia screen and position text on it.**

■ **Size, center, edit, shadow, color, and clone text.**

■ **Display text in any TrueType font installed on your computer.**

■ **Change foreground and background colors and make good color choices.**

■ **Associate text with mouse clicks, so that text elements appear one-by-one as the user clicks the mouse.**

Text is a key element of most multimedia applications, and a good working knowledge of how to enter, edit, and manipulate text is a basic requirement for anyone who wants to become multiliterate. This tutorial begins by showing you how to enter, position, size, color, shadow, clone, and edit text in a multimedia application. You will also learn how to import text from other sources, including word processors and scanners.

Creating a Directory

Before you create a multimedia application, you need to make a directory on your hard disk to put it in. Think of your hard drive as a huge filing cabinet that stores information. A directory is like a drawer in the filing cabinet. Each multimedia screen you create will be stored in a file that you keep in this directory.

To create a directory, you use the Windows File Manager. Figure 18-1 shows you how to find its icon in the Main group on the Windows desktop. If the Main group is not visible, pull down the Window menu and select Main to bring it up, then double-click the File Manager icon to launch the File Manager. Figure 18-2 provides a visual diagram of how all the files are organized on your computer. For example, if you click the icon that represents your CD-ROM drive, you will see the many directories of the *Multiliteracy CD* (assuming this CD is currently in the drive). Each directory contains the files needed to present one chapter of this book. Double-click the directory icons to inspect the contents of the individual directories.

The File Manager icon appears in the Main group on your Windows desktop.

The Windows File Manager uses a filing cabinet metaphor.

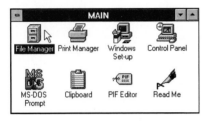

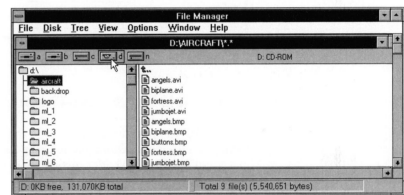

To create a new directory for your application, follow these steps:

▷ Click the icon that represents the hard disk drive in which you will create the directory for your multimedia application.

▷ Pull down the File menu and select Create Directory to bring up the dialog in Figure 18-3.

▷ For this tutorial, you need to create a directory called *multilit*. Assuming your hard drive is *C*, type **c:\multilit**

▷ Click OK. The directory should now appear in the list of directories displayed by the File Manager. If it does not, scroll to the top of the list on the left side of the File Manager and double-click on the *c:* you will find there.

▷ Close the File Manager by pulling down its File menu and choosing Exit.

18-3

The Windows File Manager's Create Directory dialog.

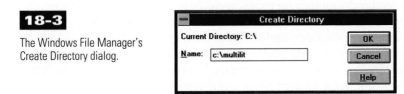

Starting a New Screen

Now you are ready to create your first multimedia screen! Follow these steps:

▶ If you do not have PODIUM running at the moment, get it started.

▶ Pull down the PODIUM Files menu and choose New Custom to make PODIUM display the File Creation dialog shown in Figure 18-4. In the File Name field, assuming your hard drive is *C*, type **c:\multilit\example.cus**.

▶ Click OK: PODIUM will create the file *example.cus* and display the custom toolbox. Because there is nothing in the file yet, the screen is blank.

The File Creation dialog lets you create a new custom screen.

The PODIUM Toolbox

The PODIUM application generator on the *Multiliteracy CD* contains a custom toolbox. It is called a **custom toolbox** because it lets you "customize" the screen. It makes multimedia application development simple and intuitive—you can design and activate your screen almost by thinking about what you want.

The custom toolbox contains nineteen icons:

Each icon represents a tool. To activate a tool, you click its icon. The cursor assumes the shape of the icon to indicate which tool is active. You mouse around the screen and click the spot where you wish to use the tool. Depending on the tool, PODIUM either opens a dialog or draws a box around the object you clicked, indicating that you can drag it around the screen to reposition or size it.

The toolbox lets you design and create all the elements of a multimedia screen, including the text and graphics that will appear on the screen, the buttons and hot spots that trigger the multimedia events themselves, and the order in which these events will be launched when the user clicks the mouse on a button or hotspot.

The toolbox is a window you can move around the screen like any other window. Press F4 to display the toolbox on your screen. To move the toolbox, position the mouse on the title bar (where it says "PODIUM Custom Toolbox"), hold down the left mouse button, and drag the window. Close the toolbox by pressing F4, which is a toggle in PODIUM that makes the toolbox come and go. Practice pressing F4 now. *When the toolbox is visible, you are an author, creating an application. When the toolbox is closed, you are a user, trying out the application.*

Entering Text

The copy of PODIUM that comes on the CD with this book is a tutorial edition. The tutorial edition lets you create the examples in this book as long as you do not stray too far from the steps in the tutorial. If later you want to make a multimedia application that has your own text in it, you will need to purchase a retail copy of PODIUM, as described in Appendix B.

Follow these steps to learn how to enter text on the multimedia screen:

▶ If the toolbox is not on your screen, press F4 to display it now.

▶ Click the icon represented by the big *T* that stands for text. If you move your mouse around the screen, you will notice that your cursor assumes the shape of a text inserter.

▶ Mouse to a spot toward the left of the center of the screen and click the left mouse button.

▶ PODIUM opens the Text Insert dialog box shown in Figure 18-5. Type **McGraw-Hill Multimedia Literacy**

▶ Click OK. Notice how your text now appears on the screen.

▶ Mouse farther down the screen, click the left button, and enter the text **Powerful**

▶ Mouse down a little farther, and enter the text **Tools**

The screen will now appear as shown in Figure 18-6.

18-5

The Text Insert dialog lets you enter text on the screen.

18-6

The inserted text appears in the PODIUM window.

Changing the Background Color

You can change the background color with the Backdrop tool. The Backdrop icon appears in the toolbox as a curtain partially opened on a stage, revealing a backdrop behind it. To change the background color:

▶ Click the Backdrop icon: the PODIUM Backdrop dialog appears.

▶ Click the Colors button and select a color.

▶ Click OK to close the dialog: the background will change to the selected color.

Try different background colors. Notice how some color combinations work better than others. On a light background, dark colors have the most impact; on a dark background, light colors stand out. Normally you should select background colors that are subdued and easy to look at. The author's favorite combination is white text on a dark blue background. Figure 18-8 shows other recommended color combinations.

18-8

Recommended color combinations.

Background Color	Suggestions for Foreground Colors
Black	White Yellow Pink Green Blue Cyan Gray Red
Blue	White Yellow Green Red Cyan Gray DarkRed Pink
DarkBlue	White Yellow Pink Green Cyan Red Gray
Brown	White Black DarkBlue Cyan Green Blue DarkRed
Cyan	Black Blue DarkBlue Brown DarkPink Pink Red
DarkCyan	White Black Yellow DarkBlue Blue Cyan Red DarkRed
Gray	Black Blue DarkBlue Pink DarkPink DarkRed Red
DarkGray	White Black Yellow Green Cyan Red DarkRed
Green	White Black Blue DarkBlue DarkPink Red DarkRed
DarkGreen	White Black Yellow Cyan DarkBlue Red DarkRed
Pink	White Black Yellow DarkBlue Cyan DarkRed Green
DarkPink	White Black Yellow Cyan Gray Green
Red	White Black DarkBlue Blue Cyan
DarkRed	White Yellow Blue Cyan Green Gray
White	Black Blue DarkBlue Red DarkRed Pink DarkPink
Yellow	Black Blue DarkBlue DarkGreen Red DarkRed

Shadowing Text

Varying the amount of drop shadow on your text can make it appear more or less bold against the screen behind it. You can change the amount of drop shadow with the Shadow tool, which appears in the toolbox as a person in a trench coat standing under a streetlight that casts a shadow at night. To change the amount of shadow of any text on the screen:

▶ Click the Shadow tool, and the mouse assumes the shape of the shadow.

▶ Mouse over the text you wish to shadow, click once, and PODIUM will open a dialog box that lets you choose the amount of shadow you want.

Try putting different amounts of shadow on the text on your screen. Notice how more shadow makes the text stand out. This is especially important in the next chapter, which will show you how to put pictures in the background behind your text. If the pictures are busy, you will need a lot of drop shadow to bring out your text.

Cloning Text

The Cloning tool is a real time-saver. Suppose you take the time to create a line of text that has a special size, font, and color, and you want another line of text with similar attributes. Instead of having to create a new line of text from scratch, you can clone the existing line, and then simply change its text with the Editing tool. To clone text:

▷ Click the Cloning tool, which is pictured in the toolbox as two stick figures side by side. (Watch closely when you click them to see how they smile when activated.)

▷ Mouse over the text you wish to clone, hold down your left mouse button, and drag the Cloning box to the location where you want the cloned text to appear on the screen.

For example, you already have the words "Powerful" and "Tools" on your screen. Suppose you want to add the word "Very" to create the phrase "Very Powerful Tools." And suppose you want the word "Very" to have the same attributes (size, color, font, and shadow) that the word "Powerful" has. Instead of specifying the attributes again, you can simply clone the word "Powerful," and then change the text to the word "Very." Here are the steps to follow:

▷ Click the Cloning tool in the toolbox: the clones will smile.

▷ Move the mouse over the word "Powerful" and hold the left button down while you drag its clone up the screen where you want the new word to appear. When you release the mouse button, the cloned word will appear.

▷ Click the Editing tool in the toolbox, and click the word "Powerful": the Edit dialog will appear.

▷ Type **Very**, then click OK. Notice how the word "Very" now has the same attributes as the word "Powerful."

Building Text

By default, all of the text you entered appears at once on the multimedia screen. Sometimes you do not want to reveal all of the text at once. For example, suppose you are making a presentation, and you want to make the items you are talking about appear one-by-one as you click your mouse button to reveal them. The Clicking tool lets you do this by associating the appearance of text fields with mouse clicks. Follow these steps:

▷ To invoke the Mouse Clicking tool, click the icon that depicts a mouse with a piece of cheese.

▷ Move your cursor over some text and click once. PODIUM opens a dialog that lets you specify which mouse click will make the text appear. Each time the user clicks the mouse, the items associated with that mouse click will appear. You can use this tool to make any number of text fields appear after any mouse click.

Clip Art Libraries

Clip art libraries usually provide a way to export graphics as BMP files. If they do not, you can use Paint Shop Pro to convert the files in the clip art libraries to BMPs. To convert a file with Paint Shop Pro, follow these steps:

▷   Pull down the Paint Shop Pro File menu and select Open.

▷   In the Type box, select the type of file you want to convert. If the file type is not listed, you will need to grab the image instead of converting it. The preceding section, "Capturing and Converting Graphics," tells you how to grab files.

▷   When the image appears in the Paint Shop Pro window, pull down the File menu and choose Save As.

▷   In the Format box, select BMP—RGB Encoded.

▷   Type the name you want the BMP to have in the File Name field. Make sure you give it a *.bmp* file extension.

▷   Click OK to save the file. Then pull down the File menu and choose Exit to leave Paint Shop Pro.

Picture Takers

Most digital video boards come with software that can snap pictures. You simply connect a video camera to the video board, point it at the picture you want to shoot, and snap the picture with your software.

PODIUM comes with a Picture Taker tool that can snap pictures from the New Media Graphics' Super VideoWindows board. The PODIUM tool greatly simplifies the process because it automatically sizes the pictures to the 640x480 grid of dots on the computer screen. To use the Picture Taker Tool:

▷   Pull down the Tools menu and select Picture Taker. The Picture Taker dialog shown in Figure 19-5 will appear.

The Picture Taker dialog lets you snap pictures from any video source.

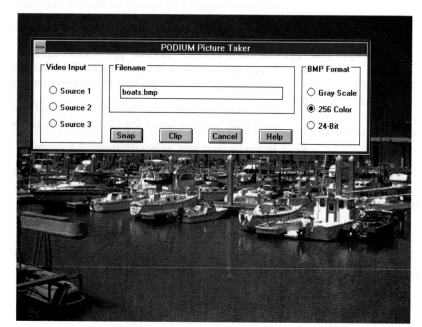

▶ Use the mouse to select your video source (up to three sources can be connected, such as a video camera, a VCR, and a television tuner), and enter a filename for the captured image.

▶ Click the Snap button: PODIUM instantly snaps the picture and saves it in BMP format.

Still Video Cameras

Still video cameras come in handy when the video source you want to use cannot easily be connected to your multimedia computer's video digitizer board. For example, it would be cumbersome and dangerous to transport your multimedia computer to shoot a picture from a mountaintop.

A reasonably priced still video camera is Canon's RC-570 (shown in Figure 19-6). Its two-inch reusable diskette can store and display up to 50 color images. It comes with auto focus, a 3× power-zoom lens, and automatic exposure.

Because the camera has a disk, many people assume the data is stored in computer readable form. It is not. The data is analog like the videotape in your VCR. As Hurter and Stone (1993) quip, "It's *still* Video!" And you *still* need to feed it into your video digitizer to make a bitmap out of it.

Canon's RC-570 still video camera.

Kodak's Photo CD

For developers who do not have their own digitizing equipment, Kodak's Photo CD may provide a cost-effective way of taking pictures for use in multimedia applications. You take the negatives or film to a nearby photofinishing service, and for a reasonable fee that averages about a dollar per picture, Kodak returns your photographs on a Photo CD disc. Images can be transferred to a Photo CD from newly developed 35mm film, older 35mm negatives that have already been used for conventional prints, and 35mm slides. While any MPC can read images off a Photo CD, double-speed CD-ROM drives are needed for multisession Photo CDs. Kodak's Photo CD was the first major product to use the multisession format, which allows more data to be added to a CD after the initial recording. This enables users of Kodak Photo CD discs to bring their discs into a Kodak dealer many times, each time adding a few more photographs to the disc.

Kodak's Photo CD Access Software uses a contact sheet metaphor.

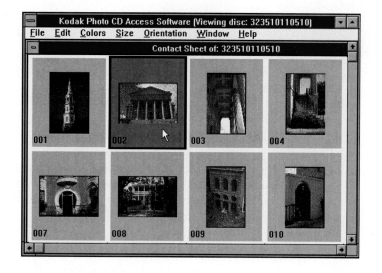

Each picture is stored in five different resolutions on the Photo CD: wallet (128 pixels by 192 pixels), snapshot (256x384), standard (512x768), large (1024x1536), and poster (2048x3072). Unfortunately, the images are not stored in the Windows BMP format, so you must convert them for use in your application. Kodak's Photo CD Access Software can export them as BMPs. Figure 19-7 shows how the software uses a contact sheet metaphor that lets you select a picture for full-screen viewing by clicking one of the miniatures. You can edit the photos by cropping or changing the size, color settings, and orientation. Another disadvantage is that the photos do not match the 640x480 grid on the computer screen. You will either need to crop the images or resize them with a tool like Paint Shop Pro. Be careful: stretching or squeezing the picture can produce undesirable results.

Digital Chalk

PODIUM has a feature called **digital chalk.** Any time the user holds down both mouse buttons simultaneously, the cursor turns into a piece of chalk with which you can draw on the screen. While drawing with chalk, the C (color) key is active. Each time you press C while drawing with the chalk, the color changes. If you hold down C continuously, you can draw a rainbow. E is the Erase key. Pressing E after you draw with chalk will erase what you just drew.

What you draw with chalk does not become part of your bitmap or alter the images on your hard drive in any way. Its purpose is to allow users to point things out during multimedia presentations. You can use the chalk on any image, including live video feeds from cameras, VCRs, and television stations.

Compressing Bitmaps

No matter how much hard disk space you have, multimedia will require you to use it wisely. Bitmaps can take up a lot of space. For example, a 640x480 bitmap with 256 colors has 307,200 pixels. When BMP file headers are added, this consumes more than 310K of space on your computer's hard drive.

PODIUM supports the Windows 3.1 **RLE** (run-length encoding) compressed bitmap format. Run-length encoding is a compression method that reduces the size of a bitmap by recording the number of times a color appears in a row, instead of the entire row of pixels. For example, if 20 pixels in a row are red, the encoding is 20R, instead of RRRRRRRRRRRRRRRRRRRRR. The more redundancy there is in a picture, the more RLE encoding can reduce its size.

You can use Paint Shop Pro to compress bitmaps. Simply open the bitmap, choose Save As, check the BMP—RLE box, and save it. Uncompressed bitmaps of 310K typically compress down to 100K, sometimes to as little as 30K.

Not all graphics editors can read compressed bitmaps. If you try to edit a compressed file with a graphics editor that cannot read it, you will need to use Paint Shop Pro to decompress the file first. To decompress a bitmap:

▶ Open the bitmap with Paint Shop Pro.

▶ Choose Save As.

▶ Check the BMP—RGB box.

▶ Save the file.

Controlling Palettes

Developers must be careful to avoid palette shifts in multimedia applications. Until all users have access to 24-bit color adapters, this is going to be a problem. At present, most multimedia computers have 8-bit adapters that can only display 256 colors at once. These colors are selected from more than 16 million colors that your computer monitor can display.

Let's begin by creating a situation in which there is a palette shift, and then take steps to correct it. To prepare for this exercise you need to copy a file from your CD-ROM onto your hard drive. You can use your Windows File Manager to do that. Follow these steps:

▶ Open the Windows File Manager from the Windows desktop.

▶ Pull down the File menu and choose Copy to make the Copy dialog in Figure 19-8 appear.

19-8

How to copy a file with the File Manager's Copy dialog.

▶ In the From field, assuming your CD-ROM drive is *D*, type **d:\problems\problem.bmp** and in the To field, type **c:\multilit\palshift.bmp**, then click OK.

After the file is copied, since it came from a read-only CD-ROM, you must change its read-only properties before you can modify its palette.

▶ Use the File Manager to list the files in your *c:\multilit* directory, and click once on the filename *palshift.bmp* to highlight it.

▶ Now pull down the File menu and chose Properties: the Properties dialog will appear.

▶ Uncheck the Read Only box, and click OK.

▶ Close the File Manager.

Now you are ready to begin the exercise.

19-9

The backdrop *photo.bmp.*

19-10

The palette shifts in *photo.bmp* when an icon with a different palette appears over it.

> ▶ Pull down your PODIUM Files menu and choose New Custom to start a new screen; create it in your *multilit* directory under the name *shift.cus.*

> ▶ Use the Background tool to set *backdrop\photo.bmp* as the background. Your screen should resemble Figure 19-9.

> ▶ Use the Picture Hanger tool to add the icon *multilit\palshift.bmp.* Notice what happens when the icon appears on top of the backdrop as shown in Figure 19-10: the palette shifts! *Note:* If you have a 24-bit color adapter, you will not see the palette shift, but if you are using an 8-bit adapter you will.

The palette shifts because *backdrop\photo.bmp* uses the standard Windows palette, while *multilit\palshift.bmp* has a custom palette. To prevent the palette shift, you need to modify *palshift.bmp* so that it also uses the standard Windows palette. Follow these steps to convert the palette of a bitmap into the standard palette.

The Decrease Color Depth dialog in Paint Shop Pro.

▶ Start up Paint Shop Pro and open the *multilit\palshift.bmp* image.

▶ Pull down the Colors menu, select Increase Color Depth, and choose 16 million colors. Wait a couple of seconds for your computer to complete the process.

▶ Pull down the Colors menu, select Decrease Color Depth, and choose 256 colors. The Decrease Color Depth dialog shown in Figure 19-11 will appear.

▶ In the Palette group, click the Standard palette.

▶ In the Reduction Method group, click Error Diffusion.

▶ Click OK and wait a couple of seconds while Paint Shop Pro completes the process.

▶ Pull down the File menu and select Save As.

▶ In the File Name field, type **c:\multilit\palshift.bmp,** then click OK. Close Paint Shop Pro.

▶ Pull down PODIUM's Controls menu and select Erase Picture Buffers to flush PODIUM's bitmap memory.

▶ Press F12 to make PODIUM reread the file. If the palette no longer shifts, as shown in Figure 19-12, you have succeeded; congratulations!

With the palette shift corrected, the *palshift.bmp* icon appears over *photo.bmp* without altering the colors in the backdrop.

EXERCISES

1. Use PODIUM to bring up *multilit\example.cus* on your screen. Press F4 and use the Picture Hanger tool to layer onto the screen every one of the icons in the *icon* directory on the *Multiliteracy CD*. Now use the grid hand tool to arrange the icons into a big square. Try your hand at making other patterns.

2. Use Paint Shop Pro to grab a screen of your choice and save it as an uncompressed BMP file. Use the File Manager to inspect the size of the file, and make a note of how large it is. Now use Paint Shop Pro to compress the bitmap by saving it as an RLE-encoded BMP. How large is it now? By what percentage did Paint Shop Pro compress the file?

3. The last section of this chapter, "Controlling Palettes," showed you how to eliminate the palette shift that occurs when you layer the bitmap *palshift.bmp* over *photo.bmp*. Repeat that section until you can control the palette shift without reading the instructions.

20

Triggering

After completing this chapter, you will know how to:

- Use the Link tool to create hypertext and connect the hypertext to one or more multimedia objects on your computer.

- Use the Trigger tool to create hyperpictures and connect the hyperpictures to multimedia objects.

- Position buttons anywhere on the screen and link them to any multimedia object on the computer.

- Edit the links to hypertext and hyperpictures, changing what will happen when the user triggers them.

- Make the backdrop of a multimedia screen trigger one or more multimedia objects.

- Launch any executable or batch file as an object in a multimedia application.

- Undo changes and delete objects from multimedia screens.

Triggers let you make multimedia applications interactive by linking objects to words or pictures on the screen. The custom toolbox allows you to link any object on your computer or network to any Text field or picture or part of a picture. When you mouse over a trigger, the cursor changes shape to indicate that it is on a hot spot; if you then click the mouse, PODIUM launches the links.

Hypertext

As you learned in Part One, linked text is called hypertext. To make hypertext, follow these steps:

▶ Pull down the PODIUM Files menu and select New Custom to bring up the Custom File Name dialog.

▶ In the File Name field, assuming your hard drive is *C*, type **c:\multilit\linkdemo.cus**, then click OK.

 ▶ Use the Backdrop tool to give this multimedia screen the *backdrop\rooster.bmp* background.

▶ Use the Text tool to put this text on the backdrop: **Speak to me!**

To make the text hyper, follow these steps:

▶ Click the Link icon, which appears in the toolbox as two links in a chain.

▶ Mouse over the "Speak to me!" text you wish to link and click once; the Link dialog in Figure 20-1 will appear.

▶ Click inside the big Edit box to position your cursor in it, then type: **audio\rooster.wav**

▶ Press F4 to put the toolbox away and become a user of your application.

▶ Mouse over the words "Speak to me!" Figure 20-2 shows how the cursor changes shape as it passes over the hot spot. If you click the hot spot, you will hear the rooster crow.

20-1

The Link dialog.

PODIUM Custom Link Editor

Editing Links to the Item:
Speak to me!

Insert or edit your links in the box below, or press Cancel
to restore them to their former contents.

audio\rooster.wav

OK   Browse...

Browse Option
○ Full Path
◉ No Drive Letter
○ No Path

Clipboard   Cancel

20-2

The cursor changes shape when you mouse over a hot spot.

You can link more than one object to a line of hypertext. Follow these steps:

▶   Press [F4] to bring up the toolbox.

▶   Use the Text tool to enter the text **Show me some pictures!**

▶   Use the Link tool to connect it to the three pictures:

> bitmaps\egg.bmp
> bitmaps\chick.bmp
> bitmaps\rooster.bmp

▶   Press [F4] to become a user again and mouse over the words "Show me some pictures!" The first picture will appear.

▶   Click the left button again: the second picture will appear.

▶   Click once more to see the third picture.

▶   Click the right button to have PODIUM back up and show the previous picture.

▶   Keep clicking the left button until you run out of pictures; PODIUM then returns you to the screen from which you triggered them.

Hyperpictures

When pictures have links, they are called hyperpictures. To put a link on a picture, follow these steps:

▶   Click the Trigger tool, which appears in the toolbox as an upward pointing arrow on a launch pad. The cursor assumes the shape of the launcher.

▶   Mouse to the beginning of the trigger you wish to create, hold down the left mouse button, then drag the Trigger box so that it encompasses the part of the picture you want to serve as a trigger.

▶   Release the mouse button: a dialog box will appear in which you can type your links, paste them from the clipboard, or browse for them. This box enables you to link any part of any picture to any combination of multimedia events, PODIUM objects, or application programs.

For example, suppose you would like the beak of the rooster in the backdrop of your *linkdemo.cus* screen to trigger the sound of a rooster crowing. Follow these steps:

▶   If the toolbox is not open, press [F4] to display it on your screen.

▶   Click the Trigger tool, then mouse over to the upper-left corner of the area you want to make your trigger. Do *not* click the mouse yet.

▶   Hold down the left mouse button, and—while holding it down—drag the mouse to the lower-right corner of the trigger: a box will appear showing the location of your trigger.

▶   Release the mouse button: PODIUM will display the Link dialog.

▶   Click once inside the big Link box to set your cursor there.

▶   Type **audio\rooster.wav**, then click OK.

▶   Press [F4] to put the toolbox away and become a user again.

Databases, spreadsheets, authoring tools, or presentation packages can be the objects of PODIUM links, as can multimedia applications made with ToolBook, Linkway, Authorware, Icon Author, PowerPoint, Compel, Freelance, Harvard Graphics, Aldus Persuasion, or WordPerfect Presentations. Simply follow the equal sign of the @os= with the command line that would launch the application from the Run dialog on the Windows Program Manager File menu.

Deleting Objects

In addition to letting you create hypertext and hyperpictures, the toolbox also lets you delete them. The Delete icon appears in the toolbox as a trash can. To delete an object:

▶ Click the Delete icon: the cursor assumes the shape of a trash can.

▶ Mouse over the object you want to delete and click once. A dialog will identify the item to be deleted and ask you to confirm that you really wish to delete it.

Undoing Deletes and Edits

Click on the Undo tool to reverse the last change you made. For example, this feature allows you to restore an object you just deleted or return an object that you just moved to its original position. To invoke the Undo tool, simply click once on the Undo icon.

E X E R C I S E S

1. When you click "Show me some pictures!" on the *linkdemo.cus* screen, you see three stages in the development of a chicken: egg, chick, hen. When the egg, chick, and hen pictures are on your screen, you can use the PODIUM Effects menu to specify different dissolve patterns, directions, and timings that add interest to the images. Try these effects.

    NOTE: The dissolves only work when you have PODIUM full screen. To pull down the Effects menu when PODIUM is full screen, press Alt-E. *E* stands for effects.

2. Reverse the order of the three images you see when you click "Show me some pictures!" *Hint:* To edit the links to "Show me some pictures!", click the Link tool, then click "Show me some pictures!" A Link box will appear that displays the links and lets you edit them.

3. Click the Undo tool to undo the changes you just made in the second exercise. Then press F4 to put the toolbox away and click "Show me some pictures!" to make sure the egg, chick, and hen appear in the proper order. If they do not, edit the links to "Show me some pictures!" until they do.

21

Waveform Audio Recording

After completing this chapter, you will know how to:

- **Record and edit waveform audio files via the digital audio hardware in your multimedia PC.**

- **Experience how the sampling rate and bits-per-sample settings affect the quality and size of the waveform audio file.**

- **Create "sound under stills" by timing the appearance of bitmaps to sounds in waveform audio recordings.**

By definition, every multimedia PC has the capability to play music from three sources: waveform audio recordings, compact disc audio, and MIDI sound tracks. In this chapter you will learn how to record waveform audio, and in the next two chapters you will learn about CD audio clipmaking and MIDI sequencing.

Sound Under Stills

Do you remember filmstrip projectors that could synchronize slides with a sound track? That technique is known as **sound under stills.** PODIUM makes it easy for you to create sound under stills.

In Chapter 20, you created a screen called *linkdemo.cus.* You can practice creating sound under stills using this screen. Follow these steps:

▶   If *linkdemo.cus* is not already on your screen, pull down the PODIUM Files menu, select Custom, and choose *linkdemo.cus.*

▶   Click "Show me some pictures!" and make sure it triggers the three bitmaps you linked to it:

    bitmaps\egg.bmp
    bitmaps\chick.bmp
    bitmaps\rooster.bmp

If the pictures do not appear, you need to complete the exercises in Chapter 20 before continuing.

To create a sound track and synchronize it with the three pictures, so the pictures appear on cue at the right time in the sound track, follow these steps:

▶   Pull down the Tools menu and select the Waveform Audio tool.

▶   Use this tool to record the commentary printed below. Make sure to hold the microphone close to your mouth and speak loudly (but do not shout):

Roosters grow through several interesting stages. Here you see how they get born: in eggs! Then they hatch out into little chicks. Eventually, they grow up and look like this. And then they start to crow!

▶   Press Play to hear what you recorded.

▶   Press Reset and record it again if you do not like it.

▶   When you are satisfied with the recording, type the following name into the Filename field: **multilit\growth.wav**

▶   Click the Save button to save the file.

▶   Press Rewind and watch the Current Location counter as you play it back once more. Write down the duration in seconds of the audio that accompanies each slide.

▶   Click Cancel to put the tool away.

▶   Press ⌷F4⌷ to bring up the custom toolbox.

   ▶   Click the Link tool, then click the text "Show me some pictures!"

A link box showing the three pictures you linked earlier will appear.

▶   Put your cursor at the very top of the box and press ⌷Enter⌷ to create a blank space.

▶   Type the name of the waveform audio recording you just created, followed by @wait=0.

▶ Put @wait= after each of the next two images, followed by the number of seconds each part of that audio took when you auditioned the recording. Do not be concerned about being 100% accurate here because you can always adjust the timing later. Your links should now read something like this:

> ! multilit\growth.wav @wait=0
> ! bitmaps\egg.bmp @wait=6
> ! bitmaps\chick.bmp @wait=5
> ! bitmaps\rooster.bmp @wait=7
> ! audio\rooster.wav

▶ Click OK to close the Link box, then press F4 to put the toolbox away.

▶ Click the words "Show me some pictures!" to try your sound under stills. If it works perfectly the first time, congratulate yourself heartily! Otherwise, use the Link tool to go back into the Link box and adjust the timings.

E X E R C I S E S

1. Use the PODIUM Waveform Audio tool to record ten seconds of your voice at 8-bits and then at 16-bits per sample. Save the first recording as *c:\multilit\8bit.wav*, and save the second recording as *c:\multilit\16bit.wav*. Use the PODIUM Files/Audio/Waveform menu to play each file. Can you hear a difference between the two recordings? Use the Windows File Manager to inspect the size of these files. How much larger is the 16-bit recording?

2. Use the same process to record some music. If you cannot connect your music source to the line input of your sound card, record it through the microphone. Does the 16-bit recording make more of a difference for recorded music than it does for your voice recording?

3. Try recording music at different sampling rates. Can you hear how the higher sampling rates result in a brighter recording? Lower sampling rates cannot record high frequencies, effectively filtering them out.

22

CD Audio Clipmaking

O B J E C T I V E S

After completing this chapter, you will know how to:

■ **Create CD audio clips by using the CD Audio Clipmaker to locate start and stop points in the music.**

■ **Copy the clips to the Windows Clipboard, and use it to paste them as links to the triggers on a multimedia screen.**

■ **Create play lists that can instruct your CD-ROM drive to play clips from any audio CD in any order.**

■ **Record CD audio clips to your hard disk drive as waveform audio files.**

We are fortunate that every piece of music recorded on an audio compact disc (CD) can be used to provide split-second access to high-fidelity music in multimedia applications. Pressed onto every audio CD is a table of contents that indicates where the different songs begin and end. Not only can you play any song, but you can also extract clips from songs, which can be as small as a 75th of a second! This split-second accuracy lets you specify the precise start and stop location for CD audio clips.

CD audio has a distinct advantage over waveform audio recordings. While waveform audio playback puts a large burden on the central processor, the CD-ROM drive has its own processor that can play music from an audio CD without putting any strain on your PC. Because the music plays independently of the central processor, you can use a multimedia application to start your favorite CD, then continue to work with your word processing or spreadsheet while the CD continues to play, providing background music.

In this chapter you will learn how to make clips from any audio compact disc and transfer them to the Windows Clipboard, from which you can paste them into any link in your multimedia application. You will also learn how to make play lists and record audio from CDs onto your hard disk drive.

Running the CD Audio Clipmaker

▶ To run the CD Audio Clipmaker, pull down the PODIUM Tools menu and choose CD Audio. This will bring up the dialog box shown in Figure 22-1.

▶ Click the Play button: the CD will begin to play.

▶ To stop the CD, press the Pause button.

▶ To try different tracks on the CD, press the Track+ and Track- buttons.

You will discover that the CD that came with this book has several audio tracks on it, including jazz, classical, and modern music.

22-1

The CD Audio Clipmaker dialog.

Locating the Clip Start Point

To make a clip, begin by setting the start point:

▶ Click on the arrows in the Clip Start control group to adjust the minute, second, and frame address.

▶ Click the Start button to rehearse it.

The minute, second, and frame addressing of audio CDs is called **Red Book** addressing. There are 75 frames per second. The CD Audio Clipmaker lets you adjust the Red Book address down to an accuracy of a 75th of a second, which lets you pinpoint the exact spot where you want your clip to start.

Setting the Clip Stop Location

To set the Clip Stop location, follow these steps:

▶ Adjust the minute, second, and frame address in the Clip Stop control group to set the clip's stop point.

▶ Press the Start button to rehearse the clip and make sure it stops where you want.

Copying the Clip to the Windows Clipboard

To copy the clip to your Windows Clipboard, press the Clip button at the bottom of the tool, and PODIUM will tell you what it has written to your Clipboard in a message similar to the one shown in Figure 22-2.

PODIUM writes the Red Book address of your CD audio clip to the Windows Clipboard.

```
┌─────────────────────────────────────────┐
│ ▭            CD Audio Clip               │
├─────────────────────────────────────────┤
│                                         │
│ PODIUM has written the following CD Audio Clip to your │
│ Clipboard, from which you can paste it into your       │
│ presentation:                           │
│                                         │
│      2.46.33  4.46.32                    │
│                                         │
│            ┌──────┐                      │
│            │  OK  │                      │
│            └──────┘                      │
└─────────────────────────────────────────┘
```

Linking the Clip to Your Multimedia Screen

It is very easy to link the clip to any item on your multimedia screen. Follow these steps:

▶ If you do not already have the *linkdemo.cus* screen in your PODIUM window, display it by pulling down the Files menu and choosing Custom.

▶ Press F4 to open the toolbox, and use the Text tool to put the following line of text on your screen:

Click here to hear a CD!

▶ Click the Link tool, then click the text "Click here to hear a CD!"

▶ When the Link box appears, press the Clipboard button. As Figure 22-3 shows, the CD audio clip gets copied into the Link box from the Clipboard.

▶ Click OK to put the Link box away.

▶ Press F4 to put the toolbox away, then click the text "Click here to hear a CD!" As soon as you click, your CD should begin to play.

NOTE: When you copy clips like this from the Clipboard, you are only copying the addresses where the clips are located on your CD, not the music itself. For the music to play, the CD must be inserted in your CD-ROM drive.

Play Lists

PODIUM has a @wait=end feature that makes it possible for you to construct play lists for compact discs. A play list is a list of songs that you want to hear one after

22-3

Pressing the Clipboard button copies the clip from the Windows Clipboard into your Link box.

PODIUM Custom Link Editor

Editing Links to the Item:

Click here to hear a CD!

Insert or edit your links in the box below, or press Cancel
to restore them to their former contents.

! 2.46.33 4.46.32

OK   Browse...

Clipboard   Cancel

Browse Option
○ Full Path
● No Drive Letter
○ No Path

---

the other. For example, suppose you want to make a play list that will automatically play all of the audio tracks on the CD that came with this book in sequence. Here are the steps to follow:

▶ If you do not already have the *linkdemo.cus* screen in your PODIUM window, display it by pulling down the Files menu and choosing Custom.

▶ Press F4 to open the toolbox, and use the Text tool to put the following line of text on your screen:

Click here for a play list!

▶ Click the Link tool, then click the text "Click here for a play list!" When the Link box appears, type the following lines into it:

Trumpet Fanfare	**57.01.55**	**57.19.17**
Jazz Funk	**57.21.18**	**57.41.36**
Latin Rhythm	**57.43.37**	**58.01.05**
Trumpet Fanfare	**58.03.06**	**58.17.34**

▶ Click OK to close the List box, then select "Click here for a play list!" Your play list will begin.

▶ If you do not want to wait until the end of a song, press the spacebar to move on to the next one.

There is no limit to the number of songs you can put in a play list. Any song can appear at any place in the list, any number of times. For example, you could make your favorite song appear more often than the other ones. Songs you do not like would not play at all. In effect, you can be your own disc jockey!

Recording Compact Disc Audio to Your Hard Drive

While compact disc technology is wonderful, it does have its drawbacks. If you want music from different CDs to play during your application, you have to keep switching CDs, because only one CD can be in your CD-ROM drive at a time. And if you publish your application, the user will need to have all of the CDs as well.

Digital Video Recording

O B J E C T I V E S

After completing this chapter, you will know how to:

- **Record and edit digital video using Microsoft's Video for Windows.**

- **Conserve disk space by compressing the digital video recording.**

- **Link digital video recordings to triggers in your multimedia application.**

- **Cut digital video windows into any multimedia screen and control palette shifts when they occur.**

- **In addition, you will gain an understanding of how digital video recording works and why it plays back better on faster computers.**

If your computer has a video board capable of capturing digital video, it probably came with a copy of Microsoft's Video for Windows. This chapter is a tutorial on recording digital video clips with Video for Windows and linking them to objects on multimedia screens. You will even learn how to cut digital video windows into the screen. Figure 24-1 shows an artist's impression of how your computer's microprocessor plays digital video.

If you do not have a video capture card with Video for Windows installed, you will not be able to make an actual recording. However, you should still read this chapter to become familiar with digital video recording techniques.

An important advantage of Video for Windows over other kinds of digital video is that it can be played back without requiring the user to have any special hardware. Therefore, even if you do not have a video capture board, you will still be able to link and play back the digital video clips on the enclosed CD-ROM when you build your multimedia application in Part Six.

24-1

An artistic impression of how microcomputers play digital video recordings. Artwork provided courtesy of Intel, Inc.

How Digital Video Works

To make a digital video recording, you must first connect an analog video source, such as a camera, VCR, or laserdisc player, to your video capture board. When you tell Video for Windows to start recording, the video capture board converts this analog video signal into digital information. Since the digital video stream contains an enormous amount of data that is too large for today's computers to store and play back in real time, it gets highly compressed to save space, down to as little as 1/200 of its original size. One or more of the video compression schemes explained in Table 24-1 may be used.

Table 24-1 Video Compression Schemes

Method	How It Works
YUV Subsampling	Divides the screen into little squares and averages color values of the pixels in each square.
Delta Frame Encoding	Shrinks data by storing only the information that changes between frames; for example, if the background scene does not change, there is no need to store the scene again.
Run Length Encoding	Detects a "run" of identical pixels and encodes how many occur instead of recording each individual pixel.

This selection assumes you plan to publish your application eventually on compact disc. On the other hand, if you know you will always be playing back this video from a hard drive, you can choose one of the hard drive targets. The hard drive setting will make your video play back more smoothly from a hard drive, but from a CD-ROM it will be very jerky, and the audio might not even play correctly.

Depending on the brand of audio capture board you have, different options may appear when you pull down the Video Compression Method menu. If you have an Intel Indeo driver installed and the Indeo option appears, choose Indeo; otherwise, choose Microsoft Video 1.

▶ To save these settings so that you won't need to change them next time, click the Save As Default button.

▶ Click OK to close the Compression Options dialog, and click OK in the Save Video File dialog. A status bar will appear showing you how far along VidEdit is in the compression process as it saves the file.

Rehearsing the Video

To test your video recording, start PODIUM, pull down the Files menu, choose the Motion option, select Video for Windows, and choose the file you just saved. If it plays back in PODIUM, you succeeded; congratulations!

Now you can make the file the object of any link on any PODIUM screen. For example, suppose you want to link it to a hypertext on your *linkdemo.cus* screen:

▶ Pull down the Files menu, choose Custom, and select *linkdemo.cus* to open the *linkdemo* screen.

 ▶ Press F4 to open the toolbox, then use the Text tool to put the following line of text on your screen:

Click here to play a movie!

 ▶ Click the Link tool, then click the text "Click here to play a movie!" When the Link box appears, type the following line into it:

multilit\movie.avi

▶ Click OK to close the Link box, press F4 to put the toolbox away, and click on the hypertext "Click here to play a movie!" The movie will play back in the center of a blue screen, which is the PODIUM default.

Cutting Video Windows into PODIUM Screens

PODIUM has a special effect called @origin=x,y that lets you position the avi window at any x,y location on the screen. If you set an origin, the screen does not clear to blue when the avi clip plays; instead, the clip cuts into whatever is already on the screen. The x,y values are percentages of the screen. They can be integers or real numbers between 0 and 100. For example, suppose you want to position your *movie.avi* clip 60 percent down and 70 percent over the screen. Use the Link tool to edit the links to the hypertext "Click here to play a movie!" to make the link read as follows:

multilit\movie.avi @origin=60,70

Trigger the link to see how it cuts into the existing screen. You might get a palette shift; do not be concerned: you will learn how to control video palettes later.

Putting Frames Around the Windows

By default, PODIUM will not draw a frame around the avi window when you set an @origin. If you want a frame around the window, use the @frame special effect as follows:

multilit\movie.avi @origin=60,70 @frame

Controlling Video Palettes

Cutting video windows into multimedia screens often causes palette shifts, because the palette in the video is different from the one on the screen. The palette shift occurs when Windows reads the video palette: the colors on the screen shift from their original palette to the new palette. Figure 24-11 shows the psychedelic appearance of such a palette shift.

24-11

A palette shift caused by the video window having a different palette than the bitmap behind it.

Video for Windows provides a method for avoiding video palette shifts. You temporarily insert the backdrop into the movie, create a custom palette for the backdrop and the movie together, apply the custom palette to the movie, and apply the custom palette to the backdrop.

In order to complete this exercise, you first need to copy the following files from the *Multiliteracy CD* to your hard drive; use the File Manager to copy them into your *multilit* directory:

palshift\video.avi
palshift\backdrop.bmp

Part Six

Creating a Simple Multimedia Application

CONTENTS

Chapter 26
The History of Flight Picture Menu

Chapter 27
1920's Barnstorming

Chapter 28
The Flying Fortress

Chapter 29
The Blue Angels

Chapter 30
Jumbo Jets

Having learned the basic tools and techniques of multimedia, you will now use them to create an actual application. Your topic, the History of Flight, was chosen for several reasons. First, almost everyone is fascinated by aircraft and the subject of flight. Second, the history of aviation can be broken down into a few well-defined historical periods that lend themselves to the design of a simple, beginning-level application. Third, Aris Entertainment was kind enough to license materials from its *MediaClips* CD-ROMs for inclusion on the *Multiliteracy CD.* These *MediaClips* CDs contain clip art, music, and digital videos of both jets and propeller aircraft. Finally, the videodisc *To Fly!* contains spectacular footage of the historical aircraft featured in the tutorial.

If you have a videodisc player attached to your multimedia computer, you will want to get a copy of the videodisc *To Fly!* to use with this tutorial. *To Fly!* was created for the IMAX theater in the Smithsonian Institution's National Air and Space Museum under a grant from Conoco, a subsidiary of Dupont. It is published by Lumivision and costs $34.95. To order a copy, phone (800) 776-5864. If you do not have a videodisc player, you can use digital video clips instead. Dupont has graciously granted permission for us to digitize the clips used in this tutorial and include them on the *Multiliteracy CD.*

NOTE: There are no end-of-chapter exercises in Part Six because of the progressive nature of its tutorial in which you build the History of Flight application.

26

The History of Flight Picture Menu

After completing this chapter, you will know how to:

- ■ **Create a directory for a simple application dealing with the History of Flight.**

- ■ **Create the opening or "home" screen for the History of Flight application.**

- ■ **Title the home screen and give it a backdrop.**

- ■ **Position the text on the History of Flight home screen.**

The simplest way to design a multimedia application is to have it begin with a screen that provides the user with a menu. When the user chooses an item from your menu, the application launches the object(s) linked to it. Then the application returns to the menu, and the user can make another choice.

The *Multiliteracy CD* contains a History of Flight bitmap. Figure 26-1 shows the four buttons on the bitmap that represent different eras in aviation history: biplanes from the 1920's, military aircraft from World War II, jet age Blue Angels, and a contemporary Boeing 747 jumbo jet. In this chapter you will learn how to make the History of Flight bitmap serve as your application's main menu. In subsequent chapters you will learn how to link objects that describe and illustrate each era.

The History of Flight bitmap has four buttons that feature different eras. Photos by David K. Brunn. © Aris Multimedia Entertainment, Inc. 1994.

Creating the Flight Directory

When you begin to develop a new application, you must create a directory for it on your hard disk. Use the File Manager to do that now, and name the directory *flight*. Follow these steps:

▷ On the Windows desktop, double-click on the File Manager icon to launch the File Manager.

▷ Pull down the File menu and choose Create Directory to bring up the Create Directory dialog.

▷ In the Name field, if your hard drive is *C*, type **c:\flight** and click the OK button. If the hard drive you wish to use is not *C*, replace the *C* with the appropriate drive letter. From now on, this tutorial will always refer to your hard drive as *C*.

▷ Close the File Manager.

Making the Home Screen

Start PODIUM if it is not already running.

▷ Pull down the PODIUM Files menu and choose New Custom to invoke the File Creation dialog.

▷ In the File Name field, type **c:\flight\history.cus**, then click OK.

PODIUM will create a blank screen called *history.cus* and display the custom toolbox on it. This will serve as the "home" screen around which this application revolves. Follow the steps in the next section to build this screen into the main menu of the History of Flight application.

1920's Barnstorming

After completing this chapter, you will know how to:

- **Link the Biplane button to a multimedia screen that presents the 1920's barnstorming era in the History of Flight.**

- **Create the text and graphics on the biplane screen, following a detailed list of instructions.**

- **Link a biplane in motion using either a videodisc or Video for Windows.**

The home screen you just created serves as a menu. When the user clicks one of the four aircraft buttons, the application branches to materials that describe the corresponding period in aviation history. In this chapter, you will create a trigger on the Biplane button and link it to materials describing the 1920's barnstorming era.

Making the Link

▷   Click on the Trigger tool icon (the one that looks like a rocket sitting on a launch pad). When you move your cursor around on the home screen, it should assume the shape of the Trigger tool. Do *not* click the mouse yet.

▷   Move the mouse carefully to position the tip of the cursor in the upper-left corner of the Biplane button.

▷   Hold the left button down as you drag the mouse to the lower-right corner of the Biplane button. A box showing the location of your trigger will appear.

▷   Release the button: PODIUM displays the Link dialog.

▷   Click once inside the big Link box to set your cursor there.

▷   Type **flight\biplane.cus** then click OK.

NOTE: If you make a mistake, you can click the Undo button in the toolbox and repeat these six steps.

Triggering the Link

▷   Press F4 to put the toolbox away and become a user of your application. Notice how the cursor changes shape as you mouse over the Biplane button, indicating that you have placed a trigger there.

▷   Click the Biplane button to trigger its link. PODIUM tells you that the *flight\biplane.cus* file linked to this trigger does not yet exist, and asks if you want to create it.

▷   Click OK. PODIUM will then create the *flight\biplane.cus* file, display it on your screen, and open the toolbox for you. The display is blank, because you have not put anything on it yet.

Entering the Biplane Text

▷   Use the Text tool to put the following lines of text on the screen; you *must* enter these lines in the order in which they are listed here to avoid getting the PODIUM "retail" message:

Barnstorming Biplanes

Biplanes were popularized by barnstormers who used them to dazzle onlookers during the 1920's.

Pictured here is the Waco Taperwing, a very acrobatic biplane.

In the 1940's, biplanes were used heavily to train civilian pilots during World War II.

Click anywhere to continue.

CHAPTER

28

The Flying Fortress

OBJECTIVES

After completing this chapter, you will know how to:

■ Link the Flying Fortress button to a multimedia screen that presents the World War II era.

■ Create the text and graphics on the Flying Fortress screen with a little less hand-holding than in the previous chapter.

■ Link a video clip showing the history of aircraft development during World War II.

This chapter is very similar to the one you just completed. In fact, all four of the historical aircraft chapters in this beginning-level tutorial have the same design. The goal is to make you so familiar with the process of linking buttons to multimedia materials that you can do it without referring to the instructions. Accordingly, each chapter will provide less hand-holding than the previous chapter until you can make these linkages on your own. Then, in Part Seven, you will learn how to implement more complex designs.

The second button on the History of Flight menu pictures the Boeing-17G "Flying Fortress," one of the most famous World War II aircraft. This chapter shows you how to create a trigger on the Flying Fortress button and link it to materials describing World War II aircraft.

To get started, follow these steps:

▶ If you do not have the History of Flight menu on your screen, pull down the PODIUM Files menu, select Custom Files, and navigate to *flight\history.cus*.

▶ Press F4 to bring up the custom toolbox.

Making the Link

▶ Click the Trigger tool icon.

▶ Position the tip of the cursor in the upper-left corner of the Flying Fortress button.

▶ Hold the left button down and drag the mouse to the lower-right corner of the Flying Fortress button. A box showing the location of your trigger will appear.

▶ Release the button: PODIUM displays the Link dialog.

▶ Click once inside the Link box to set your cursor there.

▶ Type **flight\fortress.cus**, then click OK.

Triggering the Link

▶ Press F4 to put the toolbox away and become a user of your application. Notice how the cursor changes shape as you mouse over the Flying Fortress button, indicating that you haved placed a trigger there.

▶ Click the Flying Fortress button to trigger its link. PODIUM tells you that the *flight\fortress.cus* file linked to this trigger does not yet exist, and it asks if you want to create it.

▶ Click OK. PODIUM will then create the *flight\fortress.cus* file, display it on your screen, and open the toolbox for you. The display is blank, because you have not put anything on it yet.

Entering the Flying Fortress Text

▶ Use the Text tool to put the following lines of text on the screen; you *must* enter these lines in the order in which they are listed here to avoid getting the PODIUM "retail" message:

World War II Aircraft

The allies relied on aircraft to help win World War II.

Pictured here is the famous Boeing B-17 bomber, which was nicknamed the Flying Fortress due to its heavy armament.

Click anywhere to continue.

31-7

Design of the Information Superhighway application this tutorial helps you create.

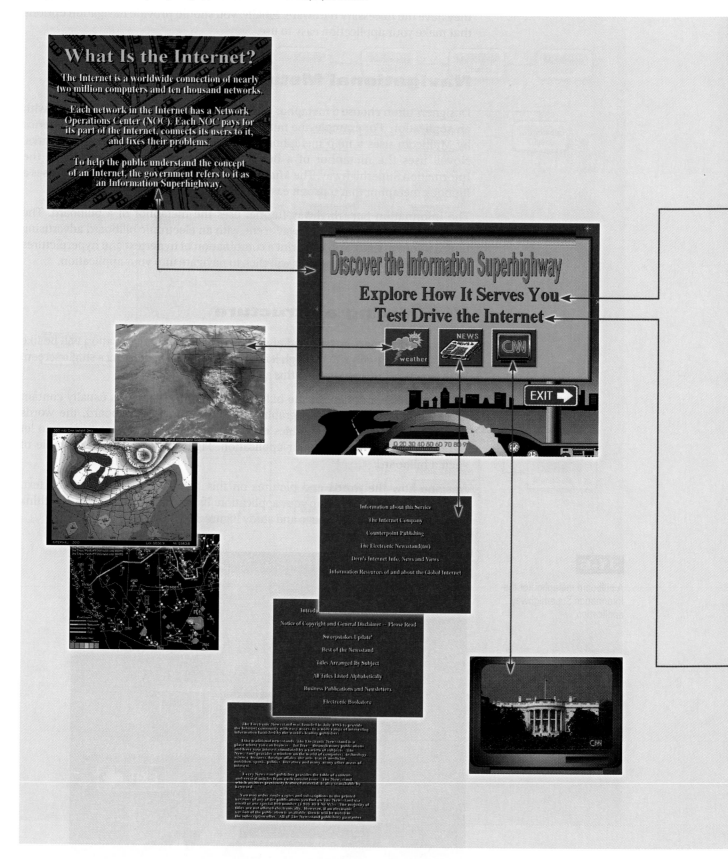

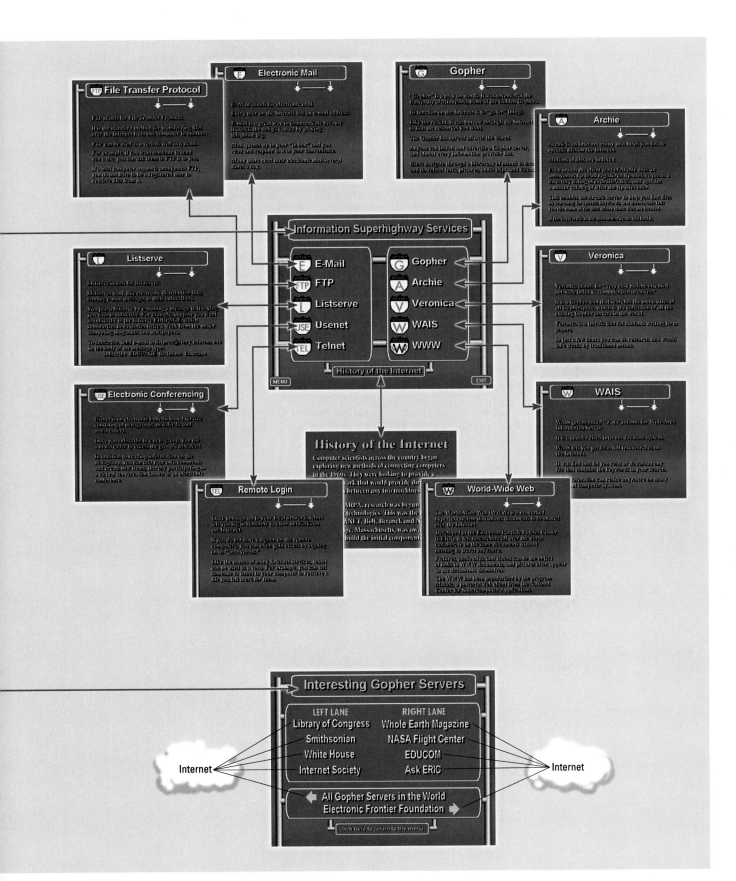

Did you imagine something like the structure shown in Figure 31-7? It is a diagram of the application this tutorial helps you create. Notice how the billboard functions as a menu. The first item, "Discover the Information Superhighway," links to a screen that defines the Internet. Clicking the mouse returns the user to the billboard. This is the simplest part of the design. The second menu item, "Explore How It Serves You," launches a submenu listing the kinds of things you can do on the Internet; each submenu item triggers a screen explaining an Internet service. "Test Drive the Internet" lets the user select interesting places to visit on the Information Superhighway, and if a real Internet connection is present, takes the user to those places.

In addition to hypertext, the billboard also contains a few hyperpictures. The Weather icon launches a series of images showing current weather conditions from the Information Superhighway's Weather Machine. The images follow a linear list design in which the mouse functions like a remote control in a 35mm slide projector; a left mouse click moves the user forward through the list, and a right mouse click moves the user backward. The News icon is linked to an electronic news feed that presents its information as a hierarchy. The Television icon is a live video feed from the CNN newsroom. Users with the necessary hardware will be able to click there to go live to CNN. Finally, the Exit sign provides a graceful way for the user to leave your application.

E X E R C I S E S

1. Draw a diagram showing the structure of the History of Flight application you created in Part Six.

2. What design paradigm(s) does the History of Flight application use? Refer to the diagram you drew in response to the previous question when doing this exercise.

CHAPTER

32

Creating the Information Superhighway Screen

OBJECTIVES

After completing this chapter, you will know how to:

■ **Create the directory and the home screen of the Information Superhighway application.**

■ **Enter the text and create the backdrop for the Information Superhighway screen.**

■ **Position the text and layer navigational icons onto the screen.**

■ **Back up your work to prevent the loss of your application in case of an accident or a problem on your hard drive.**

You must complete a few housekeeping chores before you begin to develop a new application.

35-6

telnet.cus: Remote Login.

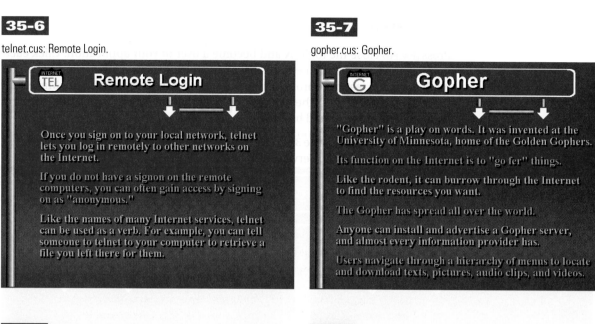

Remote Login

Once you sign on to your local network, telnet lets you log in remotely to other networks on the Internet.

If you do not have a signon on the remote computers, you can often gain access by signing on as "anonymous."

Like the names of many Internet services, telnet can be used as a verb. For example, you can tell someone to telnet to your computer to retrieve a file you left there for them.

35-7

gopher.cus: Gopher.

Gopher

"Gopher" is a play on words. It was invented at the University of Minnesota, home of the Golden Gophers.

Its function on the Internet is to "go fer" things.

Like the rodent, it can burrow through the Internet to find the resources you want.

The Gopher has spread all over the world.

Anyone can install and advertise a Gopher server, and almost every information provider has.

Users navigate through a hierarchy of menus to locate and download texts, pictures, audio clips, and videos.

35-8

archie.cus: Archie.

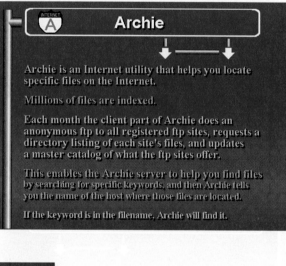

Archie

Archie is an Internet utility that helps you locate specific files on the Internet.

Millions of files are indexed.

Each month the client part of Archie does an anonymous ftp to all registered ftp sites, requests a directory listing of each site's files, and updates a master catalog of what the ftp sites offer.

This enables the Archie server to help you find files by searching for specific keywords, and then Archie tells you the name of the host where those files are located.

If the keyword is in the filename, Archie will find it.

35-9

veronica.cus: Veronica.

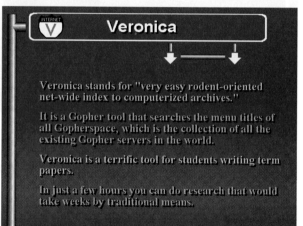

Veronica

Veronica stands for "very easy rodent-oriented net-wide index to computerized archives."

It is a Gopher tool that searches the menu titles of all Gopherspace, which is the collection of all the existing Gopher servers in the world.

Veronica is a terrific tool for students writing term papers.

In just a few hours you can do research that would take weeks by traditional means.

35-10

wais.cus: WAIS.

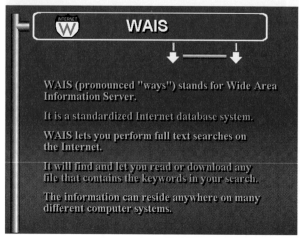

WAIS

WAIS (pronounced "ways") stands for Wide Area Information Server.

It is a standardized Internet database system.

WAIS lets you perform full text searches on the Internet.

It will find and let you read or download any file that contains the keywords in your search.

The information can reside anywhere on many different computer systems.

35-11

www.cus: World-Wide Web.

World-Wide Web

The World-Wide Web (WWW) is a networked hypertext system that allows documents to be shared over the Internet.

Developed at the European Particle Physics Center (CERN), it lets researchers all over the world collaborate on the same documents without needing to travel anywhere.

Pictures, audio clips, and videos can be the object of links in WWW documents, and pictures often appear in the documents themselves.

The WWW has been popularized by the program Mosaic, a powerful web client from the National Center for Supercomputer Applications.

Navigating

As a final touch, you should modify the *highway\services.cus* file so that the navigation buttons at the bottom of the screen work properly. Right now the Menu button takes the user back to the menu, but so does any mouse click outside of a trigger; this is the default PODIUM navigation in this situation. To complete the navigation, you should put a trigger on the Menu button and link it to the @done option, and, to provide the user a way to quit your application from this screen, link a @quit to the Exit button. Then, to prevent any mouse click outside a trigger from returning to the main menu, pull down the PODIUM Effects menu and choose Navigate.

E X E R C I S E S

1. Someone using your application to learn about the Internet may be interested in its history. A document in the *highway* directory called *history.txt* contains the history of the Internet. Use the toolbox to add the text "History of the Internet" to the *highway\services.cus* screen, then use the Link tool to link it to *highway\history.txt*. When you test the link to make sure it works correctly, you can read about the history of the Internet as well.

2. Back up the *highway\services.cus* file.

36

Interesting Gopher Servers

OBJECTIVES

After completing this chapter, you will know how to:

■ Link the menu item "Test Drive the Internet" to a trigger that will launch the Gopher Server menu.

■ Explore some interesting Gopher servers on the Information Superhighway.

■ Use the Gopher tool to find another server that interests you, and use the Windows clipboard to link it to the Interesting Gopher Servers menu.

■ Configure your Gopher connection.

■ Download objects from the Gopher to your local hard drive.

■ In addition, you will understand the Internet's domain name method of naming computers connected to the network.

As you learned by clicking on the word "Gopher" on the Internet Services screen, the Gopher is a distributed menuing system that lets you access texts, graphics, audio clips, and videos from all over the world. Before the Gopher was invented, users had to learn a complicated set of tools to cruise the Internet and download information from it. As this chapter demonstrates, it is easy to provide access to information via Gopher.

There are many fascinating Gopher servers on the Information Superhighway. Eric Braun's *The Internet Directory* (1994) lists thousands of them. Your *highway* directory contains a file called *offramps.cus* that connects to some of the more interesting Gopher servers.

Your next task is to connect the *offramps.cus* file to the "Test Drive the Internet" item on the Internet billboard. Then, if you have an Internet connection, you will learn how to use the PODIUM Gopher tool to find other interesting servers and link them to your application. If you do not already have the Billboard menu on your screen, pull down the PODIUM Files menu, choose Custom, navigate to the *highway* directory, then select *infohigh.cus.*

Linking to the Gopher Server Menu

▷ If the PODIUM toolbox is not open, press F4 .

▷ Click the Link tool, mouse over the text "Test Drive the Internet," and click the left mouse button.

▷ When the Link dialog appears, click once inside the Link box and type:

highway\offramps.cus

▷ Click OK, then press F4 to put the toolbox away.

▷ Click "Test Drive the Internet," and the Internet Test Drive menu shown in Figure 36-1 will appear. Each item in the menu is connected to a different Gopher server. If your computer has a Windows Internet connection (that is, a *winsock.dll* and the associated drivers), clicking the names of the different Gopher servers will take you to them. Otherwise, you will get a message saying you are not connected; later on, this tutorial will simulate some Gopher servers to give you an idea of what the Information Superhighway would be like if you were connected.

36-1

Menu of interesting Gopher servers.

Interesting Gopher Servers

LEFT LANE	RIGHT LANE
Library of Congress	Whole Earth Magazine
Smithsonian	NASA Flight Center
White House	EDUCOM
Internet Society	Ask ERIC

◀ All Gopher Servers in the World
Electronic Frontier Foundation ▶

Click here to return to the menu

Adding a Server That Interests You

The PODIUM software makes it possible for you to connect any Gopher server anywhere in the world to any hypertext or hyperpicture in your application. You can also link to individual text files, pictures, audio, and video clips on the Internet.

Thus, the Information Superhighway becomes a worldwide multimedia file server for your applications.

The Gopher tool, which you access from the PODIUM Tools menu, lets you cruise the Internet, find objects of interest, and link their Gopher selector strings to any hypertext or hyperpicture in your application.

Getting Connected

The rest of this chapter requires that you have a Windows Internet connection. If you do not, you can read on, but you will not be able to complete the exercises.

To get connected to the Internet, if you are at a school, college, government agency or business, get in touch with the head of computing services and ask how to get an Internet connection in your area. If you do not have someone local to ask, try phoning one of the Internet service providers listed in Table 36-1. They can tell you how to get connected in your area, even from your home.

You will need to know a little jargon to specify what you need. Here is the magic word: *winsock.dll*. Ask for a real Windows Internet connection with a "Winsock DLL." DLL stands for **Dynamic Link Library.** When vendors add capabilities to Windows, they often do so by providing a DLL. Each vendor that sells network connections can provide a *winsock.dll* that gets installed under Windows when you set up your network hardware. PODIUM follows the *Winsock* protocol and will work with any vendor's *winsock.dll*. If you do not have a *winsock.dll* installed under Windows, PODIUM's Internet services will not work.

Table 36-1   Internet Providers

Internet Provider	Locale	Phone	E-mail
AARNet	Australia	+61 6 249 4969	aarnet@aarnet.edu.au.
BARRNET	San Francisco and Far East	(415) 723-3104	info@barrnet.net
CICNet	Midwest and nationwide	(800) 947-4754	info@cic.net
Colorado Supernet	Colorado	(303) 273-3471	info@csn.org
Demon	United Kingdom	+44 81 349 0063	internet@demon.co.uk
MSEN	Michigan	(313) 998-4562	info@msen.com
NEARnet	Northeast U.S. (ME NH VT CT RI MA)	(617) 873-8730	nearnet-join@near.net
NETCOM	Major cities in United States	(800) 501-8649	info@netcom.com
Portal Communications	Worldwide through Sprintnet	(408) 973-9111	info@portal.com
PREPnet	Pennsylvania	(412) 268-7870	nic@prep.net
PSI	Worldwide	(703) 904-1207	all-info@psi.com
UUNET	Worldwide	(800) 4UU-NET3	info@uunet.uu.net
VERnet	Virginia	(804) 924-0616	net-info@ver.net
WiscNet	Wisconsin	(608) 262-4241	wn-info@nic.wiscnet.net

The faster your Internet connection, the better; if your connection is slower than 64 thousand bits per second (64kbps), multimedia will be painfully slow, and you will only be able to work efficiently with text.

Domain Names

Before you can use the Internet Gopher tool, you must give PODIUM the name of your local Gopher server. Gopher servers have names like Gopher.udel.edu, which is the author's local Gopher. This kind of name is referred to as a **domain name.** Domain names have the format:

> hostname.subdomain.first-level-domain

First level domains normally consist of one of the following:

edu	educational
com	commercial
gov	government
mil	military
net	network support centers
org	other organizations

The subdomain refers to the network to which a computer is connected, and the host name refers to the computer itself. If you do not know the domain name of your local Gopher, ask your network administrator.

Configuring Your PODIUM Gopher Connection

To configure your PODIUM Gopher connection, you must give PODIUM the domain name of your Gopher server and its port address. Do that now by pulling down the PODIUM Controls menu and selecting Configuration. In the Internet group, type the name of your Gopher server into the Host Name field, as shown in Figure 36-2.

You also need to type the port address of your Gopher server in the Port Address field. Since almost all Gopher servers are located at port 70, the port address defaults to 70.

36-2

Using the Configuration dialog to set the host name and port address of your Gopher server.

PODIUM Configuration Editor
Settings in the PODIUM.CFG configuration file in your \wnpodium directory control how PODIUM operates. You can change the configuration settings by editing the parameters below. Choose OK to save the new settings, or Cancel to ignore them.

Path:

Working Directory: C:\WNPODIUM\

PODIUM "Full Screen" Size: 640x480   Graphics Design Size: 640x480

Startup Switches
- [ ] Full Screen Only
- [ ] Automatic Sequencing
- [ ] No Hot Cursor Shape Change
- [ ] Suppress Podium Title Page
- [ ] Do Not Stretch Bitmaps

Internet Settings

Host Name:

Port Address:

[OK]   [Cancel]   [Help]

Using the Internet Gopher Tool

Pull down the PODIUM Tools menu and select Gopher. If you have an Internet connection, the Gopher menu will appear; otherwise, PODIUM will say you are not connected to the Gopher when it displays the tool. Figure 36-3 shows the Gopher tool.

You navigate the Internet by clicking menu items in the Gopher box and clicking the buttons below the Gopher box. The buttons dim when they are not active. Double-clicking on a menu item causes PODIUM to "gopher" to that menu item. To move back to the previous menu, click the Parent button. To jump all the way back to your local Gopher server, click Home.

36-3

The Internet Gopher tool.

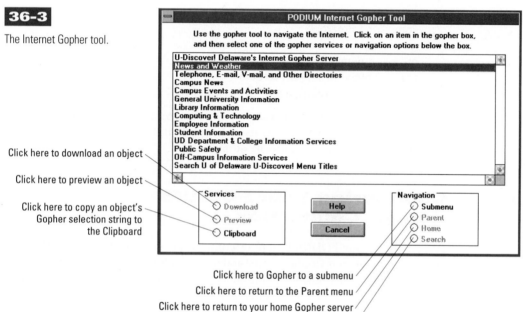

When you find an interesting item on the Gopher that you would like to link to a PODIUM hypertext or hyperpicture, highlight it by clicking it once, then click the Clipboard button. A message box will inform you that PODIUM has copied that item's Gopher selector string to the Windows Clipboard. Then close the Gopher tool by clicking the Cancel button. Figure 36-4 shows the result of clicking the Clipboard button for the University of Illinois Weather Machine.

36-4

The result of copying the selector string for the University of Illinois Weather Machine to the Clipboard.

Pasting Internet Links from the Clipboard

It is easy to paste Internet links from the clipboard. Follow these steps:

▷ Navigate to the PODIUM screen to which you wish to link the Gopher item.

▷ Create a link, using either the Link tool for hypertext, or the Trigger tool for a hyperpicture.

▷ When PODIUM displays the Link dialog in which you normally type the link, click the Clipboard button instead of typing the link. The Gopher selector string will appear, as shown in Figure 36-5. Do not make any changes to that string; you must leave it exactly the way it came from the Gopher in order for it to work.

36-5

Clicking the Clipboard button makes the Gopher string appear in the Link box.

```
┌──────────────────── PODIUM Custom Link Editor ────────────────────┐
│ ┌─ Editing Links to the Item: ──────────────────────────────────┐ │
│ │   Test Drive the Internet                                     │ │
│ └───────────────────────────────────────────────────────────────┘ │
│        Insert or edit your links in the box below, or press Cancel  │
│                to restore them to their former contents.            │
│ ┌───────────────────────────────────────────────────────────────┐ │
│ │ @gopher=        wx.atmos.uiuc.edu        70                    │ │
│ │                                                               │ │
│ │                                                               │ │
│ │                                                               │ │
│ │                                                               │ │
│ └───────────────────────────────────────────────────────────────┘ │
│                                        ┌─ Browse Option ─────────┐ │
│   ┌────────┐      ┌──────────┐         │  ○ Full Path            │ │
│   │   OK   │      │ Browse...│         │  ◉ No Drive Letter      │ │
│   └────────┘      └──────────┘         │  ○ No Path              │ │
│   ┌──────────┐    ┌──────────┐         └─────────────────────────┘ │
│   │ Clipboard│    │  Cancel  │                                     │
│   └──────────┘    └──────────┘                                     │
└───────────────────────────────────────────────────────────────────┘
```

▷ Click OK to close the Link dialog.

▷ Press [F4] to close the toolbox, and test the link by clicking the trigger to which you linked the Gopher item. There may be a brief delay, depending on the amount of traffic on the network.

Downloading Objects from the Internet

The ability to cruise the Internet, find objects of interest, and link them to your hypertexts and hyperpictures lets you use the Information Superhighway as a powerful worldwide file server. However, if you plan to publish your application for users who may not yet be connected to the Internet, you will have to download the information from the network into your application directory, and link to it directly. To download an object from the Internet, follow these steps:

▷ Navigate to the Internet with the PODIUM Gopher tool, highlight the item you wish to download with the mouse, and click the Download button.

▷ When PODIUM prompts you for the filename you wish to give the object, make sure you give it the proper file extension (i.e., *.txt* for text, *.bmp* for Windows bitmaps, *.gif* for GIF bitmaps, *.wav* for waveform audio, and *.avi* for Video for Windows clips).

E X E R C I S E S

1. The Committee on Applications and Technology of the Information Infrastructure Task Force issued a discussion paper called *What It Takes to Make It Happen: Key Issues for Applications of the National Information Infrastructure.* The document is available on the Gopher at iitf.doc.gov. The paper is in the directory called *Speeches, Documents, and Papers.* Use the Gopher tool to navigate to this Gopher server, read the document, and download it to your hard disk drive, giving it the name *highway\nii.txt.* If you do not have an Internet connection, the document is available on the *Multiliteracy CD*, and you can read it by clicking the NII-Key Issues for Applications button in the Demonstrations section, under Textbook Examples. Comments about the paper should be directed to the Committee on Applications and Technology, National Institute of Standards and Technology, Building 101, Room A 1000, Gaithersburg, Md. 20899; phone (301) 975-2667; e-mail cat_exec@nist.gov.

2. The Smithsonian Institution offers users access to an FTP site that contains a growing number of works of art, machines, aircraft, artifacts, and other holdings from its many museums. Use the Gopher tool to do a Veronica search for "Smithsonian" to find a Gopher server near you that can access this site.

3. Included here is a list of Gopher servers. Pick one that interests you, and add it to the menu of Gopher servers in the *highway\offramps.cus* file.

Bishop Museum in Honolulu	bishop.bishop.hawaii.hawaii
Carnegie-Mellon Environment Gopher	envirolink.hss.cmu.edu
Computer Solutions by Hawkinson	csbh.com
Harvard University Museums	huh.harvard.edu
Los Alamos National Laboratory	mentor.lanl.gov
Missouri Botanical Garden	gopher.mobot.org
National Institutes of Health (NIH)	gopher.nih.gov
National Science Foundation	stis.nsf.gov
Northwestern University Geology Gopher	gopher.earth.nwu.edu
Novell Netware Archives	ns.novell.com
Oak Ridge National Laboratory	jupiter.esd.orn1.gov
University of Chicago Law School	lawnext.uchicago.edu
University of Texas M.D. Anderson Cancer Center	utmdacc.uth.tmc.edu
U.S. Census Bureau	gopher.census.gov
U.S. Senate	gopher.senate.gov
Vertebrate World Server	neptune.rrb.colostate.edu

4. Back up the *highway\infohigh.cus* and *highway\offramps.cus* files.

Weather Satellite Images

O B J E C T I V E S

After completing this chapter, you will know how to:

- ☐ **Put a hyperpicture trigger on the Weather icon on the Information Superhighway screen.**

- ☐ **Link the weather trigger to a virtual slide tray of satellite images.**

- ☐ **Use left and right mouse clicks to move back and forth in the virtual slide tray.**

- ☐ **Download satellite images from the University of Illinois Weather Machine to your computer's hard disk.**

Almost everyone is concerned about the weather. Will it be sunny or cloudy, cold or hot, rainy or dry, calm or windy? How severe will an approaching storm be? Has the National Weather Service announced any warnings or emergencies in your area? All of this information is available to you on the Information Superhighway, including the latest satellite images that show the weather all over the world.

This chapter shows you how to link the Weather icon on your Billboard menu to weather satellite images and forecasts. First, you link the icon to images that were downloaded from the network and stored on your CD. Then, if you have an Internet connection, you link it to the latest satellite images, which get updated every hour.

If you do not already have the Billboard menu on the screen, pull down the PODIUM Files menu, choose Custom, navigate to the *highway* directory, and select *infohigh.cus*.

Making the Weather Icon Hyper

▷ If the PODIUM toolbox is not open, press F4.

▷ Use the Trigger tool to draw a trigger around the Weather icon on the billboard. When the Link dialog appears, enter the following three lines:

> **weather\weather1.bmp**
> **weather\weather2.bmp**
> **weather\weather3.bmp**

▷ Click OK to close the Link dialog.

Using the Virtual Slide Tray

▷ Press F4 to put the toolbox away, and click on the Weather icon: the first weather image appears.

▷ Click the left mouse button again, and the second image appears. Click once more to see the third image.

▷ Click the right button to make PODIUM back up to the second image.

▷ Click the right button again: PODIUM backs up to the first image. As Figure 37-1 illustrates, you have created a virtual slide tray that lets you show slides by clicking the left and right buttons on the mouse, just as you would press the left and right buttons on the hand control of a 35mm slide projector.

▷ Click the left mouse button twice to go to the third weather image.

▷ Click the left mouse button while viewing the last image in the virtual slide tray: PODIUM returns you to the screen that launched the images.

In the virtual slide tray, clicking the left mouse button moves you on to the next slide; clicking the right button moves you back.

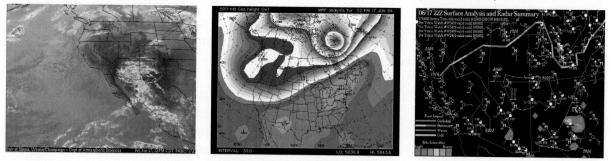

Downloading Images from the Weather Machine

If you have an Internet connection, you can gopher to the Weather Machine at the University of Illinois and download the most recent satellite images. Here are the steps to follow:

▷ Pull down the PODIUM Tools menu and choose Gopher.

▷ Select *Weather* and click the Submenu button. Note: Depending on how your local Gopher is set up, this choice may not be available on the first screen, but if you browse the Gopher menu, you will find it.

▷ Choose University of Illinois Weather Machine, then Satellite Images, then Satellite East IR. A list of GIF images will appear.

▷ Click once on the latest satellite image, which is called *00latest.gif*; see how the Download button is activated?

▷ Click the Download button, and PODIUM will prompt you for a filename. Type the path and filename you wish to give the image. Give the filename a .GIF file extension; for example, type **c:\highway\forecast.gif**, then click OK.

▷ Now you can link the image to any PODIUM hypertext or hyperpicture trigger, and when your user selects the trigger, the image will appear.

You also have the option of linking the hypertext and hyperpictures directly to the weather images on the Internet, but since the server sometimes gets too busy due to the number of people downloading these images, you could experience delays. If you want to try it, follow the steps above, but instead of clicking the Download button, click the Clipboard button to copy the Gopher selector string of the weather images to your Clipboard. Then use the Link tool to paste the selector string from the Clipboard to the hyperpicture link.

E X E R C I S E S

1. Add sound under stills to narrate the three weather images that your users will see when they click the Weather icon on the *infohigh.cus* screen. Here is a sample script on which you can base your waveform audio recording. To synchronize this script with the weather images, use the Link tool to modify the links to the Weather icon, using the @wait= option as follows:

   ! weather.wav @wait=0
   ! weather1.bmp @wait=8
   ! weather2.bmp @wait=6
   ! weather3.bmp @wait=end

   Script: *[weather picture one appears]* The satellite map shows an area of intense weather over Arizona extending into New Mexico. *[weather picture two appears]* Upper air analysis shows the effect of a stationary front that extends across the country from the southwest to the northeast. *[weather picture three appears]* The automated radar summary shows heavy echo intensities, and four severe thunderstorm watches are in effect.

2. Back up the *highway\infohigh.cus* file and the *weather.wav* file. Depending on the size of these files, you might need another blank diskette; if so, label it clearly. Form the habit of always labeling a new diskette so you can keep track of what is on each disk.

Electronic News Feed

O B J E C T I V E S

After completing this chapter, you will know how to:

■ **Put a hyperpicture trigger on the News Feed icon on the Information Superhighway screen.**

■ **Link the trigger to the Electronic Newsstand.**

■ **Browse the Electronic Newsstand and find out what it offers.**

■ **Use the Gopher to learn how to subscribe to the Electronic Newsstand.**

A growing number of newspapers and news magazines are going online. This chapter shows you how to connect the News Feed icon on the Billboard menu to an electronic news service. If you do not have an Internet connection, the CD will simulate one.

Gophering to the Electronic Newsstand

The Electronic Newsstand Gopher is located at enews.com. To connect the Electronic Newsstand Gopher to the News Feed icon, use the Trigger tool icon to draw a trigger box around the News Feed icon. When the Link box appears, if you have an Internet connection, type the following link:

> **! @gopher(enews.com)**

If you do not have an Internet connection, type:

> **! highway\enews.cus**

Testing the Electronic News Feed Connection

▸ Click OK to close the Link dialog, then press F4 to close the toolbox.

▸ Click the News Feed icon, and the Electronic Newsstand menu shown in Figure 38-1 will appear. If you have a live Internet connection, all of the choices will be active; if not, only clicking on "The Electronic Newsstand" will work. Click on it now.

▸ From the Electronic Newsstand menu (see Figure 38-2) choose "Introduction to the Electronic Newsstand," then select "Introducing the Electronic Newsstand." An article will appear on the screen describing the history of the Electronic Newsstand and how it works (see Figure 38-3).

38-1

The Electronic Newsstand.

Information about this Service

The Internet Company

Counterpoint Publishing

The Electronic Newsstand(tm)

Dern's Internet Info, News and Views

Information Resources of and about the Global Internet

38-2

The Electronic Newsstand submenu.

Introduction to the Electronic Newsstand

Notice of Copyright and General Disclaimer -- Please Read

Sweepstakes Update!

Best of the Newsstand

Titles Arranged By Subject

All Titles Listed Alphabetically

Business Publications and Newsletters

Electronic Bookstore

38-3

About the Electronic Newsstand.

This is The Electronic Newsstand

The Electronic Newsstand was founded in July 1993 to provide the Internet community with easy access to a wide range of interesting information furnished by the world's leading publishers.

Like traditional newsstands, The Electronic Newsstand is a place where you can browse -- for free -- through many publications and have your interest stimulated by a variety of subjects. The Newsstand provides a window on the world of computers, technology, science, business, foreign affairs, the arts, travel, medicine, nutrition, sports, politics, literature and many, many other areas of interest.

Every Newsstand publisher provides the table of contents and several articles from each current issue. The Newsstand, which archives previously featured material, is also searchable by keyword.

You may order single copies and subscriptions to the printed versions of any of the publications you find on The Newsstand via email or our special 800 number (1-800-40-ENEWS). The majority of titles are not offered electronically. However, if an electronic version of the publication is available, then it will be noted in the subscription offer. All of The Newsstand publishers guarantee

Dozens of magazines are available from the Electronic Newsstand. Table 38-1 lists the magazines available on the enews Gopher when this book went to press. If you have an Internet connection, you can browse these titles and even do full-text searches through the entire newsstand for key words that interest you. According to Jeffrey Dearth (1994), founder and CEO of the Electronic Newsstand and president of *The New Republic* magazine, the newsstand is accessed more than 30,000 times a day from locations all over the world.

Table 38-1 Magazines on the Electronic Newsstand

10 Percent	*Foreign Affairs*	*Nieman Reports*
American Demographics	*Foreign Policy*	*Out Magazine*
American Journal of International Law	*Free Inquiry*	*Outside Magazine*
American Quarterly	*GPS World*	*PC Graphics & Video*
Arthritis Today	*Games*	*PC Novice*
Automatic I.D. News	*Games World of Puzzles*	*PC Today*
Best Friends	*Geo Info Systems*	*Pacific Discovery*
Bio/Technology	*Growing Edge*	*Policy Review*
Blue & Gold Illustrated —	*Harvard International Review*	*Reason Magazine*
Notre Dame Football	*Health After Fifty —*	*Reviews in American History*
Body Politic	*Johns Hopkins Medical Letter*	*Rozek's*
Business Week	*Human Ecology Forum*	*Saturday Night*
CCD Astronomy	*Inc. Magazine*	*Scientist, The*
CD-ROM World	*Individual Investor*	*Skeptical Inquirer*
Cadalyst Magazine	*InsideFLYER*	*Sky & Telescope*
California Mining Journal	*International Legal Materials*	*Sloan Management Review*
Canoe & Kayak	*International Security*	*Source, The*
Christopher Street	*Internet Letter, The*	*Stage Directions*
Colloquium: A Digest for Investment	*Internet World*	*TCI: Theater Craft International*
Managers	*Journal of Democracy*	*TDR: The Drama Review*
Computerworld	*Journal of Economics and*	*TLC Monthly — The Learning*
Cornell Magazine	*Management Strategy*	*Channel Magazine*
Current History	*Journal of NIH Research, The*	*Technology Review*
Decanter	*Kennedy Institute of Ethics Journal*	*Times Higher Education*
Destination Discovery —	*Maclean's*	*Supplement, The*
The Discovery Channel Magazine	*Midrange Computing*	*Times Literary Supplement, The*
Discover: The World of Science	*Museums New York*	*Today's Traveler Magazine*
E, The Environmental Magazine	*National Review*	*Travel Holiday*
Earth Magazine	*Nature Genetics*	*Travel Matters*
Economist, The	*New Age Journal*	*Worth Magazine*
Educom Review	*New Perspectives Quarterly*	*Yankee*
Federal Employees News Digest	*New Republic, The*	*Yellow Silk*
Financial World	*New Yorker, The*	*Yoga Journal*

E X E R C I S E S

1. There are many news services on the Information Superhighway. For example, the Raleigh-based News and Observer Publishing Company operates a Gopher at merlin.NandO.net. Make an icon to represent the Gopher, put the icon on the billboard, and link the icon to the NandO news feed. If you have any questions about the NandO Gopher, send e-mail to gopher_staff@NandO.net.

2. Back up the *highway\infohigh.cus* file.

39

Cable News Network Live Video Feed

After completing this chapter, you will know how to:

- **Put a hyperpicture trigger on the Cable News Network (CNN) television icon on the Information Superhighway screen.**

- **Link the trigger to a CNN live video feed.**

- **Tune in to other channels.**

If you have a television tuner installed under Windows with a video overlay card, you can link PODIUM triggers to any television channel. Think what a tremendous resource this is, with services like C-Span broadcasting Congress and the Cable News Network (CNN) summarizing the news every half hour.

This chapter shows you how to link CNN to the Television icon on the Billboard menu. If you do not already have the Billboard menu on the screen, pull down the PODIUM Files menu, choose Custom, navigate to the *highway* directory, and select *infohigh.cus*.

Creating the Television Trigger

If the PODIUM toolbox is not open, press F4. Use the Trigger tool to draw a trigger around the TV icon, and in the Link box, type the @mci commands needed to display CNN. As you learned earlier in this book, MCI stands for the Media Control Interface, which connects multimedia devices to Windows. PODIUM's @mci option lets you send multimedia commands directly to Windows multimedia devices. If you have a device that PODIUM does not support directly, you can control it with @mci commands. The following commands assume that your TV tuner is connected to a video source named Source3, and that CNN is Channel 23. Change these values if they differ for your setup:

```
@mci=set overlay source Source3
@mci=tune overlay channel 23
@mci=tune overlay standard usa cable
@vinput=3
```

Click OK to close the Link dialog. *Note:* @vinput= is a PODIUM option that stands for video input. It makes PODIUM display the video input on your screen.

Triggering the Video

Press F4 to put the toolbox away, then click the TV icon. If you have a tuner connected, you will see CNN live. *Note:* The MCI commands given here were tested with the Super VideoWindows (SVW) tuner. Other tuners may work differently. If you do not get the channel on your screen, consult the MCI command list in the manual that came with your tuner, or contact the manufacturer.

Sizing the Video

If you have CNN playing live on your computer, press F2 to put PODIUM into a window. Did your hardware resize the video to fit the size of the PODIUM window? If so, you can resize the PODIUM window to any dimensions you wish, and the video will resize itself to fit the window. This is how stock market analysts and CIA officials watch CNN in one window so they can stay abreast of the news while they work in other windows on the screen. People have also been known to tune into football games and soap operas in one window while working in other windows.

E X E R C I S E S

1. Find a channel that interests you, such as C-SPAN. Use the Text tool to put the word "C-SPAN" on the Information Superhighway billboard screen, then link it to the C-SPAN channel using the MCI commands described earlier in this chapter as a model. Click the C-SPAN trigger to bring up C-SPAN. Then click the CNN trigger to bring up CNN. See how fast you can change the channels by clicking on these triggers.

2. Back up your *highway\infohigh.cus* file.

40

Distributing Your Multimedia Application

OBJECTIVES

After completing this chapter, you will know how to:

■ Publish your multimedia application on CD-ROM, diskettes, or the Information Superhighway.

■ Configure the installation options to make your application easy for users to install.

■ Zip and unzip applications to conserve disk space and make the applications easy to install.

■ Zip your Information Superhighway application and prepare it for publication on diskettes, e-mail, or FTP.

■ In addition, you will be able to decide when to "roll your own" CD and when to use a compact disc service bureau.

It is easy to publish applications created with PODIUM. There is a runtime version that you can distribute free of charge if your application is also free; otherwise, you must pay a modest fee for a runtime PODIUM license. PODIUM comes with an installation tool that makes it easy for users to install and run your application. You experienced this ease of use when you installed the *Multiliteracy CD* that came with this book.

Due to the number and size of the pictures, sound tracks, and video clips in the typical application, CD-ROM has become the medium of choice for multimedia publishing. Accordingly, this chapter begins by demonstrating how to package your application for distribution on CDs. You will also learn an alternative way to package, that is, to **zip** your application into a format you can publish on diskettes or distribute electronically on the Information Superhighway.

Packaging Your Application for CD-ROM

There are six steps involved in packaging a multimedia application for distribution on CD-ROM. You must:

▷ Identify the directories in which your multimedia resources are located.

▷ Copy those directories to a storage medium large enough to hold your entire application.

▷ Copy the PODIUM runtime module and help file.

▷ Use the PODIUM installation dialog to make your application easy for the user to set up.

▷ Copy the PODIUM installer to the root drive of the targeted storage medium.

▷ Test everything to make sure it all works.

An example of how you would complete these steps to prepare your Information Superhighway application for publication on a CD-ROM follows.

Step 1: Create the Directories

Your Information Superhighway application has three directories: *highway*, *weather*, and *buttons*. The first step is to create those directories on the targeted storage medium.

The targeted storage medium should be large enough to hold your entire application. It should be cleanly formatted so no other information is on it. If you plan to send your application to a CD service bureau for pressing, the targeted storage medium should ideally be removable, to facilitate your mailing it to the service bureau. Read/write optical disks are ideal for this purpose.

Use the File Manager to create the following directories on the targeted storage medium:

```
\highway
\weather
\buttons
```

Step 2: Copy the Multimedia Files

Use the Windows File Manager to copy the multimedia files to the targeted storage medium. Assuming your hard drive is *C*, your compact disc drive is *D*, and your targeted storage medium is *E*, here are the directories you need to copy:

Copy from:	Copy to:
c:\highway	e:\highway
d:\weather	e:\weather
d:\buttons	e:\buttons

Step 3: Include Runtime PODIUM

The PODIUM runtime module is called *rtpodium.exe*. It resides in the *\wnpodium* directory on the CD-ROM that came with this book. While the runtime module will run from any directory, it is customary to keep it in a *\wnpodium* directory. Therefore, you should create a *\wnpodium* directory on the targeted storage medium.

Copy the PODIUM runtime and the PODIUM help file to the *\wnpodium* directory on the targeted storage medium. Assuming your CD-ROM drive is *D* and your targeted storage medium is *E,* use the File Manager to copy the following files:

Copy from:	**Copy to:**
d:\wnpodium\rtpodium.exe	e:\wnpodium
d:\wnpodium\wnpodium.hlp	e:\wnpodium

If you do not charge a fee for your multimedia application, you may distribute the PODIUM runtime with it for free. However, if you charge for your application, you must purchase a runtime PODIUM license, as described in Appendix A.

Step 4: Configure the Installation

▷ Pull down the PODIUM Controls menu and select Installation. The Install Dialog shown in Figure 40-1 will appear.

40-1

The PODIUM Installation dialog.

PODIUM Installation Controls

Use these controls when you wish to package your PODIUM application for distribution. They create an INSTALL.CFG file you can ship with your product. It tells the PODIUM installer how to setup your application. Choose Save to save the settings, or Cancel to ignore them.

Filename of PODIUM executable (.exe) file: | rtpodium.exe

Title of Application for Startup Icon: | Information Superhighway

Application Startup Home File: | highway\infohigh.cus

Path: |

PODIUM "Full Screen" Size: | 640x480   Graphics Design Size: | 640x480

Startup Switches
☒ Full Screen Only
☐ Automatic Sequencing
☐ No Hot Cursor Shape Change

Run PODIUM From
◉ CD-ROM
○ Read/Write Drive

Save...   Open...   Cancel   Help

▷ In the Filename of PODIUM executable field, type:

rtpodium.exe

▷ In the Title of Application for Startup Icon field, type the title of your application, which is:

Information Superhighway

▷ In the Application Startup Home File field, type your application's startup file, which is:

highway\infohigh.cus

▷ Leave the Path field blank. You do not need to specify a path here, because you put directories on all your filenames.

▷ In the PODIUM "Full Screen" Size field, pull down the menu and choose the largest size to which you want your users to be able to expand your screens. PODIUM will never expand beyond the actual size of your user's screen.

▷ Leave the Graphics Design Size field set to 640x480. All of the bitmaps on the CD are designed for a 640x480 screen. Should you design graphics for some different screen size in the future, you would specify it in this field. If you want your application always to appear full screen, check the Full Screen Only box. Do not check the other startup switches for the Information Superhighway application.

▶ In the Run PODIUM From group, select CD-ROM.

▶ When you Save the configuration, put it in the root directory of the targeted storage medium. The name of the installation configuration file is always *install.cfg*. If your targeted storage medium is drive *E*, you would type:

> **e:\install.cfg**

Step 5: Copy the Installer

Now use the File Manager to copy the PODIUM installer to the root directory of the targeted storage medium.

Copy from:	Copy to:
d:\install.exe	e:\

Step 6: Test the Application

Pretend you are the user about to install your application. Make the targeted storage medium your current working directory. Run the *install.exe* program from it. If everything works properly, when the install is done, there should be an icon in your PODIUM group with the name of your application on it. Double-click on it and your application will start running. Try every nook and cranny in it to make sure it contains no errors or dead ends. Now you are ready to have your CD-ROM produced.

Rolling Your Own CD

Kodak, Philips, and Sony sell writable CD-ROM drives you can use to press your own CD. Also known as **CD-R drives** (the *R* stands for "Record"), they cost about $4,000 to $6,000. Being able to roll your own CD is convenient because your turnaround time is quick. However, unless you have more than one CD-R drive, you can only make one CD at a time, and the writable discs are expensive. When this book went to press, writable discs cost about $40. If you plan to make more than 20 copies of your CD, it will be less expensive to send your application to a service bureau and have them press it onto a CD-ROM for you.

Compact Disc Service Bureaus

Having a service bureau press a CD-ROM for you is a straightforward process. You send them your application on a storage medium they support, and they produce the CD-ROM for you, making as many copies as you request. The compact disc service bureau will tell you what storage media they support. You will save a lot of time and cost if your bureau supports the medium you used to package your application. When this book went to press, typical CD-ROM pressing costs were about $1,000 for mastering and setup, and $1.50 per disc. In large quantities, discs cost less than a dollar each.

Since CD-ROM is a read-only medium, it cannot be changed after the CD is pressed; therefore, it is wise to pay for a trial copy known as a "one-off" CD. It will cost $150 to $500 depending on how quickly you need the bureau to make it for you. Test it thoroughly to make sure your application runs from the CD exactly as intended before you pay the price for pressing multiple copies.

You can find out more about pressing CDs by contacting Disc Manufacturing Inc. They can mail you a very informative packet of materials about making CD-ROMs.

Zipping Applications for Publication

Distributing multimedia applications on diskettes or e-mailing them to users on the Internet would be unwieldy if you could not zip them into a single file. Zipping means to combine all of the files in your application into one highly compressed file that you distribute to your users. When they unzip the file, it recreates your application's directories and files on their hard drive.

The PKWARE directory on the *Multiliteracy CD* contains a shareware zip utility called *pkzip.exe*. It was produced by PKWARE, Inc. If you decide to use it, you must fill out the form printed in Appendix D and mail it to PKWARE with the fee indicated for your intended purpose.

Zipping Applications to Diskettes

When zipping multimedia applications to diskettes follow the steps given here. They use as an example the Information Superhighway application you created in this tutorial. They assume your hard drive is *C*, and your CD-ROM is *D*. If your drive letters differ, make the corresponding changes.

▶ You will need several formatted blank diskettes. Label the first one Disk 1.

▶ Use PODIUM to create the *install.cfg* file for your application. To do this, pull down the PODIUM Controls menu and select Installation. Fill in the blanks as shown in Figure 40-1, except click the Read/Write button instead of the CD-ROM button. Then press the Save button and give the file the following name, substituting a different letter if your hard drive is not *C:*

   c:\install.cfg

▶ Put Disk 1 in the disk drive and use the Windows File Manager to copy the following file from the *Multiliteracy CD* to Disk 1:

   pkware\pkunzip.exe

▶ Decide what the name of your zipped file is going to be. For this example, since it is an Information Superhighway application, let's call it *infohigh.zip.*

▶ Use a text editor, such as the Windows Notepad, to create a file on Disk 1 called *copylist.lst*. Enter the names of the files you want to zip:

   d:\install.exe
   c:\install.cfg
   d:\wnpodium\rtpodium.exe   These are the PODIUM files
   d:\wnpodium\wnpodium.hlp

   c:\highway*.*
   d:\weather*.*   These are your application directories
   d:\buttons*.*

Save the file.

From the Main Group on your Windows desktop, double-click the DOS icon to get the DOS prompt on the screen. At the DOS prompt, type the following line, substituting the letter of your CD-ROM if it is not *D:*

d:\pkware\pkzip -&P a:\infohigh.zip @a:\copylist.lst

While the files are being zipped, your computer will ask you to insert more diskettes. Keep them clearly labeled as Disk 2, Disk 3, and so on.

Now you are ready to test your application. Follow the steps below to make sure your application installs and runs perfectly. These are the instructions you will distribute for users to install your product:

■ To install the Information Superhighway application, insert Disk 1 into your disk drive.

■ From the Main Group on your Windows desktop, double-click the DOS icon to start a DOS session.

■ Change to the root directory of the hard drive to which you wish to copy the application. For example, to copy it onto drive *C,* type:

cd C:

■ To copy the application, type the following line, replacing the *a:* with the letter of your diskette drive if it is not *a:*

a:\pkunzip -do *a:*\infohigh.zip

■ When your computer finishes unzipping the files, type **Exit** and press Enter to return to Windows.

■ In the Program Manager's File menu, click Run.

■ Type the drive letter for your hard drive followed by a colon, backslash, and the word "Install." Example:

c:\install

■ When you press Enter, the computer will install your application. To run it, double-click the Information Superhighway icon that will appear in the PODIUM group on your Windows desktop.

After you solve any problems that may arise during this test, you are ready to copy the diskettes and distribute your application. You can use the DOS diskcopy command to duplicate the diskettes. Make sure you label the diskettes clearly with the name of your application and the number of each disk (Disk 1, Disk 2, and so on).

Zipping Applications for the Information Superhighway

The zipping process for distributing applications on the Internet is very similar to the diskette zipping described earlier, except that you zip to a file on your hard disk instead of on diskettes. Plus, you can take advantage of pkzip's ability to create a self-extracting archive, which simplifies the installation process for your users. Use the Information Superhighway application as an example. The following steps assume your hard drive is *C,* and your CD-ROM is *D:*

Use PODIUM to create the *install.cfg* file for your application. To do this, pull down the PODIUM Controls menu and select Installation. Fill in the blanks as shown in Figure 40-1, except click the Read/Write button instead of the CD-ROM button. Then press the Save button and give the file the following name, substituting a different letter if your hard drive is not *C:*

c:\install.cfg

▷ Decide what the name of your zipped file is going to be. For this example, since it is an Information Superhighway application, let's call it *infohigh.zip.*

▷ Use a text editor, such as the Windows Notepad, to create a file in the root directory of your hard drive called *copylist.lst.* Enter the names of the files you want to zip:

d:\install.exe
c:\install.cfg
d:\wnpodium\rtpodium.exe   These are the PODIUM files
d:\wnpodium\wnpodium.hlp

c:\highway*.*
d:\weather*.*   These are your application directories
d:\buttons*.*

Save the file.

▷ From the Main Group on your Windows desktop, double-click the DOS icon to get a DOS prompt on the screen. At the DOS prompt, type the following line, substituting the letter of your CD-ROM if it is not *D,* and your hard drive if it is not *C:*

d:\pkware\pkzip -&P c:\infohigh.zip @c:\copylist.lst

▷ To create the self-extracting archive, type:

d:\pkware\ziptoexe c:\infohigh.zip

This creates an executable file called *infohigh.exe.* When your users run it, your application will automatically copy itself to their hard drive. They can then run the install program to set up the PODIUM icon that will launch your application.

▷ The instructions in the next section will teach you how to send the zipped application through e-mail or FTP. Always test the process thoroughly to make sure all your files unzip and run correctly before you begin distributing them.

Sending Zipped Applications Through E-Mail

To send zipped applications through e-mail on hosts running Unix, follow the steps given here. If you have a non-Unix host, contact your network administrator for instructions.

▷ Transfer the *infohigh.exe* file to your Unix system. Make sure to use your communication software's binary option when you transfer it. For example, if you are using the Kermit communication software, do a *set file type binary* before transferring the file.

▷ You must "uuencode" the application unless your mailer is smart enough to know that the file is binary. Here is the command to type:

uuencode infohigh.exe infohigh.exe > infohigh.uu

▷ Address a mail message to the user to whom you wish to send the file. Include the file *infohigh.uu* at the end of the mail message. Put instructions at the beginning of the mail message that tell the user what to do with the included file. Here is a sample:

> Appended to this message is an encoded copy of the Information Superhighway application. To decode it and run it on your PC, follow these steps:
>
> 1. Copy this mail message to a file called *infohigh.uu.*
>
> 2. Edit the file *infohigh.uu* by deleting all of this message down to and including the line of equal signs.
>
> 3. Save the edited file.
>
> 4. At the Unix prompt, type the following command:
>
>   **uudecode infohigh.uu**
>
> 5. Now you will find a file called *infohigh.exe* on your system. Do a binary transfer of it to your PC, and run *infohigh.exe* from the DOS prompt of the disk drive you wish to install it on.
>
> 6. Now you will find an *install.exe* program in the root directory of the drive you ran *infohigh.exe* on. Run *install.exe* to install the Information Superhighway application.
>
> 7. To start the application, double-click on the Information Superhighway icon in the PODIUM group that will be set up on your Windows desktop.
>
> =========================

Distributing Zipped Applications via FTP

You can also distribute your application via FTP on the Internet. You can either make the application available from your local directory, or your network administrator can tell you how to copy it into a space that is accessible via anonymous FTP on the network or elsewhere on the Internet. The instructions you would send your users to download your application onto their multimedia PCs are given here. These instructions assume that your application is located in a directory called *public* that is accessible through anonymous FTP on the system oak.oakland.edu. If you do not want the public to have access to your application, put it in a directory that is not public, and tell your users how to sign on to access it. If you are running Unix, you can make the file available to others by doing a *chmod infohigh.exe 644.*

1. Sign on to your local system on the Internet.

2. FTP to oak.oakland.edu by typing:

   ftp oak.oakland.edu

3. At the prompt, logon as anonymous by typing:

   anonymous

4. The system will prompt you to enter your e-mail address as your password.

5. Change to the directory the file is stored in by typing:

   cd public

6. Set binary mode by typing:

   binary

7. Get the file by typing:

   get infohigh.exe

8. Now the file is on your Unix system. Download it to your PC with any communications program, making sure to set it to binary. For example, if you are using the Kermit communications program, do a *set file type binary* before transferring the file.

9. Run *infohigh.exe* from the DOS prompt of the disk drive you wish to install the application on.

10. Now you will find an *install.exe* program in the root directory of that drive on your PC. Run it to install the Information Superhighway application. *Note:* only the PODIUM *install.exe* and *install.cfg* files go in the root directory; all of the other files go in their own directories.

11. To start the application, double-click on the Information Superhighway icon in the PODIUM group that will be set up on the Windows desktop.

Marketability of Multimedia Titles

As for how marketable your application will be, Brian Blum (1994), President of the International Interactive Communications Society, lists five factors you should consider:

Interest

First and foremost, ask yourself if the idea or the content for the idea is interesting and unique. Is it something people will want to buy and use repeatedly?

Approach

Ask yourself what purpose multimedia is serving in this project. If you can't think of a good one, you probably want to try something else.

Technology

Does the program fully exploit the power of interactivity and multiple media to create at least slightly more value than the same content in a noninteractive format?

Design

Does the program push the creative or technological design envelope, or at least match the "state of the art" in a program on a similar topic?

Environment

Does the program immerse users in an environment, letting them forget they're using a computer?

E X E R C I S E S

1. Contact your local computer store and find out how much writable CD-ROM drives cost. Be sure to find out how much the media costs (*i.e.*, the writable CDs), as well as the hardware and software needed to press them.

2. Find out what service bureau presses CDs in your area and get prices for making a "one-off" CD, and for pressing multiple copies in quantities of a hundred, a thousand, and ten thousand.

3. Evaluate the answers to the first two questions and calculate the number of customers you would need before it becomes more cost effective to use a compact disc service bureau as opposed to rolling your own CDs.

Appendix A

PODIUM Licensing and Ordering Information

There are many ways to purchase PODIUM. Individuals who want a copy for their personal use are entitled to purchase a *Personal PODIUM* license at a substantial discount off the normal retail price. To use PODIUM for business or profit-making purposes, you must purchase a *Retail PODIUM* license. Quantity discounts make PODIUM very affordable for institutional purchasers. Both personal and institutional licensees may take advantage of *Runtime PODIUM*.

Personal PODIUM

Personal PODIUM is a fully functioning copy of the retail PODIUM product, yet it costs only $149. To qualify for *Personal PODIUM,* you must order it by yourself and pay via personal check or credit card. The *Personal PODIUM* license permits you to use PODIUM for non-profit purposes. You are on your honor to purchase a retail copy if you use PODIUM for business or commercial purposes.

To order *Personal PODIUM,* fill out the following order form and mail it to:

> The Instructional Technology Center
> 305 Willard Hall Education Building
> University of Delaware
> Newark DE 19716

Personal PODIUM Order Form

I, the undersigned PODIUM user, do hereby apply for a *Personal PODIUM* license and a fully functioning copy of the PODIUM software. I warrant that the purpose of my planned PODIUM use is personal, and I understand that if I choose to use PODIUM for profit-making purposes in the future, I must purchase a *Retail PODIUM* license.

Method of payment:

☐ Check
Make checks payable in the amount of $149 to The University of Delaware.

☐ VISA ☐ MasterCard ☐ Discover

Account Number on Card: _____

Expiration Date: _____

Printed Name: _____

Signature: _____

Address: _____

_____

City: _____ State: _____ Zip: _____

Area code: _____ Phone number: _____

Fax: _____

E-Mail: _____

Appendix B

Paint Shop Pro Order Form

Product	Quantity	Price	Total
Paint Shop Pro		$69.00 each	
Sales Tax (Minnesota residents only)		$4.49 each	
Shipping and handling - In US & Canada $5.00			
Shipping and handling - Outside of US & Canada By Air - $16.00. By Surface (allow up to 8 weeks) $5.00			
Total			
Desired Disk Size	☐ 3.5"	☐ 5.25"	

☐ VISA   ☐ MasterCard   ☐ Check **(US funds drawn on US Bank)**

☐ Purchase Order (enclosed) # _____

Card # _____

Exp. date _____ Signature _____

Name			
Company			
Street			
City		State	Zip
Country			
Day Phone			

Please return this form when you order.
JASC, Inc.
10901 Red Circle Drive
Suite 340
Minnetonka, MN 55343

Order Now By Calling
1-612-930-9171
Order number: (612) 930-9171, 9am-5pm CST
FAX number: (612) 930-9172, 24 hours

Appendix C

PKZIP Order Form

Send form to:
PKWARE, Inc.
9025 N. Deerwood Dr.
Brown Deer, WI 53223
(414) 354-8699 Voice
(414) 354-8559 FAX
(414) 354-8670 BBS

Name: _____ Date: _____

Company: _____

Address: _____

City: _____

State: _____ ZIP Code: _____ Country: _____

Daytime Phone #: _____ FAX #: _____

PKZIP,® PKUNZIP,® and PKSFX® for MS-DOS

Individual Use

☐ Diskette* with programs and documentation .... $47 $_____.____

Multiple Use

Site License for the use of PKZIP, PKUNZIP & PKSFX.
Includes one diskette* with programs and documentation.

☐ 2 to 9 computers at $36 each .... # computers ____ × 36 $_____.____
☐ 10 to 24 computers at $28 each .... # computers ____ × 28 _____.____
☐ 25 to 49 computers at $22 each .... # computers ____ × 22 _____.____
☐ 50 to 99 computers at $16 each .... # computers ____ × 16 _____.____
☐ 100 to 199 computers at $12 each .... # computers ____ × 12 _____.____
☐ 200 to 500 computers at $10 each .... # computers ____ × 10 _____.____

Write or call for pricing on quantities over 500.

☐ Extra program disk & documentation with purchase of
Site Licenses of two or more available at $8.00 each. ____ × 8 $_____.____

Shipping & Handling (Postal) US & Canada $5.00/item
Outside US & Canada $11.25/item .... $_____.____

Wisconsin residents add applicable State & County Sales Tax .... $_____.____

TOTAL ENCLOSED US FUNDS .... US$_____.____

☐ MasterCard ☐ VISA Expiration Date _____

Card Number: _____

Card Holder's Signature REQUIRED _____

* Dual Media Diskette. Includes one free upgrade to the software, when available.
PKWARE, PKZIP, PKUNZIP & PKSFX are registered with the U.S. Patent and Trademark Office.
MS-DOS is a registered trademark of Microsoft Corporation.

Glossary

A/D converter Analog to digital converter. A device that uses quantization and sampling to transform a continuous analog waveform into a digital bit stream.

algorithm A sequence of processing steps that perform a particular operation, such as compressing a digital video to store it efficiently and decompressing it upon playback.

animation Movement of a graphic object on a computer screen.

anonymous FTP A method by which computers on the Internet allow public access to certain files. These files can then be examined and downloaded by anybody. See *FTP*.

Archie An Internet utility that helps users locate specific files on the Internet. Millions of files are indexed.

aspect ratio The relative horizontal and vertical sizing of a computer display's picture elements (pixels). The typical 640x480 screen has an aspect ratio of 4:3.

avatar An agent representing the user in a virtual reality system.

bandwidth The capacity of a device to process or transmit information. The more information it can handle per second, the greater its bandwidth.

bitmap The picture formed by assigning different colors to the pixels on a computer screen; or the computer file that specifies how to color the pixels to create such a picture.

BMP The three-letter file extension for Microsoft Windows bitmaps. See *bitmap*.

bounce To mix two or more audio tracks into one.

bps Bits per second. A measurement of the speed at which data is transmitted over a communications medium.

camcorder A combination of "camera" and "recorder." A portable device that records video and sound onto videotape.

CAV Constant Angular Velocity. A type of videodisc that can hold 54,000 still frames per side, or 30 minutes of motion video. See also *CLV*.

CD-Audio The use of a compact disc (CD) to play back recorded music. Compact discs can hold up to 75 minutes of audio. Multimedia computers can access the audio in increments as small as a 75th of a second.

CD-I Compact Disc-Interactive. A multimedia delivery platform standard invented by Philips and Sony. The special players required for CD-I discs can also play CD-Audio discs.

CD-ROM XA CD-ROM Extended Architecture. Increases to as much as 19 hours the amount of audio that can be stored on a compact disc by providing lower quality recording and playback rates.

CD-ROM Compact Disc Read-Only Memory. The use of a compact disc to store computer data. CD-ROMs can hold up to 680 MB.

client A computer seeking information on your behalf from a server on a network.

CLV Constant Linear Velocity. A videodisc format that permits up to an hour of video to be recorded on each side of the disc. Most videodisc players cannot show still frames from CLV discs. See also *CAV*.

custom toolbox An object-oriented set of multimedia development tools in the PODIUM multimedia application generator.

data rate The speed of data transfer, normally expressed in bits or bytes per second. For example, the data rate of CD-ROM is 150,000 bytes per second or 150 KB; CD-ROM II is twice as fast at 300 KB.

dB   Decibel, a measurement of loudness. The higher the rating, the louder the sound. A whisper is 10dB; jet aircraft engines produce 130dB, which can permanently damage hearing.

DCT   Discrete Cosine Transform. A video compression algorithm that eliminates redundant data in blocks of pixels on the screen. It is used in JPEG (stills), MPEG (motion), and CCITT (FAX) compression standards.

digitizing   The process of converting analog audio and video signals into a digital format that can be stored, manipulated, and displayed by a computer. Digitizing is accomplished by A/D converters on scanners and audio/video capture boards. See also *A/D Converter*.

directory   An index to the files and subdirectories that are stored on a computer.

dissolve   A transition effect between two sequential images on the screen. Dissolve patterns include splits, stripes, diagonals, and fades.

DLL   Dynamic Link Library. The expandable software technology that enables vendors to add features easily to the Microsoft Windows environment.

domain name   Allows numeric IP addresses (like 140.147.2.69) to be expressed by names like "marvel.log.gov."

DSP   Digital Signal Processor. A chip designed to process digitized sound and video quickly.

DVI   Digital Video Interactive. An Intel compressed video standard for recording digital video. This format permits up to 72 minutes of full-frame full-motion video to fit on a CD-ROM. Special hardware is required to record and play back DVI.

fade   A gradual decrease in the brightness of an image or the loudness of a sound.

FAQ   Frequently Asked Question. A list of frequently asked questions and their answers.

fps   Frames per second. A measure of the recording and playback rate of digital videos.

frame   A screen full of video.

frame rate   The speed at which frames are displayed on the monitor. Broadcast television in North America and Japan is displayed at 30 fps; in Europe it is displayed at 25 fps.

freenet   An organization that provides free Internet access to people in a certain area, usually through public libraries.

FTP   File Transfer Protocol. Allows users to send a file from one computer to another.

full motion   Video played at the broadcast television frame rate. See also *frame rate*.

gateway   A computer whose role on a network is to reformat data sent from one computer into a form it can forward on to another.

Gopher   A menu-based system for accessing Internet resources, including host computers, directories, and files.

Gopherspace   The connection of all existing Gopher servers.

GUI   Graphical User Interface. Allows direct manipulation of on screen objects and events using icons, menus, toolbars, and dialog controls. Macintosh, Windows, and OS/2 Presentation Manager are examples of GUIs.

host   The main computer to which a user is connected when accessing the Internet.

hot spots   Places on the computer screen which, when selected, trigger the objects or events linked to them.

hyper   In multimedia, a prefix used to indicate that a linkage has given a new dimension to a word (hypertext), video (hypervideo), audio (hyperaudio), or part or all of a picture (hyperpicture).

IAB   Internet Architecture Board. The governing body that makes decisions about Internet standards.

IETF   Internet Engineering Task Force. A volunteer group that investigates and solves technical problems and makes recommendations to the Internet Architecture Board. See also *IAB*.

IMA   Interactive Multimedia Association. The IMA encourages the setting of industry-wide standards for multimedia hardware and software.

Information Superhighway   A popular term coined by the Clinton administration to refer to the Internet with a metaphor the public could understand. See *Internet*.

Internaut   A user who navigates the vast expanse of the Internet, much like an astronaut traverses outer space.

Internet   The worldwide network of networks that are connected to each other via the Internet Protocol (IP).

Internet address   Each computer on the Internet has a named address such as marvel.loc.gov (the Library of Congress Gopher). See also *domain name*.

ISDN   Integrated Services Digital Network. A high bandwidth digital telecommunications network being installed gradually throughout the United States. This network handles voice, video, and data; it also supports videoconferencing.

ISO International Standards Organization.

IVD Interactive Videodisc. A multimedia format in which a computer is connected to a videodisc player to provide interactive video capabilities.

JPEG Joint Photographic Experts Group, an ISO (International Standards Organization) body creating a new standard for digitizing still photographic images. The standard (which is also called JPEG) is cooperatively developed by more than 70 companies and institutions worldwide including Sony, Philips, Matsushita, and Apple. The JPEG standard permits compression ratios ranging from 10:1 to 80:1—but the greater the compression, the lower the quality of the image.

K One thousand, a unit of computer measurement. For example, 150 K means 150,000. (Purists will tell you that the K used by computer scientists actually means slightly more than a thousand, but for the measurements used in this book, a thousand is close enough and much easier to compute!)

knowbot An information retrieval tool that you can train to go out on the Internet and find things for you.

login To type your name and password to initiate a session with a host computer.

lossy Compression techniques in which decompressed images do not contain all the original information. JPEG and MPEG are lossy. The opposite is lossless compression. RLE (run-length encoding) is lossless but does not compress as much.

MIDI MIDI stands for Musical Instrument Digital Interface. The MIDI standard is a protocol by which electronic musical instruments communicate with computers and each other.

modem A datacommunications device that connects a computer to a telephone line and lets the user transfer data at speeds ranging from 1200 bits per second (bps) to 19.2 Kbps.

MPC Multimedia PC. An industry-wide specification of the minimum hardware requirements needed for multimedia. Introduced by the Multimedia PC Marketing Council in 1991, it requires a 16 MHz 286 CPU, 2 MB RAM, 30 MB hard drive, and a CD-ROM. A more powerful MPC2 standard created in 1993 requires a 25 MHz 486SX, 4 MB RAM, 160 MB hard drive, and a double-speed CD-ROM.

MPEG Motion Pictures Experts Group, an ISO (International Standards Organization) body creating a new standard for digital video. The standard (which is also called MPEG) was cooperatively developed by more than 70 companies and institutions worldwide, including Sony, Philips, Matsushita, and Apple. MPEG is expected to become the digital video standard for compact discs, cable TV, direct satellite broadcast, and high-definition television.

multiliterate Understanding the principles of multimedia, its impact on the world, and how to use it for attaining business, professional, educational, and personal objectives.

multimedia The use of a computer to combine and present text, graphics, audio, and video with links and tools that let the user navigate, interact, create, and communicate.

NIC Network Information Center. Every network on the Internet should have an NIC and a network administrator. Each NIC looks after the needs of the users connected to its network.

NOC Network Operations Center. The organization responsible for the day-to-day operations of a network.

NTSC National Television Standards Committee. The North American TV standard is named after the committee that created it.

overlay To superimpose text and graphics on still or motion video images.

PAL The European television standard that displays 25 frames per second. Used in all European countries except France; see also *SECAM*.

palette A table of colors used to paint pixels on the screen. The typical multimedia computer with SVGA graphics can display a 256-color palette.

pixel Picture element. The tiny dots that make up the computer screen are called pixels. Each pixel has a specific color and intensity level.

play list A sequence of CD-audio clips, or MIDI or waveform audio files, that play back one after another without being mixed into a new sound file.

protocol A definition of how computers communicate with each other.

Red Book The CD-Audio protocol for recording audio onto compact discs is known as the Red Book specification. The minute-second-frame CD-Audio addresses defined in the Red Book specification are known as Red Book addresses.

Resolution A measurement of the number of pixels on a display. The typical multimedia computer has a resolution of 640x480 pixels. See *pixel*.

RGB Red Green Blue. Each pixel displayed on the screen consists of a certain amount of red, green, and blue. For example, a black pixel has no red, green, or blue, while a white pixel has the maximum amount of each.

RLE   Run-Length Encoding. A lossless data compression technique that encodes the number of times a repeated data element recurs instead of recording each occurrence. For example, 12 red pixels in a row would be encoded as 12R instead of RRRRRRRRRRRR.

root directory   The primary directory on a hard disk from which all other directories branch. See also *directory*.

sampling   The process of measuring and recording the values of an analog signal at evenly spaced time intervals.

sampling rate   The number of times an analog signal is sampled each second. For example, CD-Audio is recorded at a rate of 44,100 samples per second.

SECAM   Sequential Couleur Avec Memoire. The French national standard for color TV that is also used in Russia and Eastern Europe. It operates at 25 fps.

self-extracting archive   A list of files that have been archived into a single executable file that decompresses itself automatically when the user runs it.

server   A computer on the Internet that provides information on demand to client computers. See also *client*.

shareware   Computer software distributed with no up-front cost. Users who try the software and wish to keep using it must pay a fee. Shareware is not free.

SMPTE   Society of Motion Picture and Television Engineers. Pronounced "Simptee," SMPTE refers to a time code expressed in hours, minutes, seconds, and frames. SMPTE time code is written in the form of HH:MM:SS:FF.

storyboard   A time-based outline or script for a video or multimedia production.

subdirectory   A directory inside another directory.

surf   To browse an electronic medium for information. Channel surfing means to flip through the channels on a television set, looking for something that interests you. Surfing the Internet means to browse through the interconnected menus of information servers like Gopher and the World Wide Web.

SVGA   Super VGA. A screen resolution standard created by the Video Electronics Standards Association (VESA) that delivers a screen resolution of up to 800x600 with 256-color graphics.

TCP/IP   Transmission Control Protocol/Internet Protocol. Computers use TCP/IP to connect to the Internet.

telnet   A method which allows users to log on to remote host computers on the Internet.

terminal   The computer that connects to a host. The terminal can be a personal computer.

timeout   A situation in a multimedia program in which the user must respond before a predetermined time limit expires and a default action occurs.

upload   To send a file to your host or to a remote host on the Internet. See also *host*.

Veronica   An Internet Gopher utility that lets users perform a keyword search of Gopher menus. See also *Gopher*.

videodisc   An optical disc on which video signals are recorded. Usually 12 inches in diameter, videodiscs are used for entertainment and to provide video in multimedia training applications. Videodiscs come in two formats: CAV and CLV. See also *CAV* and *CLV*.

WAIS   Wide-Area Information Servers. An Internet utility that provides full text search capability.

waveform audio   A method of creating sound by digitizing an analog audio waveform and storing the digital samples on a disk in a .WAV file, from which they can be played back on demand. WAV stands for waveform.

WWW   World-Wide Web. An Internet-wide hypermedia system accessed via the popular Mosaic software.

Market Vision. *Multimedia Applications and Markets: 5-Year Forecast.* Falls Church, VA: Multimedia Monitor, 1993.

Marshall, Nancy H. Copyright and the Scholarly Community: The Library's Responsibility to Guarantee Users' Rights. *Japan U.S. Collaboration in Enhancing International Access to Scholarly Communication: Looking Toward the 21st Century.* Tokyo University Academy Press, 1992.

McGovern, Kevin and McGovern, Leo. The Virtual Clinic: A Virtual Reality Surgical Simulator. *Virtual Reality World* (March/April 1994): 41-44.

Medina, Dina. Texture Extravaganza. *NewMedia* 3, no. 9 (September 1993): 88.

Merril, Jonathon R. Surgery on the Cutting-Edge; Virtual Reality Applications in Medical Education. *Virtual Reality World* (November/December 1993): 34-38.

Nelson, Theodor H. The Hypertext. *Proceedings of the World Documentation Federation,* 1965.

Neuwirth, Konrad. Where in the World Is Carmen Sandiego? *Ed-Tech Review* (Autumn/Winter 1994): 46-48.

Newson, Gillian. Virtual Valerie. *NewMedia* 2, no. 11 (November 1992): 42-43.

Olmstead, Jack. Video Stores Starstruck by Multimedia. *NewMedia* 2, no.11 (September 1993): 23.

Pearson, LaTresa. Multimedia Hits the Road. *Presentations* 7, no. 11 (November 1993), 29-39.

————. Releasing the Power of CD-ROM. *Presentations* 8, no. 2 (February 1994): 22-26.

Rahlmann, Reed K. Dave Grusin: The Gershwin Connection. *NewMedia* 4, no. 2 (February 1994): 56-57.

Reiger, Bob. Bob Reiger Talks About NETCOM. *Internet World* 5, no. 2 (March/April 1994): 64-70.

Reveaux, Tony. Let the Games Begin. *NewMedia* 4, no. 1(January 1994): 48-53.

Robin, Bernard; Bull, Glen; Sigmon, Tim; and Mitchell, Jason. STATE Teacher Education Server Established on Internet. *Ed-Tech Review* (Autumn/Winter 1993): 65-66.

Rosenthal, Steve. Mega Channels. *NewMedia* 3, no. 9 (September 1993): 36-46.

Shamp, Scott A. A Primer on Choosing the Medium for Multimedia: Videodisc vs. Videotape. *T.H.E. Journal* (February 1993): 81-86.

Smith, Roger. Current Military Simulations and the Integration of Virtual Reality Technologies. *Virtual Reality World* (March/April 1994): 45-50.

Smith, Stanley G., and Jones, Loretta L. Multimedia Technology: A Catalyst for Change in Chemical Education. *Pure & Applied Chemistry* 65, no. 2 (1993): 245-249.

Snyder, Joel. Diving into the Internet: The Trouble with Gopher. *Internet World* 5, no. 2 (March/April 1994): 30-34.

Stefanac, Suzanne. Sex & the New Media. *NewMedia* 3, no. 4 (April 1993): 38-45.

————. Digital Carnage: Do Violent Interactive Games Promote Real-Life Violence? *NewMedia* 4, no. 1 (January 1994): 72-77.

Stewart Publishing. *Interactive Healthcare Directories.* Alexandria: Stewart Publishing, Inc., 1993. Includes:
   Videodisc Directory.
   CD-ROM Directory.
   Computer Assisted Instruction.
   Directory of Educational Software for Nursing.

Sullivan, Eamonn. HTTP Eases Access to Internet Info. *PC Week* (January 31, 1994): 71-73.

The Cognition and Technology Group at Vanderbilt. Anchored Instruction and Its Relationship to Situated Cognition. *Educational Researcher* 19 (1990): 2-10.

Tynan, Daniel. Multimedia Goes On the Job JUST IN TIME. In John Hirschbuhl, ed. *Computers in Education.* Sixth Ed. Guilford CT: The Dushkin Publishing Group, Inc., 1993, 188-194.

Waltz, Mitzi. Four-Wheeling with Two Megs. *NewMedia* 3, no. 11 (November 1993): 39.

Wertz, Sandra. Using Copyrighted Music in Public Performances. *Tech Trends* 38, no. 5 (October 1993): 11-12.

Withrow, Frank. Guest editorial in *T.H.E. Journal* 21, no. 2 (September 1993): 10.

For Further Information

This book has mentioned many multimedia hardware and software products and online Internet resources. This section contains a list of telephone numbers, e-mail: addresses, fax: numbers, and snail-mail addresses that you can use to contact the vendors, publishers, and service providers. The list is organized according to product categories and will be especially useful for instructors wanting to obtain some of these materials for use in teaching classes.

Application Software

Authorware Professional for Windows. Macromedia. Phone: (415) 252-2000.

Band-in-a-Box. PG Music. Phone: (800) 268-6272.

Convert It! Heizer Software. Phone: (510) 943-7667.

Harvard Graphics. Software Publishing Corporation. Phone: (800) 336-8360.

IconAuthor. Aim Tech. Phone: (603) 883-0220.

Morph 2.5. Gryphon Software Corporation. Phone: (619) 536-8815.

Norton Utilities. Symantec. Phone: (408) 252-5700.

Photo CD Viewer. Eastman Kodak. Phone: (619) 693-4030.

Quest Multimedia Authoring System. Allen Communication.
    Phone: (801) 537-7800.

Studio for Windows. MidiSoft. Phone: (206) 881-7176.

Toolbook. Asymmetrix. Phone: (800) 448-6543.

Conferences and Exhibits

CeBit. Worlds largest computer show, with 700,000 attendees and 6,000 company exhibits from 54 countries. Held annually each spring in Hannover, Germany. For information, phone (609) 987-1202.

COMDEX. A huge exhibition of computer technology that occurs twice a year, once in the fall, and again in the spring. For information about COMDEX, contact The Interface Group, 300 First Avenue, Needham, MA 02194-2722. Phone: (617) 449-6600; fax: (617) 449-2674.

Ed-Media. International conference on educational multimedia and hypermedia. Sponsored by the Association for the Advancement of Computing in Education (AACE). Write P.O. Box 2966, Charlottesville, VA 22902. Phone: (804) 973-3987; fax: (804) 978-7449; e-mail: AACE@virginia.edu.

INFOCOMM. Annual exhibit of audiovisual and new media equipment sponsored by the International Communications Industries Association (ICIA). Contact the ICIA at 3150 Spring Street, Fairfax, VA 22031-2399. Phone: (703) 273-7200; fax: (703) 278-8082.

Interactive Healthcare. Annual conference dealing with the use of videodisc, CD-ROM, CD-I, and multimedia applications for medicine, nursing, allied health, continuing education, patient education, and health promotion. Contact Stewart Publishing at (703) 354-8155; fax: (703) 354-2177.

InterMedia. International Conference on CD-ROM and Multimedia. Co-hosted annually by InterMedia and *NewMedia* magazine. Phone: (800) 832-3513 or write to *NewMedia* at P.O. Box 1771, Riverton, NJ 08077-7331.

NAB Multimedia World. Annual conference dealing with multimedia, computers, consumer electronics, telecommunications, publishing, and entertainment. Sponsored by the National Association of Broadcasters and the Interactive Multimedia Association. Phone: (202) 775-4972; fax: (301) 216-1847.

National Demonstration Laboratory (NDL). Nonprofit, self-sustaining center for the demonstration of educational and informational applications of interactive video technologies. Demonstrations held at 10 a.m. and 2 p.m. Monday - Friday, by appointment only. Individuals may make an appointment for a 2-hour demo or to work with specific applications and development tools during non-demonstration hours. Phone: (202) 707-4157.

National Net. Annual conference held each spring in Washington D.C. Features prominent legislators and scientists involved in creating the Information Superhighway. Phone: (202) 872-4200 or gopher to educom.edu.

NewMedia Expo. Annual conference dealing with multimedia, computers, consumer electronics, telecommunications, publishing, and entertainment. Sponsored by The Interface Group, 300 First Avenue, Needham, MA 02194-2722. Phone: (617) 449-6600.

Virtual Reality Expo. VR trade show held several times a year in major cities. Sponsored by Mecklermedia Corporation, 11 Ferry Lane West, Westport, CT 06880. Phone: (203) 226-6967; fax: (203) 454-5840; e-mail: meckler@jvnc.net.

Education and Training Systems

ACTIV training system. Industrial Training Corporation. Phone: (800) 638-3757.

American Heart Association Advanced Cardiac Life Support training system. Actronics. Phone: (800) 851-3780.

Science 2000 interactive videodisc for 7th grade. Decision Development Corporation. Phone: (800) 835-4332.

Science Forums interactive videodiscs for grades 6 through 9. Videodiscovery. Phone: (800) 548-3472.

The Laboratory Safety Training Program, interactive videodisc. Interactive Media Communications. Phone: (617) 890-7707.

Hardware

Apple QuickTake 100 digital camera. Apple Computer. Phone: (408) 996-1010.

Audio/video switch. Radio Shack catalog number 15-1956.

Canon RC-570 Still Video camera. Phone: (516) 328-5960.

Expresso slide scanner. RasterOps. Phone: (408) 562-4065.

Heartbeat Personal Trainer. HeartBeat. Phone: (800) FUN-PLUS.

Paint Shop Pro. JASC, Inc. Phone: (612) 930-9171; fax: (612) 930-9172.

Roland Sound Canvas technology for MIDI. Roland. Phone: (213) 685-5141.

SoundBlaster waveform audio board. Creative Labs. Phone: (800) 998-LABS.

Super TV tuner board. New Media Graphics Corporation. Phone: (800) 288-2207 or (508) 663-0666, ext 177 (sales); fax: (508) 663-6678.

Super VideoWindows board. New Media Graphics Corporation. Phone: (800) 288-2207 or (508) 663-0666, ext 177 (sales); fax: (508) 663-6678.

The Typist hand-held scanner. Caere Corporation. Phone: (408) 395-7000.

Yamaha speakers. Yamaha. Phone: (714) 522-9011.

Internet Service Providers

Australia: AARNet. Phone: +61 6 249 4969; e-mail: aarnet@aarnet.edu.au.

Colorado: Colorado Supernet. Phone: (303) 273-3471; e-mail: info@csn.org.

Michigan: MSEN. Phone: (313) 998-4562; e-mail: info@msen.com.

Midwest & Nationwide: CICNet. Phone: (800)947-4754; e-mail: info@cic.net.

Northeast U.S. (ME NH VT CT RI MA): NEARnet. Phone: (617) 873-8730; e-mail: nearnet-join@near.net.

Pennsylvania: PREPnet. Phone: (412) 268-7870; e-mail: nic@prep.net.

San Francisco and Far East: BARRNET. Phone:(415) 723-3104; e-mail: info@barrnet.net.

United Kingdom: Demon. Phone: +44 81 349 0063; e-mail: internet@demon.co.uk.

U.S. (Major Cities): NETCOM. Phone: (800) 501-8649; e-mail: info@netcom.com.

Virginia: VERnet. Phone: (804) 924-0616; e-mail: net-info@ver.net.

Wisconsin: WiscNet. Phone: (608) 262-4241; e-mail: wn-info@nic.wiscnet.net.

Worldwide: PSI. Phone: (703) 904-1207; e-mail: all-info@psi.com.

Worldwide: UUNET. Phone: (800) 4UU-NET3; e-mail: info@uunet.uu.net.

Worldwide, through Sprintnet: Portal Communications. Phone: (408) 973-9111; e-mail: info@portal.com.

Multimedia and the Law

CPSR (Computer Professionals for Social Responsibility). For information about the protest against the Clipper Chip, gopher to cpsr.org.

Congresswoman Maria Cantwell. To show support of bill H.R. 3627 to liberalize export controls on encryption software, contact cantwell@eff.org.

Software Publishers Association. For statistics on software privacy and copyright infringement, phone: (202) 452-1600.

Multimedia Resources

Atlanta Vision kiosk presentation. Georgia Tech Multimedia Lab. Frederick Dyer & Mike Sinclair, co-directors. Phone: (404) 894-3539; e-mail: fred.dyer@oip.gatech.edu.

BrowseStation, movie-displaying kiosk. VStor Company. Phone: (818) 225-9505.

Disc Manufacturing, Inc. Information about pressing CDs. Phone: (800) 433-DISC.

Electronic Newsstand Gopher at enews.com.

Styles-on-Video system. Styles-on-Video, Inc. Phone: (800) 995-0352.

Videodisc recording centers. Optical Disc Corporation. Phone: (800) 350-3500.

Video Movie Guide-based kiosk. Advanced Multimedia Solutions. Phone: (206) 623-4011.

Video Viewfinder and Video Trace retail video software. Unique. Phone: (310) 396-3929.

Vienna's CITY-INFO kiosks. Vienna, Austria. Phone: (02 22) 526 94 65; fax: (02 22) 526 55 82 9.

Multimedia Titles

1993 TIME Almanac CD-ROM. Compact Publishing. Phone: (800) 964-1518.

20th Century Almanac CD-ROM. The Software Toolworks. Phone: (800) 234-3088.

A.D.A.M. (Animated Dissection of the Anatomy for Medicine) CD-ROM. A.D.A.M. Software. Phone: (800) 755-ADAM.

Anatomy & Physiology CAV videodisc. Videodiscovery. Phone: (800) 548-3472.

Beauty and the Beast CD-ROM. Ebook. Phone: (510) 429-1331.

Capitol Hill CD-ROM. The SoftwareToolworks. Phone: (800) 283-8499.

Coates Art Review: Impressionism CD-ROM. Quanta Press. Phone: (612) 379-3956.

Compton's Interactive Encyclopedia CD-ROM. Compton's NewMedia Inc. Phone: (619) 929-2500.

Consumer Information CD-ROM. Quanta Press. Phone: (612) 379-3956.

Critical Path interactive movie on CD-ROM. Media Vision. Phone: (800) 845-5870.

Desert Storm with Coalition Command CD-ROM. Compton's NewMedia Inc. Phone: (619) 929-2500.

Desert Storm: The War in the Persian Gulf CD-ROM. Time Warner Interactive. Phone: (800) 593-6334.

Dictionary for Children CD-ROM. Macmillan New Media. Phone: (800) 342-1338.

Dinosaurs! CD-ROM. Media Design Interaction. Phone: (408) 372-7141.

Dynamics of Human Anatomy interactive videodisc. Produced by the University of Delaware. Published by Lea & Febiger. Phone: (800) 882-8532.

Encarta. Multimedia encyclopedia on CD-ROM. Microsoft. Phone: (800) 426-9400.

Encyclopedia of Mammalian Biology interactive CD-ROM. McGraw-Hill. Phone: (800) 722-4726.

Exploring Ancient Architecture CD-ROM. Medio. Phone: (206) 867-5500.

Exploring Chemistry CD-ROM. Falcon Software. Phone: (603) 764-5788.

Family Health Book CD-ROM. Mayo Clinic. Phone: (800) 937-6463.

Heartbeat Personal Trainer. HeartBeat. Phone: (800) FUN-PLUS.

History series on interactive video. ABC News Interactive. Fax: (212) 456-4060.

Industrial training videodiscs. Series of interactive videodiscs. Instrument Society of America. Phone: (919) 549-8411.

Iron Helix interactive movie on CD-ROM. Drew Pictures, phone: (415) 247-7600. Distributed by Spectrum Holobyte, phone: (800) 695-GAME.

Jazz, A Multimedia History CD-ROM. Compton's NewMedia Inc. Phone: (619) 929-2500.

L.A. project videodisc from North Communications. Phone: (310) 828-7000.

Living Book series CD-ROM. Brøderbund. Phone: (415) 382-4565.

Mad Dog McCree Shooting Game video game. American Laser Games. Phone: (505) 880-1718.

Mammals: A Multimedia Encyclopedia. Multimedia CD-ROM. National Geographic Society. Phone: (800) 368-2728.

Mario is Missing! CD-ROM. The Software Toolworks. Phone: (800) 283-8499.

McGraw-Hill Multimedia Encyclopedia of Science and Technology CD-ROM. McGraw-Hill. Phone: (800) 722-4726.

Media Clips CD-ROM series of clip art and sound. Aris Entertainment. Phone: (312) 821-0234 / (800) 228-2747.

Mixed-Up Mother Goose CD-ROM. Sierra Online. Phone: (800) 743-7725.

Multimedia Beethoven CD-ROM. Microsoft. Phone: (800) 426-9400. Also available: *Multimedia Mozart, Multimedia Stravinsky,* and *Multimedia Vivaldi.*

Music Mentor with Recording Session diskette. MidiSoft. Phone: (206) 881-7176.

Musical Instruments CD-ROM. Microsoft. Phone: (800) 426-9400.

National Parks of America CD-ROM. Multicom. Phone: (206) 622-5530 / (800) 850-7272.

Nouvelles Dimensions CD-ROM. Heinle & Heinle. Phone: (800) 237-0053. Developed by linguist Dr. James Noblitt; e-mail: JIM.IAT@mhs.unc.edu.

Oceans Below CD-ROM. Amazing Media. Phone: (800) 231-3088.

Our House CD-ROM. Context. Phone: (215) 675-2899.

Peter and the Wolf CD-ROM. Ebook. Phone: (510) 429-1331.

Picture Atlas of the World CD-ROM. National Geographic Society. Phone: (800) 368-2728.

Pixar One Twenty-Eight clip art library of textures on CD-ROM. Pixar. Phone: (800) 888-9856.

Playing With Language series on CD-ROM. Syracuse Language Systems Inc. Phone: (800) 688-1937.

Science Sleuths videodisc. Videodiscovery. Phone: (800) 548-3472.

The 1993 Guiness Disc of World Records CD-ROM. The Software Toolworks. Phone: (800) 234-3088.

The '92 Vote CD-ROM. ABC News Interactive. Phone: (212) 456-4060. Other history titles available on interactive videodisc.

The Clinton Health Security Plan: What it Costs and What it Means to You on CD-ROM or diskette. Allegro New Media. Phone: (800) 424-1992.

The Doctors Book of Home Remedies CD-ROM. Compton's NewMedia Inc. $39.95. Phone: (619) 929-2500.

The JFK Assassination: A Visual Investigation CD-ROM. Medio. Phone: (206) 867-5500.

The New Grolier Multimedia Encyclopedia CD-ROM. Grolier. Phone: (203) 797-3500.

The Presidents: It All Started with George CD-ROM. National Geographic Society. Phone: (800) 368-2728.

The Puzzle of the Tacoma Narrows Bridge Collapse videodisc. Wiley Educational Software. ISBN 0-471-87320-9.

The San Diego Zoo Presents the Animals! CD-ROM. The Software Toolworks. Phone: (800) 234-3088.

The Sleeping Beauty CD-ROM. Ebook. Phone: (510) 429-1331.

The Total Heart CD-ROM. Mayo Clinic. Phone: (800) 937-6463.

The Video Encyclopedia of Physics Demonstrations videodisc. The Education Group. Phone: (310) 659-8842.

The Video Encyclopedia of the 20th Century videodisc. CEL. Phone: (800) CEL-3339.

To Fly! videodisc. Lumivision. Phone: (800) 776-5864.

Tuneland CD-ROM. 7th level. Phone: (214) 437-4858.

U.S. Atlas CD-ROM. The Software Toolworks. Phone: (800) 283-8499.

U.S. Civics CD-ROM. Compton's NewMedia Inc. Phone: (619) 929-2500.

Voyeur interactive movie on CD-I. Philips. Phone: (800) 845-7301.

War-related CD-ROMs. Quanta Press, phone: (612) 379-3956 and Compton's NewMedia Inc., phone: (619) 929-2500.

WAV Sound Effects. CD-ROM of pre-recorded waveform audio sound effects. Applied Optical Media Corporation. Price: $19.95. Phone: (610) 429-3701.

Where in the World is Carmen Sandiego CD-ROM. Brøderbund Software. Phone: (415) 382-4565.

Who Built America CD-ROM. Voyager. Phone: (800) 446-2001.

Word Tales CD-ROM. Time Warner Interactive. Phone: (818) 955-9999.

World Atlas CD-ROM. The Software Toolworks. Phone: (800) 283-8499.

Networked Resources

Computer Professionals for Social Responsibility (CPSR). For information, gopher to cpsr.org.

EDUPAGE. Triweekly digest of the week's major news items on information technology. Available by Gopher from educom.edu, or subscribe by sending an e-mail: message to listproc@ivory.educom.edu with the text: **subscribe EDUPAGE** *firstname lastname*

Electronic Frontier Foundation (EFF). Professional organization concerned with the legal, social, and political aspects of networks. To subscribe, address e-mail message to eff-request@eff.org containing the one-line message **Please add me to the mailing list**. Then add a line providing your real name, and one more line stating your e-mail: address.

FTP site for more information about networked discussion groups and listserves: At dartcms1.dartmouth.edu, in the directory *siglists,* the READ.ME file contains several thousand mailing list topics, addresses, and instructions how to subscribe to them.

George Lucas Educational Foundation. Established by film maker George Lucas to help shape his vision for a technology-enriched educational system. To subscribe to an online newsletter, send e-mail: to edutopia@kerner.com.

HOTT (Hot Off The Tree). Free monthly electronic newsletter featuring the latest advances in computers, communications, and electronics. Send subscription requests to listserv@ucsd.edu; leave the Subject line blank, and in the body of the message enter **SUBSCRIBE HOTT-LIST** (do not include first or last names following SUBSCRIBE HOTT-LIST).

Internet Resources Listserve. Sends regular updates on new happenings on the Internet. To subscribe, address an e-mail: message to listserv@vm1.nodak.edu containing the one-line message **Subscribe news your_name** where your_name is your real name, not your e-mail: address.

Nursing Network. E-mail: to nurse@nvn.com.

"Rural Datafication." For more information about the process of extending the Information Superhighway to rural America, contact Dr. Michael Staman, President of CICNet. E-mail: info@cic.net.

Whole Internet Catalog (Krol 1992) lists Internet resources covering a broad range of topics.

Professional Associations

AECT (Association for Educational Communications and Technology). The largest professional association for audiovisual and multimedia practitioners. To join, contact the AECT at 1025 Vermont Avenue NW, Suite 820, Washington, DC. Phone: (202) 347-7834; fax: (202) 347-7839.

EFF (Electronic Frontier Foundation). To join, send email to eff-request@eff.org containing three lines: Line 1: **Please add me to the mailing list.** Line 2: your real name. Line 3: your e-mail address.

HESC (Health Science Consortium). Publishes catalog of interactive instructional programs for nurses. Phone: (919) 942-8731.

ICIA (International Communications Industries Association). To join, contact the ICIA at 3150 Spring Street, Fairfax, VA 22031-2399. Phone: (703) 273-7200; fax: (703) 278-8082.

SALT (Society for Applied Learning Technology). SALT is a professional association that fosters careers in technology. While the AECT is oriented more toward the education industry, SALT focuses on industrial and military training applications. To join SALT, contact their headquarters at 50 Culpeper Street, Warrington, VA 22186. Phone: (703) 347-0055.

Publications: Catalogs, Journals, and Publishing Organizations

American Cybercasting Corporation. Publishes online versions of *USA Today*, the *Washington Post*, the *Washington Times*, and the *Los Angeles Times*. Phone: (216) 247-0770; e-mail: usa@americast.com.

American Journal of Nursing. Publishes multimedia catalog of interactive nursing programs. Phone: (800) CALL-AJN.

CD-ROM World. Journal published monthly. To subscribe, contact Mecklermedia Corporation, 11 Ferry Lane West, Westport, CT 06880. Phone: (203) 226-6967; fax: (203) 454-5840; e-mail: meckler@jvnc.net.

CD-ROMs in Print. Catalog published by Mecklermedia Corporation, 11 Ferry Lane West, Westport, CT 06880. Phone: (203) 226-6967; fax: (203) 454-5840; e-mail: meckler@jvnc.net.

Cinefex. Journal published quarterly. To subscribe, contact Cinefex at P.O. Box 20027, Riverside, CA 92516. Phone: (909) 781-1917.

Club KidSoft magazine on CD-ROM. KidSoft, Inc. Phone: (408) 354-6100.

Communications Industries Report. Monthly newspaper of the International Communications Industries Association. To subscribe, contact the ICIA at 3150 Spring Street, Fairfax, VA 22031-2399. Phone: (703) 273-7200; fax: (703) 278-8082.

Directory of Multimedia Equipment, Software, and Services. Published by the ICIA. 3150 Spring Street, Fairfax, VA 22031-2399. Phone: (703) 273-7200; fax: (703) 278-8082.

Higher Education Product Companion. Magazine published bimonthly. Free subscriptions available to qualified readers. To subscribe, contact HEPC Subscription Services, 1307 S. Mary Ave., Suite 218, Sunnyvale, CA 94087. Phone: (408) 773-0670; fax: (408) 746-2711.

Internet World. Journal published monthly by Mecklermedia Corporation, 11 Ferry Lane West, Westport, CT 06880. Phone: (203) 226-6967; fax: (203) 454-5840; e-mail: meckler@jvnc.net.

Medio Magazine. Multimedia magazine on CD-ROM. Published by Medio Multimedia Inc., P.O. Box 10844, Salinas, CA 93912. Phone: (800) 788-3866.

Morph's Outpost on the Digital Frontier. Magazine published monthly by Morph's Outpost Inc. P.O. Box 578, Orinda, CA 94563. Phone: (510) 238-4545; fax: (510) 238-9459.

Multimedia Today. Free journal to qualified readers. To subscribe, send name and address to IBM Multimedia Solutions, 4111 Northside Parkway, Atlanta, GA 30327. Fax: (404) 238-4298.

Nautilus. Multimedia magazine published on CD-ROM. For a free trial issue, phone (800) 448-2323.

NewMedia. Journal published monthly; includes annual buyer's guide. Free subscriptions for qualified readers. Write P.O. Box 1771, Riverton, NJ 08077-7331; phone: (415) 573-5170; or fax: (415) 573-5131.

NewMedia Source Book. Catalog published by Hypermedia Communications, Inc., 901 Mariners Island Boulevard, Suite 365, San Mateo, CA 94404. Phone: (415) 573-5170; fax: (415) 573-5131.

Substance.digizine. Interactive magazine published by Substance Interactive Media Inc., 444 Grove St., San Francisco, CA 94102. Phone: (415) 626-2147.

T.H.E. Journal. Free to qualified individuals in educational institutions and training departments in the U.S. and Canada. To subscribe, phone (714) 730-4011 or fax: (714) 730-3739. Mailing address: 150 El Camino Real, Suite 112, Tustin, CA 92680.

Technology & Learning. Journal published monthly, except December and the summer months. To subscribe, phone (513) 847-5900. Mailing address: Peter Li, Inc., 330 Progress Road, Dayton, OH 45449.

The Videodisc Compendium. Catalog published quarterly. To subscribe, contact Emerging Technology Consultants, 2819 Hamline Avenue North, St. Paul, MN 55113. Phone: (612) 639-3973; fax: (612) 639-0110.

Virtual Reality World. Journal published bimonthly.To subscribe, contact Mecklermedia Corporation, 11 Ferry Lane West, Westport, CT 06880. Phone: (203) 226-6967; fax: (203) 454-5840; e-mail: meckler@jvnc.net.

Virtual Reality

CrystalEyes VR hardware. StereoGraphics. Phone: (415) 459-4500.

Cybertron VR systems. Straylight. Phone: (908) 580-0086.

Flock of Birds tracking device. Ascension Technology Corporation. Phone: (802) 860-6440.

Twain-VR. Color Concepts & Images. Phone: (702) 831-7451 or (800) TWAIN-VR.

VActors. SimGraphics Engineering. Phone: (213) 225-0900.

Credits

Figure 2-1: © 1994, USA Today. Reprinted with permission.

Figures 2-2, 11-1, 11-2, 11-4, 11-7, 11-8, 13-6: Photos by Jack Buxbaum.

Figures 2-4, 2-6, 2-7: Courtesy of Educorp, a division of Gazelle Technologies, Inc.

Figures 2-5, 19-7: Courtesy of Eastman Kodak Company.

Figures 2-8, 2-9, 2-10 2-11: Courtesy of Pixar.

Figure 2-12: Photos and art by (left to right, top to bottom): Roger Goldingay; Chris Kitze; Ira Rubin; Chris Kitze; Alan Gornick, Jr.; Chris Kitze; Tom Atwood; Roger Goldingay; Chris Kitze; David K. Brunn; Mediamix; Chris Kitze; NASA; Ira Rubin; David K. Brunn; Chris Kitze. © Aris Multimedia Entertainment, Inc. 1994.

Figure 3-1: Courtesy of MusicWriter.

Figure 3-2: Courtesy of IBM Corporation.

Figure 3-3: Photo of Capitol by Roger Goldingay. © Aris Multimedia Entertainment, Inc. 1994.

Figure 3-4: Courtesy of Union Pacific Railroad.

Figure 3-5, 9-7, 9-8, 9-9, 9-10: Courtesy of Allen Communication.

Figures 3-6, 3-7, 3-8: Courtesy of AT&T.

Figure 3-9: Courtesy of Industrial Training Corporation.

Figures 3-10, 3-11, 3-12, 3-13: Courtesy of Chrysler Corporation

FIgures 3-14, 3-15, 3-16: Courtesy of Styles-on-Video, Inc.

Figures 3-17, 3-18: Courtesy of Frontier Media Group.

Figures 4-1, 4-2, 4-3: Courtesy of Ebook, Inc.

Figures 4-4, 4-5: Courtesy of National Geographic Society.

Figures 4-6, 4-7, 4-8: Courtesy of Amazing Media

Figures 4-9, 4-10, 4-11: Courtesy of Falcon Software, Inc.

Figures 4-12, 4-13: Courtesy of Syracuse Language Systems.

Figures 4-14, 4-15: Courtesy of Heinle & Heinle, Inc.

Figures 4-16, 4-17, 4-35, 4-36: Courtesy of Brødurbund Software, Inc.

Figures 4-18, 4-19, 4-20: Courtesy of Multicom Publishing, Inc.

Figures 4-21, 4-22, 4-23, 4-24, 5-8, 5-9: Courtesy of Medio Multimedia, Inc.

Figure 4-25, 4-26: Courtesy of MidiSoft Corporation.

Figures 4-27, 8-4, 8-5, 8-6, 8-7: Courtesy of Compton's NewMedia, Inc.

Figure 4-28: Courtesy of The Education Group, Inc.

Figures 4-29, 4-30: Courtesy of Videodiscovery, Inc.

Figures 4-31, 4-32: Courtesy of KidSoft, Inc.

Figures 4-33, 4-34: Courtesy of Macmillan New Media.

Figure 4-37: Courtesy of 7th Level, Inc.

Figures 4-38, 4-39: Courtesy of Time Warner Interactive.

Figures 5-1, 5-2: Courtesy of Gryphon Software Corporation.

Figures 5-3, 5-4, 5-5: Courtesy of Drew Pictures.

Figures 5-6, 5-7: Courtesy of Phillips Interactive Media of America.

Figures 5-10, 5-11: Courtesy of Straylight Corp.

Figures 5-12, 5-13: Courtesy of StereoGraphics Corporation, San Rafael, CA.

Figure 5-14: Courtesy of Ascension Technology Corporation.

Figures 6-1, 6-2: Courtesy of CITY-INFO.

Figure 6-3, 6-4, 6-5: Courtesy of Oregon Department of Human Resources.

Figure 6-6, 6-7, 6-8, 6-9: Courtesy of Georgia Tech Multimedia Lab.

Figure 6-10: Courtesy of Quanta Press.

Figures 7-1, 7-2, 7-3, 7-4: Courtesy of the The BOHLE Company.

Figures 7-5, 7-6: Courtesy of High Techsplanations, Inc.

Figures 7-7, 7-8, 7-9: Courtesy of HeartBeat Corporation.

Figures 8-1, 8-2, 8-3: Courtesy of Grolier Electronic Publishing, Inc.

Figures 8-8, 8-9, 8-10, 8-11, 8-12: Courtesy of McGraw-Hill, Inc.

Figures 9-1, 9-2: Courtesy of Microsoft Corporation.

Figures 9-3, 9-4: Courtesy of Software Publishing Corporation.

Figures 9-5, 9-6: Courtesy of Macromedia, Inc.

Figure 11-3,13-3: Courtesy of Creative Labs, Inc.

Figures 11-5, 11-6: Courtesy of New Media Graphics Corporation.

Figure 13-4: Courtesy of Turtle Beach Systems, Inc.

Figure 16-1: Courtesy of American Laser Games, Inc..

Figures 19-4, 19-11: Courtesy of JASC, Inc.

Figure 19-6: Courtesy of Canon U.S.A., Inc.

Figures 23-1, 23-2, 23-3, 23-4: Courtesy of PG Music Inc.

Figure 24-1: Courtesy of Intel, Inc.

Figures 26-1, 26-5, 27-1, 28-1, 29-1, 30-1: Photos by David K. Brunn. © Aris Multimedia Entertainment, Inc. 1994.

Logos in Chapter 10:

Windows: Courtesy of Microsoft Corporation

Ultimedia: Courtesy of IBM Corporation

CD-I: Courtesy of Philips Consumer Electronics Company.

Logos in Chapter 17:

Morph's Outpost: Courtesy of Morph's Outpost on the Digital Frontier

Internet World, CD-ROM World, and Virtual Reality World: Courtesy of Mecklermedia Corporation

T.H.E. Journal: Courtesy of T.H.E. Journal

Technology & Learning: Courtesy of Peter Li Education Group

Videodisc Compendium: Courtesy of Emerging Technology Consultants

CeBIT: Courtesy of CeBIT

AACE: Courtesy of the Association for the Advancement of Computing in Education

Interactive Healthcare: Courtesy of Stewart Publishing, Inc.

Index

@ commands
    @mci=, 319
    @origin=x,y, 246–247
    @os=, 221
    @wait=, 221, 226–227, 230–231,
        254, 255
    navigation options, 296
    videodisc special effects, 254
. (period) for @wait=key feature,
    255
7th Level, 72–73
8-bit color vs. 24-bit color, 213,
    214
8-bit sound vs. 16-bit sound, 13,
    136
20th Century Almanac, 114
64 KB buffer, 14
'92 Vote, The, 53
640x480 display, 14, 134–135
1920's barnstorming tutorial
    segment, 262–265
*1993 Guinness Disc Of Records,
    The*, 114–115
1993 TIME Almanac, 113–114

AARNet, 306
ABC News Interactive, 53, 60
access issues for the Information
    Superhighway, 92–93, 180
accessories, 136–140, 147–148
ACTIV training system, 38–39
actors, virtual, 86
Actronics, 100
A.D.A.M. CD-ROM, 102
Addams, Jane, 116
Adobe Photoshop, 80
Advanced Multimedia Solutions,
    32
advertising applications, 40–42
AECT, 188
agents for virtual shopping, 33
AimTech, 123
Allegro New Media, 105
Allen Communication, 124–126
Allen, Mike, 122
alliances and mergers, 8–9
Amazing Media, 50–51
American Association for the
    Advancement of Science,
    105
*American Heart Association
    Advanced Cardiac Life
    Support*, 100
American Journal of Nursing
    catalog, 101

Anatomy & Physiology, 102
anatomy applications, 100–101,
    102
anchored instruction, 46
animation applications, 78
annual reports on CD-ROM, 41
Apple, 130, 145, 165, 180
applications
    business and industry, 31–45
    CD-ROM titles, 346–349
    development packages,
        117–126, 343
    education, 46–75
    encyclopedic resources,
        107–116
    entertainment, 76–87
    government, 88–98
    medicine and nursing, 99–106
    as objects of links, 221–222
    parameters for links, 221
    publishing multimedia appli-
        cations, 320–329
Applied Optical Media, 24
approach and marketability, 328
Archie, 300, 302
Aris Entertainment, 22–23, 257
Arnold Arboretum, 116
art. *See* graphics
art education applications, 47–48
Arthur's Teacher Trouble, 71, 72
Ascension Technology, 86
Asymmetrix, 121
AT&T, 37–38, 165
Atkinson, Bill, 33
Atlanta Olympic bidding appli-
    cation, 93–96
Atlanta Vision, 95–96
atlases on CD-ROM, 56–57
audio. *See* music; sound;
    waveform audio
audio CDs, 24–25, 228–232
audio connections, 151–153
audio mixing, 151–153
audio speakers, 136–137
audio/video switch, 154–155
author.bmp, 207
authoring systems, 122–126
author vs. user in PODIUM, 198
Authorware Professional,
    122–123
*Authorware Professional for Win-
    dows Reviewer's Guide*, 123
auxiliary input devices, 143–145,
    148–149

back.bmp, 296
Backdrop icon, 202, 206–207
backdrops
    color, 202
    graphics backdrops, 206–207
    History of Flight tutorial,
        260–261, 264, 268, 271, 275
    Information Superhighway
        home screen, 289–290
    Information Superhighway
        Services menu, 299
    triggers in, 221
    videodisc slides, 254
background music, 228
backing up your work, 291
Band-in-a-Box, 233–237
bandwidth, 14
Barlow, John Perry, 159
barnstorming tutorial segment,
    262–265
BARRNET, 306
.bat files as link objects, 221–222
BCE Telecom, 173
Beauty and the Beast, 71
Bernstein on CD-ROM, 65
bibliography, 340–342
biology education applications,
    49–51
Biplane button, 263
Bishop Museum, 116
bit, 13
bitmaps
    See also .bmp files
    BMP format, 205
    compressing, 212–213
    defined, 18
bits per sample, 225
Black and White, 77
blackout training application,
    37–38
Blockbuster, 32
Blue Angels button, 271
Blue Angels tutorial segment,
    270–273
*Blueprint for Delivery of Govern-
    ment Services Using Infor-
    mation Technology*, 181
blues with Band-in-a-Box,
    235–237
.bmp files, 205
    See also bitmaps
    backdrops, 207
    Information Superhighway
        application icons, 290
    navigation icons, 296
    saving screen captures as, 209

BMP format, 205
books
    bibliography, 340–342
    multimedia vs., 3
borders around digital video
    windows, 247
Braun, Eric, 304
BRI ISDN, 164
broadband ISDN, 164
Brøderbund Software
    Living Books series, 70–71
    *Where in the World Is Carmen
        Sandiego?*, 57–58
BrowseStation, 32
building text, 203–204
business and industry applica-
    tions, 31–45
buttons
    creating, 220
    History of Flight menu,
        258–259, 263, 267, 271, 275
    Information Superhighway
        Services menu, 300, 303
    navigation options, 296
buying. *See* shopping
byte, 11

cable television multimedia
    mergers and alliances, 8–9
Caere scanner, 16, 17, 143
California Museum of
    Photography, 116
California's public service kiosks,
    89–91
cameras
    digital, 144–145
    video, 23, 210–211
campaigning, virtual, 96
Canadian Security Intelligence
    Service, 172
Canon RC-570, 211
Cantwell, Maria, 173
Capitol Hill, 53
capturing
    See also recording
    digital video, 240–244
    digital video palette, 242
    screen images, 208–209
Carpal Tunnel Syndrome, 97
car rental applications, 34–35
catalogs, 187–188, 350–351
CATV multimedia mergers and
    alliances, 8–9
CAV format, 27, 252
CD Audio Clipmaker, 228–232
CDI350 portable player, 131

CD-I, 81–82, 131
CD-I Viewer, 131
CD-ROM, 13
CD-ROM discs
    See also Multiliteracy CD
    audio CDs, 24–25, 228–232
    clip art libraries, 19–23
    magazines on disc, 186–187
    multimedia titles, 346–349
    packaging applications for,
        321–323
    pressing equipment, 323
    read-write optical disks, 141
    service bureaus, 323–324
    sound effects, 24
CD-ROM drives
    64 KB buffer, 14
    installed base, 4
    MPC and MPC2 specifica-
        tions, 12
    multisession capability, 13,
        211
    purchasing, 136
    transfer rates, 12, 13
    writable drives (CD-R), 142,
        323
CD-ROMs in Print, 187, 188
CD-ROM World, 185
CeBit, 189
CEL, 59–60
cellular networks, 166
censorship, 173
centering text, 200
central processors, 7, 12, 134, 240
chalk, digital, 212
checklists for multimedia com-
    puter buyers, 146–149
chemistry education applica-
    tions, 51–53
child pornography, 170–171
chips (processors), 7, 12, 134, 240
choruses in Band-in-a-Box, 236
Chrysler, 40–42
CICNet, 160, 306
Cinefex, 186
cinema applications, 77–79
    interactive movies, 79–82
    movies vs. multimedia, 3
    virtual reality, 82–86
CITY-INFO kiosks, 89
civics education applications, 53
ClariNews, 9
Clark, William, 174
Clicking tool, 203–204
Cliffhanger, 78
Clinton Health Security Plan, The,
    105
clip art, 18–23, 210
Clipboard, 230, 308–309
clipmaking
    See also recording
    CD audio, 228–232
    videodisc, 251–255
Clipper Chip, 172–173
Cloning tool, 203.
    See also copying
closing the custom toolbox, 198
Club KidSoft, 68–69, 72
CLV format, 27, 252
CMC Research, 49
cnn.bmp, 290

CNN live video feed, 318–319
Coates Art Review:
    Impressionism, 48
color
    background, 202
    capturing digital video
        palettes, 242
    digital chalk, 212
    displays, 134–135
    palette shifts, 213–215,
        247–249
    recommended combinations,
        202
    scanners, 143
    of text, 201
Colorado Supernet, 306
Color Concepts & Images, 86
Color tool, 201, 202
COMDEX, 189
com domain, 307
communication options,
    142–143, 147–149
communications, wireless, 166
Communications Industries
    Report, 186
compact discs. *See* CD-ROM
    discs; CD-ROM drives
Compact Publishing, 113–114
components, 133–145
    auxiliary input devices,
        143–145, 148–149
    buyer checklists, 146–149
    communication options,
        142–143, 147–149
    multimedia accessories,
        136–140, 147–148
    printers, 145, 147–149
    read/write storage, 140–142,
        147–149
    system unit, 134–135, 147–148
Composer Quest, 64
compressing
    applications for the Internet,
        325–326
    applications to diskettes,
        324–325
    bitmaps, 212–213
    digital video, 239, 245–246
Compton's Interactive Encyclo-
    pedia, 109–112
Compton's NewMedia
    Compton's Interactive Encyclo-
        pedia, 109–112
    Desert Storm with Coalition
        Command, 61
    Jazz, A Multimedia History, 65
    patent, 174–175
    The Doctors Book of Home
        Remedies, 100
    U.S. Civics, 53
    Vietnam, 207
    war CD-ROM titles, 60
Compuserve copyright suit, 176
computer manuals as unwanted,
    3–4
computers
    See also hardware
    buying complications, 127
    configuring a multimedia
        computer, 150–155
    home computer market
        growth, 6
    home market, 6
    iCOMP index for processors, 7

MPC and MPC2 specifica-
    tions, 11, 12
multimedia components,
    133–145
multimedia computer buyer
    checklists, 146–149
processors, 7, 12, 134, 240
telecomputers, 165
U.S. multimedia market
    growth, 4
Computer Technology Research
    (CTR), 1, 3, 31
conferences and exhibits,
    189–191, 344
configuring
    Gopher connection, 307
    multimedia computers,
        150–155
connections
    audio wiring, 151–153
    Internet, 143, 305, 306–307,
        345–346
    videodisc players, 140
    video wiring, 154–155
Conoco, 257
consumer information applica-
    tions, 97
content definition for multimedia
    applications, 281, 283
Context, 72
Continental Cablevision, 179
converting graphics, 210
copying
    See also inserting; pasting
    CD audio clip addresses, 230
    CD audio to hard disk, 231–232
    cloning text, 203
    Gopher selector strings, 308
    video segments, 244
copyright issues, 176–178
corporate mergers and alliances,
    8–9
corporate training applications,
    36–39, 38–39
costs
    CD-ROM pressing, 323
    Information Superhighway
        services, 179
CPSR, 172
creating
    buttons, 220
    custom screen, 198
    directories, 197
    entering text, 199
    hyperpictures, 219–220
    hypertext, 218–222
    twelve-bar blues, 235–237
Creative Backgrounds and
    Textures, 19–20
Crecine, Pat, 94
Crews, Kenneth, 178
Critical Path, 81
CrystalEyes VR, 84–85
custom toolbox, 198
Cybersex Machine, The, 86, 170
Cybertron, 83–84

Dataquest, 4
D.C. Heath, 60
Decision Development, 66–67
default navigation options, 294
    disabling, 296–297

defragmenting hard disks, 240,
    243
Delete icon, 222
deleting
    digital video sections, 244–245
    hypertext and hyperpictures,
        222
    undoing, 222
    video segments, 244
    waveform audio sections,
        224–225
Delft University, 170
delta frame encoding, 239
Demon, 306
deregulation of telecommuni-
    cations, 171–172
Desert Storm: The War in the
    Persian Gulf, 60
Desert Storm with Coalition
    Command, 61
designing multimedia applica-
    tions, 278–286
desktop video conferencing
    applications, 33–34
Dictionary for Children, 69–70
Diet Coke commercials, 79
digital audio boards, 12, 13, 136,
    137, 140
digital cameras, 144–145
digital chalk, 212
digital recasting, 79
digital video
    capturing, 240–244
    compression, 239, 245–246
    dropped frames, 240, 243–243
    editing, 244–245
    future trend, 163
    hard disk preparation, 240
    History of Flight tutorial, 265,
        269, 272–273, 276
    live video feed, 26, 318–319
    overview, 27, 239–240
    palette shifts, 247–249
    playing, 246
    positioning on screen, 246–247
    purchasing boards, 139
    recording, 238–250
    taking pictures, 210–211
    Video for Windows, 130–131,
        138, 238–250
Digital Video Interactive (DVI),
    130–131
digitized pictures, 23
Dinosaurs!, 50
directories
    creating, 197
    for History of Flight applica-
        tion, 259
    for Information Superhighway
        application, 288
    packaging applications for
        CD-ROM, 321
Directory of Multimedia Equip-
    ment, Software & Services,
    187, 188
discipline-based art education, 48
"Discover the Information
    Superhighway" hypertext,
    292–294
distributing multimedia applica-
    tions. *See* publishing mul-
    timedia applications
Doctors Book of Home Remedies,
    The, 100

Dodds, Philip, 174
domain names, 307
done.bmp, 296
double-speed CD-ROM drives, 136
Dow Jones, 9–10
downloading
    Internet objects, 309
    Weather Machine images, 312–313
DPI (dots-per-inch), 145
Drew Pictures, 79
drop shadows for text, 202–203
Dr. T's Music Software, 64
DuPont, 257
DVI, 130–131
DX processors, 134
Dyer, Frederick B., 95, 96
Dynamics of Human Anatomy, 102

ease of use issues, 179–180
Ebook, 47–48, 71
editing
    cloning text, 203
    digital video, 244–245
    links, 220–221
    text, 200–201
    text in dialog boxes, 221
    undoing, 222
    waveform audio recordings, 224–225
Editing tool. *See* editing
Ed-Media, 190
education
    access issues, 180
    anchored instruction, 46
    applications, 46–75
    effectiveness of multimedia, 3
    Fair Use in, 176–178
    multimedia market growth, 8
    multimedia's impact, 10
    resources, 345
    training applications, 36–40, 100–102, 104–105, 345
Education Group, 66–67
edu domain, 307
EDUPAGE, 191
effectiveness of multimedia, 3
EFF (Electronic Frontier Foundation), 159, 172–173, 191
Electric Image Animation System, 80
Electric Power Research Institute, 39
Electronic Conferencing screen, 301
Electronic Library of Art series, 47–48
electronic mail, 172–173, 300, 301, 326–327
Electronic Mail screen, 301
Electronic Newsstand, 314–317
electronic publishing, 9–10
    brochures, 40–42
    distributing multimedia applications, 320–329
    as multimedia frontier, 159
electronic text, 16, 18
electronic town meetings, 92
elementary education applications, 68–70

e-mail, 172–173, 300, 301, 326–327
Emerging Technology Consultants
    The Videodisc Compendium, 185
employment and the Information Superhighway, 181
employment opportunity kiosks, 91–92
Encarta, 112
encryption, 172–173
Encyclopedia Britannica, 116
encyclopedic resources, 107–116
Enduring Vision, The, 60
enews.com, 315
entering text, 199
entertainment, interactive vs. passive, 29
entertainment applications, 76–87
    cinema, 77–79
    interactive movies, 79–82
    video games, 79
    violence in games, 79, 169–170
    virtual reality, 82–86
entitlement issues, 178–179
environment and marketability, 328
erotic imagery, 170–171
Esrey, William, 179
Ethernet cards, 142
eWorld, 180
Excel, 118, 119
.exe files as link objects, 221–222
exhibits and conferences, 189–191, 344
exit.bmp, 290, 296
exit for Information Superhighway application, 295–297
Expert Systems Environment, 90
Exploring Ancient Architecture, 82–83
Exploring Chemistry, 52–53
Expresso slide scanner, 144
external audio mixing, 151, 152

Fair Use, 176–178
Falcon Software, 52–53
Federal Electronic Communications Privacy Act, 172
files
    compressing, 212–213, 239, 245–246, 324–326
    converting clip art, 210
    digital video capture file, 241
    graphics formats, 205–206
File Transfer Protocol, 191, 300, 301, 327–328
financial services applications, 35
Fitzsimmons, Edward A., 180
flatbed scanners, 144
Flock of Birds, 86
Florsheim merchandising kiosk, 31
Flying Fortress button, 267
Flying Fortress tutorial segment, 266–269
Font icon, 201
font selection, 201
forecast.bmp, 290

foreground color, 202
foreign language applications, 54–56
fragmented hard disks, 240, 243
frame.bmp, 207
frames (borders) around digital video windows, 247
frames (video)
    dropped, 240, 243–243
    grab feature of video overlay cards, 138
Frank, Stanley, 174
freedom of speech, 159, 172, 173
frontiers. *See* future developments
FTP, 191, 300, 301, 327–328
full-motion video. *See* digital video
future developments
    keeping up, 157, 183–193
    multimedia frontiers, 158–161
    societal issues, 168–182
    technology, 162–167

Galleria 21 virtual shopping mall, 33
games. *See* entertainment applications
Gates, Bill, 10, 166
gateways, 172
Gazell Technologies, 19–20
Geist, Christopher, 170
General Magic, 33
Generic Fault Analysis, 39–40
Genigraphics, 118
geography education applications, 56–59
George Lucas Educational Foundation, 193
Georgia Tech Multimedia Lab, 96
Gershwin Connection, The, 131
GIF format, 205
Gilder, George, 165, 166
glossary, 336–339
Godwin, Mike, 170–171
Goldilocks & the Three Bears, 54, 55
Gopher
    connection configuration, 307
    copying selector strings to Clipboard, 308
    defined, 304
    downloading objects from the Internet, 309
    Electronic Newsstand connection, 315–316
    Interesting Gopher Servers menu, 304–310
    menu link, 300
    resource definition screen, 302
    servers, 310
    Weather Machine connection, 312–313
Gore, Al, 159, 172, 180–181
gov domain, 307
government applications, 88–98
graphics
    See also photographs; video
    backdrops, 206–207
    clip art, 18–23, 210
    compressing bitmaps, 212–213

converting files from clip art libraries, 210
digital chalk, 212
file formats, 205–206
hanging pictures, 207–208
hyperpictures, 23–24, 219–222
overview, 18–24
palette shifts, 213–215
Photo CD, 13, 19–20, 211–212
positioning, 208
screen captures, 208–209
sound under stills, 226–227
standards, 205–206
taking pictures, 210–211
Grolier's *Multimedia Encyclopedia*, 108–109
Grusin, David, 131
Gryphon Software, 77–78
Guinness Disc of Records, 1993, 114–115

hairstyle imaging system, 42–44
hand-held scanners, 143
Hand tools, 200, 208
hanging pictures, 207–208
    buttons, 220
    icons, 290–291
hard disks
    defined, 12
    fragmented, 240, 243
    MPC and MPC2 specifications, 12
    recording CD audio, 231–232
    recording digital video, 240–244
    requirements, 12, 140, 240
    waveform audio file size, 225
hardware, 127–155
    See also computers; *specific types of hardware*
    auxiliary input devices, 143–145
    buyer checklists, 146–149
    buying complications, 127
    CD-ROM pressing equipment, 323
    communication options, 142–143
    competing multimedia standards, 128–132
    configuring a multimedia computer, 150–155
    for desktop video conferencing, 33
    MPC and MPC2 specifications, 11, 12
    multimedia accessories, 136–140
    multimedia components, 133–145
    printers, 145
    read/write storage, 140–142
    resources, 345
    system unit, 134–135
Harriman Dispatching Center, 36–37
Harvard Graphics, 119–121
HDTV (High Definition Television), 163–164
healthcare and medical applications, 93, 99–106
HeartBeat Personal Trainer, 104–105
Hefner, Christie, 171

Heinle & Heinle, 55–56, 121
HEPC Subsription Services, 186
HESC catalog, 101
Hi8 Camcorder, 145
hierarchy design paradigm, 280
High Definition Television
    (HDTV), 163–164
high-end system checklist,
    148–149
*Higher Education Product
    Companion*, 186
highlighting triggers, 220
Historical Text Archives, 62–63
history education applications,
    59–63
History of Flight tutorial, 257–276
    1920's barnstorming segment,
        262–265
    Blue Angels segment, 270–273
    buttons, 258–259, 263, 267,
        271, 275
    directory for, 259
    Flying Fortress segment,
        266–269
    home screen, 259–260
    jumbo jets segment, 274–276
    picture menu, 258–261
    self-assessment, 276
H-Net project, 62
HNSOURCE, 62
holographic technology, 165
home.bmp, 296
home market
    Gates' growth prediction for,
        10
    healthcare CD-ROMs, 100–101
    network market growth, 6
    shopping, 9, 33
home screen
    History of Flight application,
        258–261
    Information Superhighway
        application, 287–291
HomeVision, 35–36
hospitals video conferencing
    network, 104
host name, 307
HOTT, 192–193
Hull-House, 115–116
Hundt, Reed E., 180
hybrid design paradigm, 281, 282
hype about multimedia, 1
hyperaudio, 26
Hypermedia Communications,
    187–188
hypermedia programs, 121
hyperpictures, 23–24, 219–222
hypertext, 18, 218–222, 292–294
hypervideo, 28

IBM, 32
    Digital Video Interactive (DVI),
        130–131
    Expert Systems Environment,
        90
    Multimedia Today, 184
    Person to Person, 34
    Power Visualization System
        (PVS), 78
    Ultimedia, 130
ICIA, 186, 187, 188–189
iCOMP index for computer
    processors, 7

IconAuthor, 123
icons
    navigation icons, 296
    pasting on screen, 290–291
Illich, Ivan, 195
IMA, 131–132, 174
images. *See* graphics; photo-
    graphs
Index Medicus, 105
Industrial Light & Magic, 78
Industrial Training Corp., 38
industry and business applica-
    tions, 31–45
INFOCOMM, 189
information services and the
    mass market, 10
Information Superhighway, 3
    See also Internet
    access issues, 92–93, 180–181
    artwork access, 48
    connections, 143
    costs, 179
    delays in development, 132
    employment impact of, 181
    entitlement issues, 178–179
    as multimedia frontier, 159
    need to know about, 11
    protectionism, 173
    regulatory issues, 171–173
    sizing issues, 181–182
    tutorial, 277–329
    usability issues, 179–180
    zipping applications for,
        325–326
Information Superhighway
    Services menu, 298–303
Information Superhighway
    tutorial, 277–329
    backing up your work, 291
    CNN live video feed, 318–319
    design, 278–286
    distributing multimedia appli-
        cations, 320–329
    Electronic Newsstand feed,
        314–317
    Exit sign, 295–297
    home screen, 287–291
    Information Superhighway
        Services menu, 298–303
    Interesting Gopher Servers
        menu, 304–310
    Internet definition screen,
        292–294
    weather satellite link, 311–313
inkjet printers, 145
inner city decay, 181
inserting
    See also copying; pasting
    text, 199
    waveform audio sections, 225
installer for PODIUM runtime
    version, 323
Instructional Technology Center,
    The, 332, 333
Intel, 7, 130–131
Interactive Healthcare, 190
Interactive Healthcare Directories,
    100
Interactive Media Communica-
    tions, 39
interactive movies, 79–82
interactive multimedia merchan-
    dising, 31–33

interest and marketability, 328
Interesting Gopher Servers menu,
    304–310
InterMedia conference, 189
internal audio mixing, 151–153
Internet
    See also Information Super-
        highway
    access issues, 92–93, 180–181
    and art education, 48
    as campaign tool, 96
    compressing applications for,
        325–326
    connections, 143
    crime solving uses, 93
    distributing applications via
        FTP, 327–328
    domain names, 307
    downloading objects, 309
    electronic town meetings, 92
    encyclopedic resources, 115–
        116
    history resources, 62–63
    knowbots, 166
    overview, 292
    regulatory issues, 171–173
    rural datafication, 160
    service providers, 306, 345–346
    and sex, 170, 171
    Windows connection, 143,
        305, 306–307
    wireless communications, 166
Internet Directory, The, 304
Internet Resources Listserve, 191
Internet Test Drive menu,
    304–310
Internet World, 184
Introductory Games, 54
Iron Helix, 79–81
ISDN, 164

Jacobson, Linea, 170
JASC Inc., 334
Jazz, A Multimedia History, 65
Jeep and Eagle Adventure, The, 40
*JFK Assassination, The: A Visual
    Investigation*, 61–62
Jones, Loretta L., 52
Jumbo Jet button, 275
jumbo jets tutorial segment,
    274–276
Jurassic Park, 78
Just Grandma and Me, 70–71
just-in-time training applica-
    tions, 39–40

K, defined, 13
Kapor, Mitch, 159
KB, defined, 14
Kennedy assassination on
    CD-ROM, 61–62
kilobyte, 14
Kindersley, Dorling, 64
Kinko's videoconferencing
    service, 34
kiosks, 31–32, 89–92
knowbots, 166
Kodak
    Photo CD, 13, 211–212
    Photo CD Access Software,
        19–20, 212
Krol, Ed, 192

*Laboratory Safety Training
    Program, The*, 39
language education applications,
    54–56
L.A. Project, 90
laser discs. *See* videodiscs
laser printers, 145
launching
    Band-in-a-Box, 234–235
    VidCap, 240–241
Laurel, Brenda, 195
LC MARVEL, 115
LD-V8000 videodisc player, 140
learning. *See* education
Leclerc, Jean-Claude, 181
legal issues, 174–178
legal resources, 346
libraries of clip art, 19–23, 210
Library of Congress online
    service, 115
licensing *Runtime PODIUM*, 333
life support skills training,
    104–105
linear list design paradigm, 279
linking. *See* triggering
Link tool
    CD audio clips, 230
    digital video, 246
    editing links, 220–221
    hypertext creation, 218–219,
        292
    Information Superhighway
        Services menu links, 299,
        300
    Interesting Gopher Servers
        menu links, 305, 309
    pasting Internet links from
        Clipboard, 308–309
    sound under stills, 226–227
    videodisc clips, 253
    weather images, 313
Listserve, 300, 301
live video feeds, 26, 318–319
Living Books series, 70–71
logo.bmp, 207
Los Angeles Times, 10
low-budget system checklist, 147
Lucas newsletter, 193
Lumivision, 252, 257

McCaw Cellular Communica-
    tions, 166
McCaw, Craig, 166
*McGraw-Hill Multimedia
    Encyclopedia of Science
    and Technology*, 112–114
Macmillan, 69–70
Macromedia, 80, 122–123
magazines. *See* periodicals
*Mammals: A Multimedia
    Encyclopedia*, 49–50
Mannington Resilient Floors,
    43–45
Mario is Missing!, 68–69
marketability issues for applica-
    tions, 328
Markey, Edward, 173
Marshall, Nancy H., 178
Martin, Mick, 32
MARVEL, 115
mass market applications, 42–45

Mayo clinic, 100–101
MB (megabytes), 11, 134
MCI (Media Control Interface), 129–130, 319
MECC, 72
Mecklermedia Corp., 184, 185, 187, 188
MediaClips, 22–23, 257
Media Design Interactive, 50
MediaFest, 176
Media Vision, 81
medicine and nursing applications, 93, 99–106
Medio, 61–62, 82–83, 186–187
Medio Magazine, 186–187
MEDLINE, 105
meg, 134
megabytes (MB), 11, 134
megahertz, 12
megapixels, 14
memory (RAM), 11, 12, 134, 138
memory retention, 1, 3
menu design paradigm, 279
menu tutorials
  History of Flight, 258–261
  Information Superhighway Services, 298–303
  Interesting Gopher Servers, 304–310
merchandising impact of multimedia, 9, 31–33
Mercury Center, 10
mergers and alliances, 8–9
Metcalfe, Bob, 173
MHz, 12
mice, 135, 203–204
microprocessors, 7, 12, 134, 240
Microsoft
  Encarta, 112
  Excel, 118, 119
  MCI, 129–130
  multimedia music series, 64
  Office Professional, 119
  PowerPoint, 118–119
  SoftImage purchased by, 78
  Teledesic, 166
  "Utopia," 180
  Video for Windows, 130–131, 138, 238–250
MIDI
  defined, 13, 26
  MPC standard vs. "real" MIDI, 139
  overview, 13, 26
  purchasing equipment, 139–140
  sequencing, 233–237
  standard development, 129
  synthesizers, 13
MidiSoft, 63–64
mid-range system checklist, 147–148
mil domain, 307
mixed media, multimedia vs., 3
Mixed-Up Mother Goose, 72
mixing audio, 151–153
modems, purchasing, 142
monitors. *See* video displays
Morph 2.5, 77–78
morphing, 77–78
Morph's Outpost on the Digital Frontier, 184

Mortal Kombat, 79
Mosaic and Internet overload, 181
mouse, 135
Mouse Clicking tool, 203–204
mouse pens, 135
movies
  cinema applications, 77–79
  interactive, 79–82
  multimedia vs., 3
  virtual reality, 82–86, 160, 351
moving
  custom toolbox on screen, 198
  digital video position, 246–247
  graphic position, 208
  text position, 200
  triggers, 220
MPC standards, 11–14
MPEG standard, 130, 163
MSEN, 306
Multicom, 58–59
Multiliteracy CD
  Arthur's Teacher Trouble demo, 71
  Authorware Professional demo, 122
  backdrops, 207
  Band-in-a-Box, 233–237
  clip art demo, 18–19
  digital video demo, 27
  directories of, 197
  Exploring Ancient Architecture demo, 82
  Exploring Chemistry excerpts, 52
  Harvard Graphics demo, 121
  hyperaudio example, 26
  hyperpictures demo, 23, 24
  hypertext demo, 18
  hypervideo demo, 28
  Iron Helix demo, 80–81
  Just Grandma and Me demo, 70–71
  L.A. Project video, 90
  live video feed demo, 26
  MediaClips excerpts, 257
  MIDI examples, 26
  Morph 2.5 demo, 78
  navigational metaphor, 283
  Nouvelles Dimensions demo, 56
  Paint Shop Pro, 208
  pkzip.exe file, 324
  PowerPoint demo, 119
  Quest 5.0 for Windows demo, 126
  songs, 232
  Studio for Windows demo, 63
  The National Information Infrastructure: Agenda for Action, 159
  The Puzzle of the Tacoma Narrows Bridge Collapse, 66
  The Video Encyclopedia of Physics Demonstrations demo, 67
  ToolBook application demo, 121
  waveform audio demo, 24
  waveform audio instructions, 221
  Word Tales demo, 74
multimedia
  See also resources
  components, 3

defined, 3
as emerging technology, 166
importance of, 3–4
keeping up with events, 183–193
market growth, 4–8
need to know about, 11
societal issues, 168–182
titles, 346–349
world changes from, 8–10
multimedia accessories, 136–140, 147–148
multimedia applications
  application development packages, 117–126
  business and industry, 31–45
  CD-ROM titles, 346–349
  education, 46–75
  encyclopedic resources, 107–116
  entertainment, 76–87
  government, 88–98
  medicine and nursing, 99–106
  publishing and distribution of, 320–329
Multimedia Audobon's Mammals, 49
Multimedia Beethoven, 64
multimedia CD-ROM titles, 346–349
multimedia components. *See* components
Multimedia Mozart, 64
Multimedia PC Marketing Council, 11
Multimedia PC (MPC) standards, 11–14
multimedia production services growth, 5
Multimedia Stravinsky, 64
Multimedia Today, 184
Multimedia Vivaldi, 64
multi multimedia, 129–132
multisession CD–ROM, 13, 211
murder, 169
Murray, Alan, 178–179
Museum of Paleontology, 115
museums online, 115–116
music
  See also MIDI; sound; waveform audio
  CD audio, 24–25, 228–232
  education applications, 63–65
  sheet music kiosks, 31–32
Musical Instruments, 64
Music Mentor with Recording Session, 63–64
MusicWriter's NoteStation, 31–32
My Own Stories, 72

NAB Multimedia World, 190
names of Internet domains, 307
National Air and Space Museum, 115, 257
National Center of Supercomputer Applications, 181
National Demonstration Laboratory (NDL), 190–191
National Geographic Society, 49–50, 56, 60, 115
national health insurance on CD-ROM, 105

National Information Infrastructure, The: Agenda for Action, 159
nationalism, 173
National Museum of American Art, 115
National Museum of Natural History, 115
National Music Publishers Association, 176
National Net, 190
National Parks of America, 58–59
national security applications, 93
Nautilus, 186
navigational metaphor for multimedia applications, 283
navigation buttons, 296, 303
navigation defaults, 294
  disabling, 296–297
navigation options, 296
NEARnet, 306
Nelson, Ted, 18
NETCOM, 306
net domain, 307
Netherlands Foreign Investment Agency, 40
network cards, 142
network design paradigm, 281
networked resources, 191–193, 349
New Grolier Multimedia Encyclopedia, The, 108–109
New Image Industries, 42–44
NewMedia Expo, 189–190
New Media Graphics, 138, 210
NewMedia magazine, 184
NewMedia Source Book, 187–188
news.bmp, 290
newspapers, online, 9–10
Newton, 165
New York Times, 10
next.bmp, 296
NightWatch, 170
Noam, Eli, 179
Noblitt, James, 55
Noll, Landon Curt, 96
North Communications' kiosks, 90–91
Nouvelles Dimensions, 55–56, 121
NTSC video format, 140
nursing and medicine applications, 93, 99–106
Nursing Network, 105

obscenity, 170–171
Oceans Below, 50–51
OCR software, 143
Office Professional, 119
Olympic bidding applications, 93–96
Online Journal of Current Clinical Trials, 105
online services, 9–10, 105, 115–116
opening
  Band-in-a-Box, 234–235
  custom screen, 198
  VidCap, 240–241
Optical Data Corp. patent, 174
Optical Disc Corp., 27

optical disks. *See* CD-ROM discs; videodiscs
order forms
    Paint Shop Pro, 334
    PKZIP, 335
    PODIUM, 330–333
Oregon's public service kiosks, 90, 91–92
org domain, 307
Our House, 72

packaging applications for CD-ROM, 321–323
Paint Shop Pro, 208–210, 334
palettes
    controlling palette shifts, 213–215, 247–249
    digital video, 242, 247–249
PAL video format, 140
paradigms of design, 279–281, 282
parameters for linked applications, 221
pasting
    See also copying
    buttons on screen, 220
    icons on screen, 290–291
    Internet links from Clipboard, 308–309
    pictures on screen, 207–208
    video segments, 244
patent issues, 174–175
PCMCIA cards, 142
PCs. *See* computers
PDAs, 165
pen computing, 165
period (.) for @wait=key feature, 255
periodicals
    CD-ROM magazines, 186–187
    Electronic Newsstand magazines, 317
    online newspapers, 9–10
    recommended resources, 184–186, 350–351
personal computers. *See* computers
personal digital assistants, 165
Personal Journal, 9–10
Personal PODIUM, 331
Person to Person, 34
Peter and the Wolf, 71
Petit, Bernard, 55
Philips, 81–82, 131
photo.bmp, 207
Photo CD, 13, 211–212
Photo CD Access Software, 19–20, 212
photographs
    See also graphics
    as backdrops, 207
    digital cameras, 144–145
    video cameras, 23, 210–211
PhotoQuest, 40–42
Photoshop, 80
PhotoVR, 83–84
physics education applications, 65–66
physiology applications, 102
Picture Atlas of the World, 56, 115

Picture Hanger tool
    pasting buttons, 220
    pasting icons, 290–291
    pasting pictures, 207–208
picture menu (History of Flight), 258–261
pictures. *See* graphics; photographs
Picture Taker tool, 210–211
PictureTel Corp., 33
.pif files as link objects, 221–222
pilot training applications, 40
Pioneer, 140, 162
Pixar One Twenty-Eight, 20–22
pixels, 14
PKWARE Inc., 335
PKZIP, 324–327, 335
Playboy, 171
playing
    audio CD play lists, 230–231
    Band-in-a-Box sequences, 237
    digital video, 246
    videodisc slide show, 253
    video playback frame rates, 240
Playing with Language series, 54, 55
PODIUM, 121
    alternatives to, 195
    CD audio clipmaking, 228–232
    custom screen creation, 198
    custom toolbox, 198
    default navigation options, 294
    digital video operations, 246–248
    disabling default navigation options, 296–297
    Gopher connection configuration, 307
    graphics operations, 205–216
    History of Flight tutorial, 257–276
    live video feed, 319
    navigation defaults, 294
    navigation options, 296
    ordering information, 330–333
    Personal PODIUM, 331
    Retail PODIUM, 332
    Runtime PODIUM, 320, 321–328, 333
    text operations, 196–204
    triggering operations, 217–222
    tutorial edition vs. retail copy, 199, 204, 260
    videodisc clipmaking, 251–255
    virtual slide tray, 312
    waveform audio recording, 223–227
pointing devices, 135
pornography, 170–171
Portal Communications, 306
Porter, Marsha, 32
positioning. *See* moving
PowerPoint, 118–119
Powers of the U.S. Government, 60
Power Visualization System (PVS), 78
PREPnet, 306
preschool education applications, 72–74
presentation packages, 118–121

Presidents, The: It All Started With George, 60
pressing equipment for CD-ROMs, 323
preventive medicine, 104–105
printed text, 16
printers, 145, 147–149
privacy issues, 172–173
processors, 7, 12, 134, 240
professional associations, 188–189, 350
programs. *See* applications
Project Sage, 165
protectionism, 173
PSI, 306
public service kiosks, 89–92
publishing
    electronic, 9–10
    electronic brochures, 40–42
    as multimedia frontier, 159
    organizations, 350–351
publishing multimedia applications, 320–329
    CD-ROM packaging, 321–323
    CD-ROM pressing equipment, 323
    CD-ROM service bureaus, 323–324
    compressing applications for the Internet, 325–326
    compressing applications to diskettes, 324–325
    distributing applications via FTP, 327–328
    marketability issues, 328
    overview, 320
    sending applications through e-mail, 326–327
purchasing. *See* shopping
Puzzle of the Tacoma Narrows Bridge Collapse, The, 66, 177

quality of waveform audio recordings, 225
Quanta Press, 48, 60, 97
Quebec Internal Department of Communications, 173
Quest 5.0 for Windows, 36–37, 124–126
QuickTake, 145
QuickTime, 130

Racket Selector Co., 44–45
Radio Shack, 154–155
RAM, 11, 12, 134, 138
RasterOps, 144
rate, sampling, 225
RC-570 camera, 211
RCA's videodisc development, 162–163
reading education applications, 70–72
read-write optical disks, 141
read/write storage, 140–142, 147–149, 165
real estate applications, 35–36
recording
    See also capturing
    CD audio clipmaking, 229–230
    CD audio to hard disk, 231–232
    digital video, 238–250

videodisc clipmaking, 251–255
    waveform audio, 223–227
Regen Hut application, 37–38
regulation issues, 159, 171–173
Remote Login screen, 302
Reno, Janet, 179
replacing waveform audio sections, 225
requirements
    hard disks, 12, 140
    MPC and MPC2 specifications, 12
    RAM, 11, 12, 134
    video displays, 12, 134–135
resizing. *See* sizing
resources
    application development packages, 117–126, 343
    bibliography, 340–342
    catalogs, 187–188, 350–351
    conferences and exhibits, 189–191, 344
    education and training systems, 345
    glossary, 336–339
    Gopher servers, 310
    hardware, 345
    Internet service providers, 306, 345–346
    legal, 346
    magazines on CD-ROM, 186–187
    multimedia, 346
    multimedia titles, 346–349
    networked resources, 191–193, 349
    periodicals, 184–186, 350–351
    professional associations, 188–189, 350
    publishing organizations, 350–351
    virtual reality, 351
Retail PODIUM
    order form, 32
    tutorial version vs., 199, 204, 260
RLE compression format, 212–213, 239
RoadReady kiosks, 90
Roland Sound Canvas, 140
Rothenberg, Martin, 54
Royal British Columbia Museum, 116
royalties
    and clip art, 18
    Fair Use, 176–178
    Runtime PODIUM license, 333
rtpodium.exe, 321–322
Runtime PODIUM, 320, 321–328, 333
rural datafication, 160
Ryder Touch-TV Moving Center, 35

SABREvision, 34
safeguarding national interests, 93
SALT, 188
sampling waveforms, 24, 25, 224–225. *See also* waveform audio

*San Diego Zoo Presents The
     Animals!, The,* 50
SAS Airlines pilot training, 40
Saudi Arabia, 173
Sa.Vant, 39
saving
     Band-in-a-Box files, 237
     screen images in BMP format,
          209
scaling. *See* sizing
scanned text, 16, 17
scanners
     flatbed, 144
     hand-held, 143
     overview, 16, 17
     slide, 144
Science 2000, 66–67
science education applications
     biology, 49–51
     chemistry, 51–53
     general science, 66–68
     physics, 65–66
Science Forums, 67
Science Sleuths, 67–68
screens
     capturing, 208–209
     creating a new screen, 198
     cutting digital video into,
          246–247
     History of Flight home screen,
          259–260
     Information Superhighway
          home screen, 287–291
     Information Superhighway
          Services menu, 299–300
     Information Superhighway
          Services resource defini-
          tions, 301–302
     Internet definition screen,
          293–294
     linking instructions to, 221
SCSI, 141
selecting
     fonts, 201
     styles in Band-in-a-Box, 236
sequencer, 233
sequencing with Band-in-a-Box,
     233–237
service bureaus for pressing
     CD-ROMs, 323–324
service providers for Internet,
     306, 345–346
sexuality
     cybersex, 86, 170
     societal issues, 170–171
Shadow tool, 202–203
shareholder reports on
     CD-ROM, 41
shareware, 208
sheet music kiosks, 31–32
shopping
     checklists for multimedia
          computer buyers, 146–149
     home shopping, 9, 33
     for multimedia hardware,
          127–155
     multimedia's impact on, 9,
          31–33
     virtual shopping, 33
Sierra Online, 72
SimGraphics Engineering, 86
Sinclair, Mike, 96

Sizer tool, 200
sizing
     choruses in Band-in-a-Box,
          236
     digital video capture size, 243,
          244
     Information Superhighway,
          181–182
     live video feed, 319
     text, 200
slides
     sound under stills, 226–227
     videodisc, 253
slide scanners, 144
Smithsonian Institution, 115, 257
Smith, Stanley G., 52
snooper software, 172
societal issues, 79, 168–182
SoftImage, 78
software. *See* applications
Software Publishers Association
     copyright suits, 176
Software Publishing, 119–121
Software Toolworks, The, 50, 53,
     57, 68–69, 114–115
Sony, 131
sound
     See also music; waveform
          audio
     cards, 12, 13, 136, 137, 140
     digital video audio, 241–242
     hyperaudio, 26
     linking to graphics, 219–220
     overview, 24–26
Sound Blaster
     mixing software, 152–153
     waveform audio board, 137,
          140
speakers, 136–137
special effects for videodisc slides
     and clips, 254–255
Spectrum Holobyte, 79–81
speed
     CD-ROM drives, 136
     CD-ROM transfer rates, 12, 13
     of Internet connections, 307
     processors, 12, 134
     video playback frame rates,
          240
Staman, Michael, 160
standards, 128–132
     CD-I, 131
     CD-ROM XA, 13
     Digital Video Interactive (DVI),
          130–131
     for graphics, 205–206
     HDTV, 163–164
     lack of, 127, 128–129
     MCI, 129–130
     MIDI, 129, 139
     MPC and MPC2, 11–14
     MPEG, 130, 163
     multi multimedia, 129–132
     QuickTime, 130
     Ultimedia, 130
     videodisc formats, 140
     Video for Windows, 130–131
Stargazer, 8
start point for clips, 229, 253
StereoGraphics, 84–85
still video cameras, 211
stop point for clips, 230, 253

Story Book Weaver, 72
Straylight, 83–84
structure of multimedia applica-
     tions
     design paradigms, 279–281,
          282
     navigational metaphor, 283
     visualizing a structure,
          283–286
styles in Band-in-a-Box, 236
Styles-On-Video system, 42–44
subdomains, 307
Substance.digizine, 187
Substance Interactive Media, 187
superimposition, 78
super VGA, 134–135
Super VideoWindows board,
     138, 210
Supreme Court's *Miller* ruling,
     171
surgery, 93, 103
Survey of Western Art, A, 47
SVGA, 134–135
Swivel 3D, 80
SX processors, 134
synthesizers, 13
Syracuse Language Systems, 54,
     55
system unit, 134–135, 147–148

TCP/IP protocol, 143
teachers, Fair Use for, 176–178
teaching. *See* education
Technological Horizons in
     Education, 185
technological underclass,
     180–181
Technology & Learning, 185
technology and marketability,
     328
technology developments,
     162–167
     keeping up with changes, 157,
          183–193
telecommuting, 9
telecomputers, 165
telephone services
     multimedia mergers and
          alliances, 8–9
     regulatory issues, 171–172
     telecomputers, 165
     video dial tones, 164
television
     cable multimedia mergers and
          alliances, 8–9
     HDTV (High Definition
          Television), 163–164
     market growth vs. multimedia
          market growth, 6
     multimedia mergers and
          alliances, 8–9
     multimedia vs., 3
     shopping, 9
     telecomputers, 165
     tuners on cards, 138, 139
     video dial tones, 164
telnet, 300, 302
tennis rackets on CD-ROM,
     44–45
Terminator II, 77
terminology, 336–339

Test Drive menu, 304–310
testing
     Electronic Newsstand connec-
          tion, 315–316
     Exit sign, 296
     History of Flight application,
          264–265, 268–269, 272–273,
          276
     Information Superhighway
          Services menu, 301–302
     your CD-ROM application, 323
text, 196–204
     See also hypertext
     associating appearance with
          mouse clicks, 203–204
     background color, 202
     centering, 200
     cloning, 203
     coloring, 201
     editing, 200–201
     editing in dialog boxes, 221
     entering, 199
     font selection, 201
     History of Flight tutorial,
          260–261, 263–264, 267–268,
          271, 275
     hypertext, 18, 218–222,
          292–294
     Information Superhighway
          home screen, 288–289, 290
     Information Superhighway
          Services menu, 299–300
     Internet definition screen,
          293–294
     positioning, 200
     shadowing, 202–203
     sizing, 200
     types of, 16–18
Text Editor tool. *See* editing
T.H.E. Journal, 185
Thinking Software, 86, 170
Thorn-EMI, 31
TIME Almanac, 1993, 113–114
time/timing
     CD audio clips, 229–230
     digital video recording,
          243–244
     sound under stills, 227
Time Warner Interactive, 60,
     73–74
To Fly!, 252, 257
Token Ring cards, 142
Tokyo Olympic bidding applica-
     tion, 95
ToolBook, 121
toolboxes, custom, 198
Total Heart CD-ROM, The, 100
town meetings, electronic, 92
trackballs, 135
TrackPoint, 135
training applications
     See also education applica-
          tions
     corporate, 36–39
     just-in-time, 39–40
     life support skills, 104–105
     medical, 100–102
     pilots, 40
     resources, 345
Transmission Control Protocol/
     Internet Protocol, 143
travel applications, 34–35
trends. *See* future developments

triggering, 217–222
  applications as link objects, 221–222
  backdrop triggers, 221
  buttons, 220
  CD audio clips, 230
  CNN live video feed, 319
  default navigation options, 294
  deleting objects, 222
  design paradigms, 279–281
  digital video, 246
  disabling default navigation options, 296–297
  editing links, 220–221
  Electronic Newsstand connection, 315
  highlighting triggers, 220
  History of Flight menu buttons, 263, 267, 271, 275
  hyperpictures, 219–220
  hypertext, 218–219
  Information Superhighway Services menu links, 300–302
  moving triggers, 220
  navigation buttons, 296
  pasting Internet links from Clipboard, 308–309
  sound under stills, 226–227
  undoing deletes and edits, 222
  videodisc clips, 253–254
  weather image links, 312, 313
Trigger tool
  button creation, 220
  Exit sign activation, 296
  History of Flight menu buttons, 263, 267, 271, 275
  hyperpicture creation, 219–220
  weather icon, 312
TriplePlay, 54
Tulare Touch, 90–91
Tuneland, 72–73
Turtle Beach, 152–153
tutorial edition of PODIUM vs. *retail PODIUM*, 199, 204, 260
tutorials
  See also History of Flight tutorial; Information Superhighway tutorial
  CD audio clipmaking, 228–232
  default navigation options, 294
  digital video recording, 238–250
  graphics operations, 205–216
  History of Flight application, 257–276
  Information Superhighway application, 277–329
  MIDI sequencing, 233–237
  text operations, 196–204
  triggering operations, 217–222
  videodisc clipmaking, 251–255
  waveform audio recording, 223–227
TV tuners on cards, 138, 139
Twain-VR, 86

twelve-bar blues, 235–237
Typist, The, 16, 143

UBI consortium, 8–9
Ultimedia, 130
Unabom case, 93
Unchained Melody, 176
underclass, technological, 180–181
undoing in PODIUM, 222
Undo tool, 222
Union Pacific, 36–37
U.S. Atlas, 57
U.S. Civics, 53
U.S. Government Consumer Information Center, 97
U.S. Supreme Court's *Miller* ruling, 171
University of Delaware, 102, 121
University of Illinois Weather Machine, 312–313
University of Toronto, 173
University of Waterloo, 171
usability issues, 179–180
USA Today, 10
usenet, 300, 301
user vs. author in PODIUM, 198
US West/Time Warner partnership, 8
"Utopia," 180
uudecode, 327
uuencode, 326
UUNET, 306

VActors, 86
VCRs and videotapes, 27, 179
VERnet, 306
Veronica, 300, 302
VGA, 134
VidCap, 240–246
VidEdit, 244–246, 248–249
video
  See also digital video; videodiscs
  hypervideo, 28
  live video feeds, 26, 318–319
  types of, 26–27
  videotape, 27
  wiring connections, 154–155
video adapters, 8-bit vs. 24-bit, 213, 214
video/audio switch, 154–155
video cameras, 23, 210–211
video conferencing, 7, 33–34, 104
video dial tones, 164
video digitizing boards, 23
Videodisc Clipmaker, 252–253
Videodisc Compendium, The, 185
Videodiscovery, 67–68, 102
videodisc players, 5, 140
videodiscs
  backdrops from slides, 254
  browsing, 252
  CAV vs. CLV, 27

  clipmaking, 251–255
  development of, 162–163
  formats, 140, 252
  history education, 59–60
  linking clips, 253
  overview, 27, 251
  slides, 253
  special effects, 254–255
  as textbook replacements, 10
  total in *Videodisc Compendium*, 6
  for tutorial exercises, 252, 257
video displays
  8-bit vs. 24-bit color, 213, 214
  640x480 resolution, 14
  color displays, 134–135
  MPC and MPC2 specifications, 12
  requirements, 12, 134–135
Video Encyclopedia of Physics Demonstrations, The, 66–67
Video Encyclopedia of the 20th Century, The, 59–60
Video for Windows, 238–250
  See also digital video
  overview, 130–131, 238–240
  palette shifts, 247–249
  playback frame rates, 240
  VidCap program, 240–246
  VidEdit program, 244–246
  video overlay card compatibility, 138
video games, 79, 169–170
video merchandising applications, 32
Video Movie Guide, 32
video-on-demand costs, 179
video overlay cards, 137–138
videotape, 27
videotape recorders (VCRs), 179
Vienna's CITY-INFO kiosks, 89
Vietnam, 207
viewing Photo CDs, 19–20, 212
vinyl flooring demo CD-ROM, 43–45
violence in video games, 79, 169–170
virtual actors, 86
virtual campaigning, 96
virtual reality, 82–86, 160, 351
Virtual Reality Expo, 190
Virtual Reality World, 185
virtual shopping, 33
virtual slide tray, 312
virtual surgery, 103
Virtual Valerie, 170
voice recognition, 165
Voluntary Hospitals of America, 104
Voyager, 60
Voyeur, 81–82
VR (virtual reality), 82–86, 160, 351
VStor Co., 32
VTEL, 104

WAIS, 300, 302
Wall Street Journal, 9
warfare, 60–61, 93
Warner Brothers, 31
Washington Post, 10
waveform audio, 223–227
  See also music; sound
  bits per sample, 225
  editing recordings, 224–225
  file size, 225
  hyperaudio, 26
  overview, 24, 25
  quality of recordings, 225
  recording, 224
  sampling rate, 225
  sound under stills, 226–227
  .wav files, 24, 25
Waveform Audio tool, 224
.wav files, 24, 25
WAV Sound Effects, 24
weather satellite link, 311–313
Weisinger, Eileen, 81
Where in the World Is Carmen Sandiego?, 57–58
Who Built America?, 60
Whole Internet Catalog, 192
Wiley Educational Software, 66
Wilson, Pete, 90
Windows Internet connection, 143, 305, 306
winsock.dll, 143, 305, 306
Winter Garden, The, 22
wireless communications, 166
wiring
  audio connections, 151–153
  video connections, 154–155
WiscNet, 306
Word Tales, 73–74
World Atlas, 57
World Book Encyclopedia, 116
World-Wide Web (WWW), 300, 302
writable CD-ROM drives (CD-R), 142, 323
WWW, 300, 302

XA enhancements to CD-ROM, 13
Xerox, 39–40

Yamaha MS202 speakers, 136–137
YUV subsampling compression, 239

zipping
  See also compressing
  applications for the Internet, 325–326
  applications to diskettes, 324–325
  PKZIP order form, 335
  sending zipped applications via e-mail, 326–327